Foreword

PHOTO: Tangle Photography

My father's lifelong interest in and enthusiasm for all things to do with aviation began in 1910 and lasted well into his 90s. In the days when I was flying a Bell Jet Ranger, one had to make sure that there was enough fuel for him to have a trip round his property and indeed the local countryside before putting it away.

Only the lucky few can turn a hobby into a business as my old man did. To go from teaching himself to fly to the ability to fly supersonically to New York, or see a man walk on the moon, in one man's lifetime is quite a contrast. This work charts that history, particularly the early days of the Sopwith company, in some detail.

The company started serious production in what was essentially a skating rink and became, in its latter days, half the British aircraft industry. In the early days of the company, my father said that there was no single designer but a team who each made a contribution, the drawings often being finished after the aircraft had flown! Later on, however, with the arrival of Sydney Camm in the 20s, that all changed.

Sydney's genius with the pen and drawing board was still in evidence up to the time of the Harrier's first flight.

It seems remarkable that Sydney Camm and Stanley Hooker, who were both well past pensionable age, succeeded in creating a successful vertical take-off and landing aircraft where the financial might of the United States and the Soviet Union had failed to come up trumps.

While Sir Thomas Sopwith is naturally associated with the Sopwith and Hawker companies, it should not be forgotten that Hawker Siddeley encompassed many other companies, not least of which was Avro who of course produced the all-conquering Lancaster bomber during the Second World War.

I suspect it would take many volumes to do justice to the whole of the group which, nonetheless, started at Brooklands and Kingston.

Tommy Sopwith, April 2014

56

48

66

Author's introduction

Early aeroplanes have held a fascination for me ever since, as a small boy, I first read a battered copy of Biggles of 266 by Captain W E Johns. The idea of pilots sitting exposed in wood and canvas machines, battling to the death thousands of feet above the earth without even a parachute filled me with a curious awe.

The more I learned of the Great War's horrors, the more my admiration for those early pilots grew. The risks were incredible yet they still climbed into those open cockpits and took to the skies to fight – not much more

than a decade after man's first powered flight.

Spend any time at all studying aviation during the Great War and one name will crop up again and again: Sopwith. The dynamic Kingston-upon-Thames company, its wealthy and charismatic founder Tommy Sopwith and dashing Australian chief test pilot Harry Hawker were behind the war's most famous fighter, the Sopwith Camel.

Yet the pilots and aeroplanes of the devastating 'war to end all wars', even the Camel, have begun to recede quietly into the

pages of deep history. With the 100th anniversary of the Great War approaching, I felt that the time was right to bring the triumphs and tragedies of Sopwith and its machines back to the fore once more. In so doing, I have attempted to retell the story of those desperate times when a service revolver in the cockpit was not merely for self defence.

I hope you enjoy this glimpse back into those wondrous and terrifying days at the dawn of aviation.

Dan Sharp

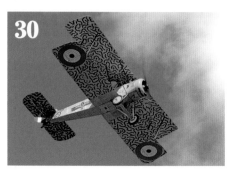

30

114

96

Contents

Front cover:
Combat over Messines by Mark Postlethwaite.
Australian pilot Lieutenant Patrick Gordon Taylor in
his Sopwith Pup, A7309, of 66 Squadron RFC shoots
down a German reconnaissance Albatros C.VII on
the morning of June 7, 1917, while the Battle of
Messines Ridge plays out below. For the full story
see Chapter 8.

Author: **Dan Sharp**

Designer: **Leanne Lawrence**

Reprographics: **Jonathan Schofield** and
Simon Duncan

Group production editor: **Tim Hartley**

Production manager: **Craig Lamb**

Marketing manager: **Charlotte Park**

Publisher: **Dan Savage**

Commercial director: **Nigel Hole**

Published by: Mortons Media Group Ltd,
Media Centre, Morton Way,
Horncastle, Lincolnshire LN9 6JR
Tel: 01507 529529

Printed by:
William Gibbons and Sons, Wolverhampton

Credits:
The author is indebted to David Hassard
of the Kingston Aviation Heritage Trust
(www.kingstonaviation.org) for his tireless
support and expert advice, and Paul Le Roy
(www.flickr.com/photos/minicountryman)
for his excellent photographs.
    For invaluable assistance and generosity,
the author would like to thank: Clive Barker,
Daniel Brackx, Brooklands Museum, Tim
Callaway, Phil Curme, John Davies, Michael
Goodall, Roger Gunn, Romain Hugault, Cyrille
Manileve, Mark Postlethwaite, Alexander
Power, Dave Roberts, James Robinson, Lynn
Roseman, Clive Rowley, John Sharratt, Tangle
Photography, Tommy Sopwith and John Ward.

ISBN: 978-1-909128-38-5

Chapter 1

A day at the RACES

Wealthy young businessman, motorsports enthusiast and aviator Thomas Octave Murdoch Sopwith pictured in 1911 aged 23.

When **Thomas Sopwith** left engineering school he already had a taste for fast cars and motorboats. It was an age of engineering marvels and another new toy soon caught his eye – the aeroplane. One young man's enthusiasm for powered flight was about to change the course of British history…

Engineering ran in Thomas Sopwith's family. His grandfather, also called Thomas, had been a friend and contemporary of steam engine pioneer George Stephenson and Tarmac inventor John Loudon McAdam.

He made good money, though not spectacular sums, surveying railway lines in France and Belgium and acting as principal agent for the world's largest lead mines in Northumberland. His son, Thomas's father and another Thomas, joined him in the business and went on to operate lead mines in Spain – which brought in rather a lot more money.

Thomas Sopwith was born in 1888, the only boy to parents who already had seven girls. His father doted on him but was often away from their London home on business in Spain so they mainly spent time together during family holidays.

His father often leased an estate on Lismore in the Inner Hebrides from the Duke of Argyle and the two spent many happy hours sailing around the island together. They were out with a friend on July 30, 1898, when a loaded hunting rifle lying across 10-year-old Thomas's knees went off and shot his father dead.

The accident stunned Sopwith and haunted him for the rest of his life. His father was buried five days later and left an estate worth £51,721 – about £5.7 million in today's money. With most of his sisters already married, most of the money was divided between Sopwith and his mother.

Less than a year later, Sopwith was enrolled as a boarder at the Cottesmore School at Hove – which he hated. He became a keen cyclist and spent as much time as he could at the local cycle shop away from his teachers and fellow pupils – learning about gears, chains and bearings.

It had been intended that he would graduate from Cottesmore to the Royal Naval College after two years but his poor academic performance meant the navy would not take him so instead he went to the Seafield Park engineering college at Lee on Solent near Portsmouth where he could pursue his burgeoning interest in the internal combustion engine.

Orville Wright becomes the first man to take flight in a controlled heavier-than-air machine on December 17, 1903, at Kill Devil Hills, near Kitty Hawk, North Carolina, US. Thomas Sopwith was 15 and studying mechanical engineering at college in Lee on Solent at the time. Seven years later Orville was trying to take Sopwith to court for patent infringement.

A Mercedes racer similar to the one driven at 100mph around the Brooklands race circuit by Tommy Sopwith in 1908. Sopwith was a keen sportsman with a restless passion for the latest and fastest machines – including motor cars, motorcycles, yachts and aeroplanes.

Charles Rolls, pictured centre, founder of luxury car maker Rolls-Royce, was a friend and mentor of Tommy Sopwith but died after his aeroplane crashed while landing. He was the first British man to die in a plane crash and only the 11th internationally.

He was 15 when Orville Wright made the world's first powered heavier-than-air flight at Kitty Hawk but when he left college at 16 it was cars – an invention that had only been available in England for seven years in 1904 – that held a particular fascination for him.

Though still a teenager, he established a successful motor trade consultancy business with his childhood friend Phil Paddon and got stuck in with motor sport. He won the 1904 Hatfield 100 Mile Reliability Trial for three-wheeled motorised vehicles in a Pearson 6½hp machine. The same year he bought his first motorcycle.

Two years later, in 1906, he was the youngest driver to compete in the first ever Isle of Man Tourist Trophy Race in a two-cylinder Peugeot – an event won by 28-year-old Rolls-Royce founder Charles Rolls.

He became friends with Rolls, who introduced him to ballooning and the pair went up in Rolls' balloon Venus on June 24. Within a few months Sopwith had bought his own balloon with Paddon from brothers Eustace and Oswald Short who were building them at Battersea in London. They christened it the Padsop and on September 8, 1906, Sopwith went up in it and stayed aloft for 21 hours, 15 minutes, drifting 22 miles from Chelsea to Eynsford in Kent.

In November, he and Paddon took off in strong winds and were soon in danger of being blown out to sea. They resorted to tearing open the envelope to allow the hot air to escape and when they came down they were dragged through three fields before finally coming to a stop.

After this, Sopwith decided to give ballooning a rest and he next took up ice skating instead, rapidly becoming very proficient at it. He joined Britain's first ice hockey club, Princes in Hammersmith, and was in goal during the team's match against C P P Paris in 1908 and throughout the 1909-10 season. This latest pursuit reached its peak in January 1910 when the team won gold at the world's first European Ice Hockey Championships in Switzerland, precursor to the present day Ice Hockey World Championships.

During 1909, he had also become joint owner of a 166 ton schooner, the Neva, and hired mechanic Fred Sigrist, who he had heard of through the motor trade, to work on it. Sigrist became a full time Sopwith employee the following year.

Meanwhile, Charles Rolls and the Short brothers had been pursuing their interests

Seven men hold back Tommy Sopwith's Bleriot XI during a demonstration in the US on May 26, 1911. Sopwith's visit to America amounted to a publicity tour with numerous high profile stunts and displays attracting the attention of the press and the envy of American aviation pioneers.

both personal and business in aviation. The Wright brothers had been demonstrating their aircraft at Le Mans in France in 1908 and the French had begun to construct their own aeroplanes.

A number of British pioneers, including 34-year-old Alliot Verdon Roe (A V Roe – founder of Lancaster bomber building Avro, a contraction of his name) had come close to success with their fledgling aircraft and the first powered flight in Britain had been made on October 16, 1908, in the British Army Aeroplane No. 1 by its American designer Samuel Franklin Cody at Farnborough.

Rolls had informed the balloon-building Shorts that aeroplanes were the future of flight. Oswald Short then persuaded Eustace

A Martin & Handasyde Type 4B monoplane similar to the one bought and flown by Thomas Sopwith.

and his other brother Horace that this was the business opportunity of the century. He told Eustace: "This is the finish of ballooning. We must begin building aeroplanes at once."

Having obtained the rights to build Wright Flyers under licence in 1909, the newly formed Short Brothers company built its first aircraft for Rolls. Once the machine was delivered, Rolls, a founder member of the Royal Aero Club in 1903 when it was entirely concerned with balloons, made more than 200 flights.

On July 10, 1910, the tail of his Shorts-built Wright Flyer broke off while he was performing a display at Hengistbury Airfield, Southbourne, Bournemouth, and he was killed in the ensuing crash. He was the first British man to die in an aeroplane crash and the 11th internationally.

The death of his friend did little to endear Sopwith to the idea of taking flight in an aeroplane but just over two months later, on September 18, he learned that an American, John Bevins Moissant, had flown a Bleriot monoplane with his mechanic as a passenger across the English Channel. Something about this feat fired Sopwith's imagination, and he was in need of a new plaything, so he went down to Brooklands. The motor racing circuit in Surrey, on which Sopwith had driven a Mercedes racer

"*This is the finish of ballooning. We must begin building aeroplanes at once.*"

at 100mph in 1908, had also now become an aerodrome. Hilda Hewlett, 46, the first British woman to hold a pilot's licence, had bought a French aircraft built by Henri Farman and was running the country's first flying school with business partner Gustav Blondeau.

It was Blondeau who took Sopwith up in the Farman, which was nicknamed Blue Bird, for two circuits within the confines of the banked racetrack. Within a month Sopwith had bought his own aeroplane.

It was a Howard T Wright (no relation to the American brothers) Avis monoplane fitted with a 40hp ENV engine and it cost £630 – the equivalent of £62,842 today. ENV was an Anglo-French enterprise that had only begun in 1908 its name derived from the shape of its engines – the V8's pistons were slanted in a 'V' shape or in French, 'en V'.

Rides for the paying public were all part of the Sopwith show in the US. Here he prepares to take Mrs Chudoba for a spin in his Burgess Wright Model F on September 19, 1911.

Aviation pioneer Samuel Franklin Cody was an American who, in his 40s, settled in Britain and ended up building Britain's first powered aeroplane. He was a fierce and determined competitor when it came to cash prizes for flying feats and regularly flew against Sopwith.

Young Australian mechanic Harry Hawker was another pupil at the Sopwith School of Flying. He proved to be a gifted pilot and joined the school's staff soon after. He later became a pivotal figure in the Sopwith Aviation Company and after his untimely death his name survived in H G Hawker Engineering, later Hawker Aircraft, manufacturer of the Hawker Hurricane.

The commander of the Royal Flying Corps and later the RAF, Hugh Trenchard, was taught to fly an aeroplane at the Sopwith School of Flying in 1912.

After taxiing the aircraft around Brooklands a few times to get a feel for it, Sopwith took his first flight on October 22. The machine hopped up and soared for 900ft before Sopwith pulled back too hard on the control stick, stalled it, and crashed it into the ground.

A report in *Flight* magazine stated: "After a few straight runs he guided the machine into the air in great style. But after 200 or 300 yards it rose suddenly to a height of 40ft or so and, for a moment, looked like falling backwards – so steep was the angle. Fortunately, he righted it but, in landing, came down sideways, smashing the propeller and chassis and damaging one wing."

After repairs, he was flying again on November 4, making circuits within the Brooklands track, though the following day he was forced to stop practicing when one of his engine cylinders cracked. He kept at it throughout the month, trading in his monoplane for a Howard Wright biplane with a 60hp engine on November 21.

By now he was able to fly with ease and regularly took up passengers including one of his sisters, May. When he was awarded his Aviator's Certificate by the Royal Aero Club he was only the 31st person in Britain to receive one.

EYES ON THE PRIZE

Aviation was an exciting and glamorous new form of transport and the activities of Sopwith, now aged 22, and his fellow pioneers was regularly attracting the attention of the national press in 1910. In addition, a number of big companies tried to get in on the act by setting challenges and offering large cash rewards to the aviators who could complete them.

Sopwith, who had spent a considerable sum on his aircraft, decided to try for these prizes to see whether he could recoup some of the money. First up was the British Michelin Cup. The original Michelin Cup, a French-backed international trophy accompanied by a 20,000 franc cash sum, had been won in 1908 by Wilbur Wright.

The British Empire version, newly established for the 1909-1910 season alongside an American version, offered a trophy and a £500 prize annually for five years to the pilot of a British machine that could make the longest nonstop flight. Sopwith's effort of 107 miles in three hours, 12 minutes at Brooklands on November 24 was eventually trumped by 43-year-old Samuel Franklin Cody, now a rival of Sopwith, who did 185.46 miles in four hours, 47 minutes in a machine of his own design.

He was more successful however with a second competition – the Baron de Forest £4000 Prize for "the longest flight from England across to and on the Continent".

Aviation pioneer Alliott Verdon Roe with the wreck of his first triplane design, the Roe I. Roe was appointed as secretary of the Royal Aero Club by Charles Rolls and was in his early 30s when he began designing and building some of Britain's first successful aeroplanes. He would later lend his name to A V Roe and Company, later known as Avro Aircraft.

Fred Sigrist was hired by Sopwith in 1909 to work on the *Neva*, his 166 ton schooner. He started work as a full time Sopwith employee the following year and would later become works manager of the Sopwith Aviation Company.

He set off from Eastchurch on December 18 at 8.30am and flew over Canterbury before heading out above the ocean.

His compass gave out shortly after he'd lost sight of the English coastline and the sun then moved behind a cloud so he was unable to use it as a guide. He was alone, doing 50mph in a flimsy open-framed machine about 1000ft above the vast and featureless ocean.

After 22 minutes at sea he finally sighted land and made a beeline for it. He had imagined himself flying over to Paris and landing triumphantly amid the stunned pioneer aviators who were based there but now the wind was picking up and his instruments were largely useless.

Now flying over hilly terrain, he was forced to settle for landing wherever he could – which turned out to be a field near Beaumont in Belgium, nine miles from the French border.

He rolled to a stop in front of a solitary Belgian peasant. Recalling the moment years later, Sopwith said: "The old man turned, looked at me, then turned his back and went on hoeing his bloody potatoes." He had flown 169 miles, though thought

he'd done 177 at the time, in three hours and 40 minutes and the £4000 prize was his. He was presented with it on January 31, 1911, and the following day King George V sent him an invitation to fly over to Windsor Castle.

Having driven over to scout out a suitable landing site, he then made the flight and was welcomed on touching down by cheering crowds. The King, Prince Henry, Prince George and Prince John met him on the East Lawn and he presented Sigrist and his sister May to them.

As a famous and increasingly full time pilot, Sopwith decided to make a further investment in a pair of new aircraft – a Martin & Handasyde Type 4B monoplane and a 70hp Bleriot XI that he bought in France.

Having won a prize in Britain, he looked further afield and realised that there was even better money to be made in the US – specifically a £10,000 (£1 million in today's money) prize for the first flight from New York to the American west coast.

The cash had been put forward by newspaper baron William Randolph Hearst – the man whose life story was the basis for the lead character in Orson Welles's Oscar-winning film Citizen Kane – and it inspired dozens of European aviators to try their luck.

Better still, Sopwith's eldest sister Violet, 44, had married a US Army general, Edward Burd Grubb Jr, so he had contacts and somewhere to stay if needed. Grubb, who in his youth had led a regiment in the Union Army known as 'The Yahoos' against the Confederates during the American Civil War, was 69-years-old and in the process of losing his fortune thanks to a bad investment.

He had little time for Sopwith, and certainly wasn't keen about the prospect of his wife taking flight with her "kid brother" but nevertheless the young pioneer had his Howard Wright and the new Bleriot shipped over.

Sopwith arrived himself on a separate ship in early May, 1911, and was pictured in the New York Herald. He made further headlines on May 17 when he flew the Howard Wright around Philadelphia's City Hall. The following day the newspapers said he was to make an attempt on the world flying endurance record but it never happened. Instead, he spent time enjoying the media attention and giving joyrides in his aircraft at $50 a time. One passenger, on June 25, was Henry Taft, brother of the then US President William Howard Taft – best known for being the most obese American leader in history at 24 stone.

As he attracted more column inches in the newspapers, Sopwith also attracted the attention of the Wright brothers who were in the midst of a 'patent war' – attempting to sue other pioneer aviators, particularly Glenn Curtiss, who they accused of infringing their patents. Sopwith later said: "The Wright brothers were a very curious pair, quite different – Wilbur the thoughtful,

Thomas Sopwith's first aircraft, bought in 1906 before the first powered flight in Britain, was a balloon that he called the Padsop – a combination of his name with that of co-owner Phil Paddon. It was a Short Brothers design.

imaginative man who did all the hard work and had all the ideas. Orville, rather brash, not very nice, who I had a lot of trouble with. When I went to America in 1911, Orville came storming around to me and said: 'You can't fly here because you are breaking all our patents'."

To avoid legal trouble he bought a Burgess Wright Model F aeroplane from the brothers for $5000, which he immediately disliked, but used for his joyrides in the US thereafter. He carried on flying his other types too however, winning $14,000 at the Chicago Aviation Meeting on August 12.

The Model F was wrecked during a crash on September 10 but Sopwith went and bought another to replace it.

> ## "The old man turned, looked at me, then turned his back and went on hoeing his bloody potatoes."

GOING TO SCHOOL

With the cash he'd won, less expenses, Sopwith established the Sopwith School of Flying at Brooklands – launching it in February 1912. His new Model F and his original Howard Wright were fitted out with dual controls and his Bleriot monoplane was used for advanced training. A fourth machine, another Howard Wright, was also used.

One of the first pupils was Boer War veteran Major Hugh Trenchard, who had returned to England two years earlier after leaving his position commanding the Southern Nigeria Regiment, a British colonial unit, due to a liver abscess.

Finding life in England tedious and clashing continuously with his superiors, Trenchard, then aged 39, had been urged to take up flying by one of his old comrades from Nigeria, Captain Eustace Loraine, who

had recently learnt to do it himself.

His commanding officer reluctantly agreed to give him a three month leave of absence so he could undergo flight training and he travelled to London on July 6, 1912, only to be told that Loraine had been killed in a plane crash only the day before. In order to join the Royal Flying Corps, established three months earlier, Trenchard had to pass through the Central Flying School, set up only two months earlier.

The school had an upper age limit of 40 however, and Trenchard's 40th birthday was on February 3, 1913. Time was running out. He rented a room in Weybridge and walked down to Brooklands where he was faced with a number of competing flying schools. Perhaps because of the publicity surrounding his numerous flying feats, Trenchard picked Sopwith, reportedly saying, on meeting him: "You Sopwith? Can you teach me to fly in 10 days?"

Over the course of the next 12 days, Trenchard, who later became known as the 'father of the RAF' spent many hours in the air and on July 18, having spent one hour and four minutes flying aeroplanes, either on his own or with an instructor ready on the dual controls, earned his Royal Aero Club Certificate. He was still only the 270th person to get one.

Another pupil whose name would earn enduring fame in later years was young Australian Harry Hawker. He had been working as a motor mechanic since he was 12 and having spent some years maintaining a fleet of cars for a rich businessman by 1911 he had saved up £100 which he used to travel to England.

Once arrived, he struggled to get a job without prior references until he was taken on by Fred Sigrist to work for the Sopwith school. Sopwith made him pay for his own tuition, albeit at a discounted rate, and on September 12, 1912, he was presented with Royal Aero Club Certificate number 297.

But it was not in flying schools and instruction that Sopwith and Hawker's future lay. Having become disenchanted with some of the lacklustre flying machines he saw being built and flown around him, Sopwith became determined to see if he could do better. ■

Tommy Sopwith teaching himself how to pilot an aeroplane in his Avis-engined Howard Wright 1910 monoplane. He is pictured at Brooklands between mid October and November 4, when he sold the aircraft – buying a Wright biplane instead.

King George V sent Sopwith an invitation to fly over to Windsor Castle on February 1, 1911. After making the flight, the aviator was welcomed by the king, Prince Henry, Prince George and Prince John.

Chapter 2

Making AEROPLANES

The early types and the first customers

While Tommy Sopwith was getting his flying school off the ground, two captains and a lieutenant of the British Air Battalion Royal Engineers were sent to attend a flying competition at Rheims, Le Grand Concours d'Aviation Militaire de Reims, on October 1, 1911. They were amazed at what they saw.

The French Ministry of War had become interested in the potential of aeroplanes as early as 1910, but trials in September that year had demonstrated that the only available flying machines were all designed for sports and were largely unsuitable for military applications.

The great powers of Europe were heavily engaged in an arms race by 1912. Britain, Germany and France had all increased military spending dramatically and it was against this backdrop that Tommy Sopwith had an enterprising idea. Why not break into the aeroplane-building business?

Therefore, colonial engineer General Pierre Auguste Roques and military ballooning specialist Colonel Auguste Édouard Hirschauer organised the government-sponsored Rheims event to encourage the numerous fledgling aircraft manufacturers to come up with machines capable of flying 'minimal performance' missions in support of the French army.

The rules were published in October 1910, a full year before the event, stating that only French-made machines would be eligible and that they should be able to travel 186 miles carrying a 661lb load, excluding oil, water and fuel. They also had to have three seats, dual controls and to be able to reach a speed of 37mph.

The winning manufacturer would get 100,000 francs in cash – a huge sum – plus a firm order for 10 aircraft at 40,000 francs apiece. Additional bonuses would be paid for machines that could meet the full requirement, but go faster than specified.

The money was such that nearly every manufacturing concern in France registered to participate. Some firms were

The first Sopwith aeroplane ever built was the Hybrid in 1912. While it may appear ungainly to modern eyes, it had many innovative features, such as an enclosed cockpit and a cut-out section in the upper wing to improve visibility for the pilot. *DH/MG/Brooklands*

The Sopwith Bat Boat was ordered by the RNAS and the German navy – this example is the German Bat Boat II. *DH/MG/Brooklands*

established just to compete. In the meantime, the French military bought up nearly 200 of the machines it had previously deemed 'unsuitable' to begin training pilots.

Seventy-one machines from 42 firms were registered, but accidents and mechanical failures turned the competition into a 'course à la mort' or 'death race'. Men fell from their aeroplanes in mid-air, fuel tanks exploded and there were numerous crashes. Eight aviators suffered serious injuries and two were killed – although this did not stop the competition. The founder of the Nieuport company, Édouard Nieuport, had already died from injuries he suffered during a heavy landing while preparing for the Rheims trials. His company, however, won the competition and the prize.

The French government also gave cash and an order for six machines to Breguet, while Deperdussin received money and an order for four aircraft.

In contrast, the British government at this time had no official interest in the potential of heavier-than-air craft. A factory making military balloons had been established 29 years earlier at Chatham in Kent along with a training school, which moved to Farnborough in 1894. The factory moved there too in

1904 and Samuel Franklin Cody was hired as the school's chief instructor for kites in 1906.

In 1907, Cody was paid to build his British Army Aeroplane No. 1, but his contract was allowed to lapse in April 1909. The balloon-building Army Aircraft Factory was authorised to repair the small number of British military aeroplanes that had been accumulated by 1910, and shortly thereafter one of its engineers, Geoffrey de Havilland, began turning the remains of a crashed Bleriot XII, owned by the Army, into a new aircraft – the S.E.1.

A handful of extra aeroplanes was bought and on April 1, 1911, the Air Battalion, Royal Engineers was formed from the balloon section of the Royal Engineers.

A trio of Air Battalion officers who had witnessed the splendour, the tragedy and the sheer raw potential exhibited at Rheims, not to mention the vast sums being invested, reported to their superiors back in England in early November.

It was now obvious that other nations were taking military aeroplanes very seriously and Britain's armed forces had only 19 – none of which were airworthy. Action was desperately needed, so the following month a set of requirements was published for a British military aircraft competition.

The winning machine, built by any nation, had to top 55mph, carry a load of 350lb for three hours, climb to 1000ft in five minutes and reach a ceiling of 4500ft. Aircraft also had to have two seats and be easy to dismantle and transport.

The top prize was £4000, second was £2000. The best aircraft made in Britain, excluding the engine, would get a £1500 prize – possibly on top of the £4000 if it also proved to be the overall winner. There were two Britain-only second prizes of £1000 and three third prizes of £500. Ten others got £100.

No date was set for the contest itself, but aircraft had to be delivered to Larkhill, Britain's first military aerodrome, for testing before July 15, 1912.

In the meantime, plans for a dedicated British air force were hastily drafted. In April 1912, the Government issued a lengthy 'memorandum' that made clear its urgent desire to catch up with other nations' progress in developing military aircraft.

It said: "The Government have been impressed by the evidence which has been placed before it regarding the state of aerial navigation in this country, compared with the progress made by other great naval and military powers.

> *"Without doubt aeroplanes have now become an important adjunct to the equipment of an army in the field"*

"The necessity for an efficient aeronautical service in this country is not less urgent than in the case of the other powers. The efficiency of the aeroplane for the purpose of military reconnaissance has been proved both in foreign manoeuvres and in actual warfare in Tripoli" – the Italians having carried out the world's first aerial reconnaissance and bombing missions there during the Italo-Turkish War in late 1911 – "and without doubt aeroplanes have now become an important adjunct to the equipment of an army in the field."

It went on to announce the formation of the Royal Flying Corps (RFC), which would have both naval and army branches, and would absorb the men and material of the Air Battalion, Royal Engineers, which would cease to exist.

"SOPWITH" SCOUT BIPLANE.   ALDERSHOT.

Emerging from the Sopwith factory in November 1913 was the type on which much of the company's later success would be founded – the St.B. Pictured here is a production version known as the Type SS or 'Tabloid'. The 'SS' may have stood for 'Speedy Scout'.

The Army Aircraft Factory would be renamed the Royal Aircraft Factory and would train mechanics, repair and rebuild RFC aircraft, test British- and foreign-made engines and aircraft, carry out experimental work and continue making balloons.

The aircraft to be flown by the RFC – of which there were to be 84 organised into seven squadrons for the Army – would be bought from private companies both in Britain and overseas. The Army would need 364 pilots and these would need to be rapidly recruited and trained. The navy was given latitude to sort out its own requirements internally. It was a start.

LARKHILL AND THE HYBRID

The official search for Britain's first approved military aircraft began on August 2, 1912. A total of 32 aircraft had been registered to participate by 21 different manufacturers, but more than two weeks after the original deadline had elapsed three of the firms had still failed to show up.

There were three judges. Firstly, Brigadier David Henderson, one of the architects of the RFC 'memo' and a former director of military intelligence during the Boer War. He had learned to fly aged 49 in 1911, making him the world's oldest pilot.

Captain Godfrey Paine was the second.

He was an experienced navy man who had served aboard several ships before being placed in command of a destroyer flotilla in 1909. Having watched some of his men become the first Royal Navy pilots, he earned his own pilot's licence just two and a half months before the trials, and was put in charge of the newly established military Central Flying School.

Lastly, there was Mervyn O'Gorman who had been superintendent of the Army Aircraft Factory since 1909 and was now in charge of the Royal Aircraft Factory. He reported directly to the Master-General of Ordnance at the War Office – a system intended to bypass the military traditionalists who did not believe in the value of aircraft.

In practice, it gave him unrivalled power to make decisions about what aircraft the military would use. He was a keen motorist, but never learned to fly himself.

Acting as secretary was Major Frederick Sykes, who had been appointed as the first officer commanding the Army wing of the RFC. He was another Boer War veteran who had been attached to the ballooning section of the Royal Engineers since 1904, and had earned his Royal Aero Club certificate in June the previous year.

Also present was Tommy Sopwith. He had, just two months earlier, won yet another high-profile competition – the gold cup at the *Daily Mail*-backed First Aerial Derby event, witnessed by 45,000 spectators – but this time he wasn't flying on his own account, having been hired as a test pilot for the Coventry Ordnance Works (COW) team.

Earlier in the year, too late to enter the Larkhill trials, but nevertheless spurred on

The Hybrid may have been the first Sopwith aeroplane, but it was this machine that really got the company off the ground. The Type D or 'Three-Seater' was designed and built towards the end of 1912, but was leaps and bounds ahead of the primitive types displayed just a few months earlier at Larkhill. *DH/MG/Brooklands*

by the financial opportunity they represented, Sopwith had begun working on his own aeroplane design with the aid of his flying school staff, particularly Fred Sigrist.

While this was taking shape, they also modified Sopwith's American Burgess-Wright Model F. Sigrist inserted a Green C.4 four-cylinder unit and rebuilt it.

The altered machine was flown for the first time on May 2, again on May 3 and a third time on May 5 when Freddie Raynham, then only 18 and newly hired by Sopwith as the chief pilot, manager and instructor of his flying school, flew it to third place in a cross-country handicap race.

A month later, on June 8, its engine had been swapped again for an ABC and Raynham used it to defeat his boss in the Shell Speed Trophy race, which took place shortly before the 'main event' on the day of the first Aerial Derby.

This practical experience in modifying and customising an existing model paid dividends in the construction of the machine that emerged from the Sopwith sheds at Brooklands for testing on July 4. Described by *Flight* magazine as being "Mr Sopwith's new biplane after the fashion of the Burgess-Wright, but with a 70hp Gnome tractor", it was actually a largely original design. Its wings were modelled on those of the Burgess-Wright, but there the resemblance ended. Instead of two propellers at the back it had just one at the front and the pilot sat in an enclosed section of forward fuselage – even though the rearward fuselage was just an open skeletal frame.

> ## "Sopwith had S E Saunders make a hull to which he intended to attach wings and create a flying boat"

This was the first true Sopwith aircraft, later to become known as the Hybrid. It flew quickly first time out with the 24-year-old company owner himself at the controls – a true 'big boy's' toy, with exciting commercial possibilities. Unfortunately, eight days later, two of Sopwith's employees managed to crash it into a sewage farm – necessitating a rebuild that took two and a half months.

Intrigued by the possibilities, however, and still regarding himself as being as much a champion yachtsman as an aviator, Sopwith retained the services of boatbuilder S E Saunders of Cowes, on the Isle of Wight, to build a hull to which he intended to attach wings and create a flying boat.

Then came the Larkhill trials. Sopwith was meant to fly the two COW biplanes entered, but one never got off the ground after suffering a sheared magneto coupling, while the other simply failed to climb at anything

like a satisfactory rate. In fact, none of the entrants – including such luminaries as A V Roe, Louis Blériot, Frederick Handley Page and the ubiquitous Samuel Franklin Cody – impressed. Two examples of the winning machine, Cody's Cody V biplane, were bought by the military, but one disintegrated in mid-air the following year, causing the survivor to be grounded.

What did impress Sopwith, however, was the Royal Aircraft Factory's B.E.2. The factory's trials judge, O'Gorman, who was not meant to be building aircraft – just maintaining existing ones – had quietly been producing in-house designs and was keen to show them off even though they were ineligible for the trials. The B.E.2 biplane was another of de Havilland's designs.

Smaller than the Sopwith Hybrid and more delicate, it had a broadly similar layout. Its propeller was at the front, but it had just a single neat pair of wheels at the front and a fuselage covering that extended all the way to the tip of the tail, which sat on the ground.

Hanriot company pilot Gaston Dubreuil tinkers with the engine of his Hanriot VIII during the French military trials at Rheims in October 1911. Dozens of machines took part and several pilots were killed – such was the rush to win lucrative French government contracts.

In the months before the first true Sopwith aeroplane was built, the fledgling aviation company made substantial modifications to Sopwith's American Burgess-Wright Model F, including replacing the engine and adding a partially enclosed cockpit for the pilot.

A WINNING DESIGN

Realising that his company had the skill and talent to produce a similarly successful design, Sopwith decided that there was too much competition and not enough scope for profit in running a flying school and resolved to focus on building aircraft.

He employed a draughtsman, R J Ashfield, and set out to sell some aeroplanes. Sopwith already had many naval contacts through his yachting – the Royal Aero Club and Royal Navy officers who had been trained through his school. As a result, he had little difficulty in persuading the navy to buy the Hybrid for the princely sum of £900 – £87,000 in today's money. It was given the Admiralty number 27.

A second machine was then ordered by the navy, swiftly built and delivered to the fledgling Naval Flying School at Eastchurch on the Isle of Sheppey, Kent, on November 22. This was not a second Hybrid, however, but a new design dubbed the Type D.

It was the first new Sopwith design since Tommy's trip to Larkhill and it was a very different beast. It was smaller and lighter and bore more than a passing resemblance to de Havilland's B.E.2 in size and layout, despite being a three-seater. The example delivered to the navy became No. 33.

As production progressed, Sopwith leased a roller skating rink at Kingston-upon-Thames – turfing out the skaters. Three Type Ds were then built as 'stock' for the business, and by early 1913, six newly hired carpenters and fitters were working on Type Ds. In addition, a hull commissioned from Saunders was having its wings added to create the Bat Boat Type 1.

An earlier attempt at a flying boat, the original Bat Boat, had been made the year before, but proved unsuccessful. At the Aero Show at London's Olympia centre on February 2, 1913, the completed Bat Boat Type 1 sat alongside a Type D on the Sopwith stand and was greatly admired for the workmanship of its hull, so much so that the Admiralty decided to buy one.

When the next Type D was ready, naval pilots came to collect it – on March 1, 1913. It was accepted as H M Aircraft No. 103 and flown away. Another Type D was finished on May 8 and flown to

FARMAN BIPLANE DESCENDING AFTER GOOD FLIGHT IN A 30 MILE-AN-HOUR-WIND

A Maurice Farman S.7 biplane competing at the Larkhill trials in August 1912. Its manufacturer won £100 from the Government just for having a machine able to participate. The S.7's fragile open structure was typical of the machines demonstrated at Larkhill.

Farnborough for War Office tests. From there it went back to Brooklands and then on to Hendon for the fifth London Aviation Meeting where it proved that it could out-climb all-comers – soaring into the clouds more than 7400ft up. The second Type D was then also bought by the Admiralty as No. 104. The third was retained as a company demonstrator.

The as-yet undelivered Bat Boat Type 1, meanwhile, had problems. It could not be made to take off from the water near Cowes during tests. In the end, it was wrecked by high winds after being left beached overnight and Sopwith quickly got work started on two – one to fulfil the Admiralty order and another with wheels to compete in the Mortimer Singer Prize competition, for which an undercarriage was mandatory. These were known as BB2 and BB3.

BB3 flew on May 25, but required further alterations, which kept it grounded until early June.

The Admiralty meanwhile had ordered three floatplane versions of the Type D, which were to be fitted with French-made 100hp Anzani radial engines rather than the type's usual 80hp Gnome Lambda rotary.

On May 27, the Admiralty went a step further and commissioned an enormous pusher floatplane, described as a 'special gun-carrying hydro-biplane' for £2650 – it was given the Sopwith designation Type S, and would have been a radical departure from the company's 'mainstream' products had it ever been completed. BB2 was delivered to the Navy on June 8 and became No. 38, serving until September 1914.

With his manufacturing business now well and truly taking flight, Sopwith hired more staff. It was just as well because on August 8, the company was presented with its biggest order yet from the War Office – for nine two-seater Type Ds, this altered version becoming the Type D2. This made

the previously built machines D1s.

Even as the workflow increased, Sopwith continued to devote much of his time to sporting competitions and one in particular, another *Daily Mail* contest this time offering a £5000 prize, caught his eye.

The Circuit of Britain Race required competitors to follow a set course around Great Britain and complete it within 72 hours, starting on August 16. Pilots and aircraft had to be entirely British or from the British Empire.

There were just four takers who coughed up the £100 entry fee – Cody, Short Brothers' collaborator Francis McClean, pioneering aviator James Radley, in partnership with ex-Bristol Aeroplane Company designer Gordon England, and Sopwith, with another new floatplane design. This one was based on the naval Type D1, but with a British-made Green engine to comply with the rules.

Freddie Raynham pictured in 1911 – a year before he became chief test pilot for Sopwith, aged just 18. Sopwith himself was only 23. The company's chief engineer Fred Sigrist was 27.

The Bat Boat amphibian was the first aeroplane capable of taking off from land or sea. *DH/MG/Brooklands*

An early example of the Royal Aircraft Factory B.E.2. Its neat design and fully covered fuselage influenced the development of the next Sopwith machine, the Type D 'Three-Seater'.

Cody was killed before he could compete, when his floatplane broke up at 500ft and crashed, McClean's Short S.68 wasn't ready in time and the Radley-England partners were unable to obtain a suitable engine – leaving Sopwith as the only game in town.

Hawker and fellow Aussie and Sopwith employee Harry Kauper took off in the modified Type D and managed 240 miles before Hawker collapsed due to a mysterious illness. The *Daily Mail* rescheduled to August 25, by which time Hawker had recovered, but the other competitors remained unable to take part. So, Hawker and Kauper tried again, and despite managing 1043 miles over two and a half days of flying, with stops every hour or so, came to grief 15 miles north of Dublin. Then they crashed. Kauper's arm was broken, but Hawker escaped unscathed.

The *Daily Mail* gave Sopwith £1000 as a consolation prize and the wrecked machine's Green engine was salvaged and fitted into a new airframe which was destroyed four days after it was finished when Hawker crashed it.

It was rebuilt and taken on by the Admiralty as No. 151. Sopwith received its first export order on October 14, when the Greek government ordered three floatplanes

Gaston Dubreuil takes his Hanriot up during qualifying at Rheims in October 1911. A number of the machines built to participate could not even get airborne.

– having chosen the company on the advice of the British Admiralty. These were Anzani-powered floatplanes, but pushers with the propeller to the rear and uncovered tail frames. The Admiralty ordered two of these for itself shortly afterwards.

More orders came in on November 17 – for two Bat Boats. One was for the Admiralty and the other the German navy. In the latter order, it was specified that the aircraft should be "in Germany not later than the end of March 1914". Although similar to the original, these Bat Boats were to be fitted with engines almost twice as powerful and substantially redesigned – making them Bat Boat IIs. Back in October, aware that de Havilland had been working on fast single-seater 'scouts' at the Royal Aircraft Factory, Harry Hawker commissioned the construction of his own small scout, although with two seats. He called it the St.B and Sigrist helped with the

design which featured an 80hp Gnome rotary engine and a wingspan of just 25ft. What emerged from the hard-pressed factory on November 27 was a world beater.

The Sopwith team took the St.B to the Royal Aircraft Factory at Farnborough on November 20 for performance tests.

These showed that the new aircraft had fuel for two hours and 30 minutes of flying, a 92mph top speed and a climb rate of 1200ft per minute – in other words it outperformed every other British type.

Aeroplane magazine devoted its entire front page to the St.B on December 4 and called it the 'Tabloid' because, like the Tabloid first-aid kit that was popular at the time, it had so much goodness in such a small package. By the beginning of 1914, the Sopwith Aviation Company was thriving. It had a full order book and had just produced Britain's best aircraft. The year ahead looked to be full of promising opportunities. ∎

Chapter 3

War with GERMANY

The first Sopwith aircraft to see action

Soaring on the winds of success it seemed that there was nothing but clear skies ahead for Sopwith in 1914. Then Bosnian Serb nationalist Gavrilo Princip shot dead the heir to the Austro-Hungarian Empire, Archduke Franz Ferdinand, and everything changed…

At the beginning of 1914 the Sopwith Aviation Company had a world-beating new product to sell – the Type SS. *DH/MG/Brooklands*

At the beginning of the 'war year', only five other organisations in Britain had made more aircraft than Sopwith. It had built 18 aircraft with several orders still to fulfil.

The fifth largest manufacturer was the government-financed Royal Aircraft Factory with 24 machines built since 1911. In August 1913 its role had been redefined by the War Office in more ambiguous terms to allow it a design function and it could build prototypes of those designs. These were then contracted out to private firms for serial production.

Ahead of the Royal Aircraft Factory were Avro with nearly 50 aircraft made, Short Brothers with more than 50, British and Colonial (Bristol) with 76 and Airco with 100.

Sopwith had no need to build others' designs as orders for its own privately designed machines kept coming. The War Office ordered nine Sopwith Type SS 80hp single-seat scouts for £1075 each on January 9.

The Type SS was essentially a single-seat version of Harry Hawker's St.B 'Tabloid' but with a modified tail and independent suspension for each wheel at the front.

At the end of January, the Admiralty placed an order for another large seaplane following on from the Type S of the previous May, the Type C. Powered by a single Salmson 200hp Canton Unné engine, this was to be one of the biggest military aircraft in Britain with a wingspan of 66ft and torpedo dropping equipment patented by the commander of the Royal Navy's air department, Captain Murray Sueter. The price was £2740 – equivalent to a quarter of a million pounds today.

Another new Admiralty type being worked on in January was a one-off widened offspring of the St.B/Type SS line known as the Sociable. It had been ordered by the 39-year-old First Lord of the Admiralty himself, Winston Churchill, who specified that the aircraft should be "roomy" and fitted with side-by-side leather upholstered seats. It also boasted dual controls – the object being that Churchill could be taught to fly. It first flew at Brooklands on February 17, though not with Churchill on board.

He went up in it for the first time with Lieutenant Spenser Grey in control on February 21 but strong winds cut the flight short before the new Sociable could go higher than 600ft. Churchill visited the Navy's Calshot aerodrome in Hampshire two days later to get a closer look at some of the new Anzani-engined Sopwith floatplanes and flew in the Sociable, RNAS aircraft No. 149, again on February 25.

It probably made a change for Churchill, who had spent the first 10 years of the 20th century as a politician during a time of national unrest. He had helped to establish the first job centres – Labour Exchanges – in 1909 before becoming Home Secretary and being forced to deal with miners' strikes, the unruly early stages of the suffragette movement and the Siege of Sidney Street, a gun battle in London's East End that he witnessed first-hand.

Now he was ordering new battleships and

SOPWITH OF GERMANY

During the fourth meeting of the Sopwith Aviation Company's board on February 11, 1914, the company's directors agreed to form a new company in Germany in partnership with Essen-based flying school operator Kondor Deutsch.

This would be known as Sopwith FluggWerk GmbH and 20% of profits made during the first year would be handed over to deal brokers Delacombe and Maréchal.

The war broke out before Sopwith FluggWerk could be properly established and Kondor went on to become one of 14 firms to build a version of the Taube or 'Dove' – Germany's first mass-produced aircraft.

being taught the basics of flying an aeroplane. His third flight with Lieutenant Grey took place on February 28 when the pair went for a much longer jaunt. Exactly what he thought of these early flights went unrecorded but despite never really learning how to fly he continued to enjoy the experience as a passenger for the rest of his life.

Grey crashed the Sociable on March 25 while flying from Hendon to Eastchurch with a Lieutenant Aldwell as his passenger. Rescuers took 20 minutes to drag the unconscious and concussed but otherwise uninjured Grey from the wrecked fuselage. Aldwell was fully conscious but suffered a fractured skull and broken thigh – rendering him similarly unable to get out of his seat until help arrived. It was the first major accident involving a military Sopwith and it would not be the last.

The same month, Tommy Sopwith decided that his company should take part in the 1914 Schneider Cup contest. The competition had been first held the year before, arranged by Jacques Schneider, the 33-year-old French heir to a huge industrial and armaments manufacturing empire. Its goal was to promote the development of seaplanes which Schneider felt were the future of aviation.

Sopwith Type HT Anzani-engined floatplane. All three examples built served with the Navy.
DH/MG/Brooklands

During his early career as an aircraft manufacturer, Tommy Sopwith was a shameless self-publicist and emblazoned his name in large letters on the side of aircraft such as this, the side-by-side two-seater prototype Type SS, the St.B.

Archduke Franz Ferdinand, heir to the Austro-Hungarian Empire, sits in the back seat of a 1910 Gräf & Stift Double Phaeton open-topped sports car with his wife on June 28, 1914, during his visit to Sarajevo. They were assassinated just a few hours later. Only the day before, Harry Hawker had walked away from a crash that destroyed the Sopwith Schneider racer.

As the great powers of Europe mobilised for war, the Sopwith Aviation Company was busy putting the finishing touches to this slimline Type SS in readiness for the Gordon Bennett Aviation Trophy competition, planned to take place at Rheims on September 19-28. When war broke out it was pressed into service as RNAS No. 1215. *DH/MG/Brooklands*

There was a £1000 cash prize plus a rather handsome 22.5in trophy featuring a silver wave crashing over Neptune and his three sons with a winged female personification of the spirit of flight swooping down to kiss one of them. It was set on a marble pedestal and Schneider called it the Coupe d'Aviation Maritime Jacques Schneider.

> *"Pixton was offered the best Champagne but asked for a bottle of Bass instead"*

There had been no British competitors in the 1913 event held on the Mediterranean off the coast of Monaco. All four entrants were French and all four used landplanes with temporary floats fitted.

Sopwith resolved that his entry for 1914 would be different. It was, after all, another

great opportunity to promote the company, which was rapidly becoming the go-to manufacturer for the Royal Navy.

Why not showcase Sopwith seaplanes to the world? The speedy St.B design was chosen as the basis for the Sopwith Schneider racer but with a set of floats and lightweight 100hp Monosoupape Gnome engine fitted.

The aircraft was completed by mid-April, crated up and shipped out to Monaco. It arrived on April 16, ready for the contest itself four days later. The French scoffed at the little biplane – the race's smallest and least powerful entrant – and ridiculed Sopwith and his team as they carried out tests and prepared the racer's engine.

Nevertheless, on the day of the race, the French team with their two Nieuport monoplane seaplanes struggled to keep up with pilot Howard Pixton as he took the Sopwith racer around the Schneider Cup's prearranged course at an average of 85.5mph. One by one they, and the other contestants, fell back or dropped out before the triumphant Pixton crossed the finishing line.

It was a severe blow to French national pride, since the French had regarded

themselves as the undisputed world leaders in aviation and the Schneider Cup itself was a French contest. Jacques Schneider himself offered to buy Pixton whatever drink he liked afterwards to celebrate – expecting him to call for the most expensive Champagne. He was somewhat nonplussed when the Mancunian asked for a bottle of Bass.

DECLARATION OF WAR

Throughout May, the Sopwith Aviation Company Ltd continued to develop and produce aircraft to fulfil orders already taken and Harry Hawker returned from the demonstration trip to his native Australia.

The first fatal Sopwith accident happened on May 12. Lieutenant C W Wilson of the Royal Flying Corps took off from Farnborough in a Sopwith Type D three-seater, No. 324, bound for Brooklands. He returned half an hour later, just as Captain E V Anderson of the Black Watch was taking off with Air Mechanic Carter in a second Type D, No. 325. Neither saw the other until it was too late and they crashed in mid-air, both stricken machines tumbling back to the ground.

The only survivor was Lieutenant Wilson, who suffered a broken jaw and serious bruising.

On June 20, Hawker entered the 100hp Schneider aircraft, now converted to a landplane, in another Daily Mail backed contest – the First Race from London to Manchester and back. However, he was forced to retire with a return of the mystery illness that had plagued him on previous occasions. Fumes had been blamed before and this time it was air pressure on the ear drums, but in truth no one knew what was causing it.

A week later, on June 27, he took the Schneider machine up for another ride. He pulled a loop at 1000ft before the aircraft suddenly went into a spin and plunged towards the ground. It ploughed into the top of a tall tree, shearing off branches as its wings folded back and its landing gear was pushed violently up into the fuselage. Then it dropped like a stone. Hawker got out without a scratch and hitched a lift to the aerodrome on the back of a motorcycle.

At 10am the following day, almost exactly

A Zeppelin similar to the one RNAS pilot Reggie Marix destroyed in its hangar.

A small number of Sopwith Type SSs were crated up and shipped to France with the British Expeditionary Force. This example is seen with the lower portion of its engine fairing removed.

1000 miles away in the capital of Bosnia and Herzegovina, Sarajevo, 50-year-old Archduke Franz Ferdinand and his wife Sophie, 46, climbed into the back of a 1910 Gräf & Stift Double Phaeton open-topped sports car and it moved off in a motorcade.

Ten minutes later, a bomb landed on the Gräf & Stift's folded-back convertible cover, bounced off and landed in the street – before exploding under the next car along and wounding 20 people.

The motorcade sped off at top speed, leaving the wrecked car behind, but Franz Ferdinand and his wife later decided to visit those injured by the bomb in hospital.

Afterwards, they were heading out of Sarajevo when their driver Leopold Lojka took a wrong turn down a side street. He realised his mistake and started to reverse out of it. Then he spotted a man brandishing a gun getting up from his seat outside a nearby cafe and approaching the car.

Panicking, Lojka's foot missed the accelerator pedal and the gunman got within 5ft of the almost stationary car. He fired two shots into it. The first hit Franz Ferdinand in the jugular and the second hit Sophie in her stomach. Within 20 minutes both were dead.

The assassin, Serbian nationalist and Black Hand secret society member Gavrilo Princip had been arrested at the scene. But it was too late and an inexorable chain of events had been set in motion.

Serbia was blamed for the assassination and Germany assured Austro-Hungary of its backing if it went to war over it. Russia stepped in on Serbia's side.

As the international situation continued to spiral out of control, nobody in Britain realised what was about to happen. On July 16, Sopwith unveiled another new type, a floatplane designed for the 1914 Circuit of Britain race due to take place in the middle of August. A slimline Type SS was also devised for the Gordon Bennett Aviation Trophy competition, planned to take place at Rheims on September 19-28.

On July 28, Austro-Hungary declared war on Serbia, and Russia, as expected, mobilised in its defence.

Germany declared war on Russia on August 1 and the following day it invaded Luxembourg. The day after that, August 3, Germany declared war on France and then invaded Belgium to outflank the French army. Britain declared war on Germany in support of both the Belgians and the French. It was August 4, 1914. The genteel atmosphere of

Reginald 'Reggie' Marix claimed a widely publicised victory when he flew Type SS No. 168 to Düsseldorf and destroyed Zeppelin Z IX in its hangar. As he flew away, his aeroplane was repeatedly hit by ground fire and eventually ran out of fuel due to bullet holes in the tank.

Naval pilot Spenser Grey was the Sopwith Sociable's regular pilot. After war had been declared, he also flew it in France against German forces.

The production model Type SS 'Tabloid' as viewed from the front.

friendly competition and sportsmanship at Brooklands quickly evaporated when it was taken over as a military camp. The Bristol Flying School, the largest there, was forced to turn over all of its aircraft to the RFC, and the airfield was placed under armed guard. The Sopwith sheds there remained under the company's control, however.

As the British Expeditionary Force (BEF) prepared to depart for France, Sopwith workers laboured over the next batch of machines ordered.

These included 10 of the Type 806 pusher gunbus, a land-based version of the machines ordered by Greece; six of the pusher floatplanes actually ordered by the Greeks but taken over for British service as the Type 880; 24 Type D3 Spinning Jennies, a development of the now unnecessary Circuit of Britain aircraft resembling a wheeled Type 807; and 13 Type SSs. Some Sopwith staff were members of the Territorial Army and were called up, so further workers had to be recruited.

SOPWITH'S ZEPPELIN KILLER

The BEF's airborne contingent consisted of RFC squadrons 2, 3, 4 and 5 plus an aircraft park. While none of the squadrons was equipped with Sopwith types, the aircraft park had four Sopwith Type SS Tabloids packed into crates – numbers 362, 386, 387 and 611. These arrived in Boulogne on August 19 and two of them had been fully assembled by the end of the month.

The early phase of the war saw three massive German armies, 1.3 million men, hammering down on the hastily mobilised French forces numbering about 1.25 million

with only a relatively small 80,000-strong British contingent. The Allies' primary objective to begin with was a delaying action to prevent the capture of Paris before sufficient French reinforcements could arrive.

The BEF tried to make a stand against the huge German First Army at Mons in Belgium on August 23. It was an attempt to prevent the Germans from swinging an enormous 'right hook' into the Allies and it was only partially successful.

There were 160,000 Germans advancing on British positions and although the British inflicted heavy casualties, the sheer weight of numbers, combined with the sudden retreat of the French Fifth Army, which exposed the BEF's flank, forced a withdrawal. The Germans gave chase and the British engaged

> ### "Spratt chose to pop off a shot or two from the cockpit of his Sopwith Type SS"

in a series of hurried and costly rearguard actions that would continue until September 28. It was during the first of these, the Battle of Le Cateau on August 26, that the two Sopwith Type SSs that had been assembled made their first military flights.

The battle saw the assembled British rearguard remorselessly pummelled by

German artillery firing from concealed positions. They stood their ground but suffered horrendous casualties – more than 5000 men killed out of 40,000 and another 2600 taken prisoner.

After the battle the two assembled Sopwith machines, along with the other two still in their crates, were distributed to 3 and 4 Squadrons.

The first use of an RFC Sopwith machine against an enemy aircraft took place on August 29, when a German machine overflew 4 Squadron's base at Compiègne and dropped three bombs on it. Second Lieutenant N C Spratt jumped into his Type SS, No. 387, and took off, chasing the German and "running rings around him". This "put the wind up" the enemy pilot but the SS was unarmed and it is not recorded whether Spratt chose to pop off a shot or two with his service revolver from the cockpit.

Four days later, late on September 2, Spratt had a second go when another enemy aircraft overflew the squadron's encampment, this time at Serris.

He chased the German but by the time he came back it was dark and, trying to land, he somersaulted the machine. He walked away from the crash but the SS wasn't so fortunate. It was crated up and stuck on a trailer, never to be used again.

The BEF was retreating from Mons and had no time to make repairs.

Meanwhile the Navy, which had a far larger collection of Sopwith machines, was also putting them to use on the Western Front in an attempt to prevent German Zeppelins from flying over the coast towards Britain.

Three RNAS squadrons, 1, 2 and 3, were

The first Sopwith machines built under licence by another company were these gunbuses built in Lincoln in 1914 by Robey & Co. *DH/MG/Brooklands*

Sopwith's Howard Pixton lounges on the wing of his racing seaplane offshore at Monaco ahead of his attempt to take the Schneider Cup. Pixton was chosen to fly because Harry Hawker was away in his native Australia at the time of the competition.

formed with around 12 aircraft each and the first included the original Sopwith Type D delivered in 1913 – No. 33 – and Type D No. 906, which had been Sopwith's Brooklands runabout until the Navy bought it when war broke out.

The unit was sent to Ostend on August 27 but was soon withdrawn to Dunkirk, however, as the Germans advanced.

Both Sopwith machines were flying reconnaissance missions on September 9 and again on September 15. These were not particularly successful, having sighted no enemy troops, so the unit's leader, Wing Commander Charles Rumney Samson, decided to set up a forward base near the fortress city of Antwerp – directly in the path of the German advance.

The idea was to launch a bombing attack against Zeppelin sheds at Düsseldorf and Cologne. No. 906 flew a reconnaissance mission with a B.E.2, No. 50, at 11am on September 16 and on September 18 a pair of Type SSs, Nos. 167 and 168, joined them. Churchill's one-off Sopwith Sociable, No. 149, now repaired from its crash in March, arrived the following day fitted with an additional fuel tank and bomb dropping gear.

This small band of aircraft minus No. 167, which had crashed, was launched into action on September 23 but only 27-year-old Flight Lieutenant Charles Herbert Collet flying No. 906 managed to find his target.

Having flown the 200 miles from Antwerp to Düsseldorf, he glided down from 6000ft to try to locate the gigantic Zeppelin shed which was shrouded in mist. He sighted it a quarter of a mile away while flying at just 400ft and made straight for it. His first 20lb bomb fell short and exploded, but although both of the next two hit the shed they failed to go off.

Turning smartly about, Collet sped away and returned to base. The Sociable and Type D No. 168 ran out of fuel and were forced to land for a refill before flying home. The B.E.2, flown by the force commander Major Eugene Louis Gerrard, had a fuel system failure but landed near some Belgian troops and was back at the airfield by 1pm having been speedily fixed.

Type D No. 103 became the first Sopwith to

be fired on by the enemy when it was flown from Dunkirk on September 24 to attack a German airfield at Roeulx in northern France. Its crew dropped grenades on four sheds and a bomb on a railway line. The next day it also became the first Sopwith to be hit by enemy bullets – two through the wing – during an attack on the same target.

By the end of September, the RNAS force of 18 aircraft on the Western Front included eight Sopwiths.

The advancing Germans began shelling Antwerp's outer forts on September 28 and by October 8 they were hitting targets within Antwerp itself. The RNAS air base, between the forts and the town, was in danger of being overrun as the enemy broke through the outer defensive ring and silenced the forts.

A last assault on the Zeppelin sheds was launched the following day. Lieutenant Commander Spenser Grey flew Type SS No. 167 to Cologne but was unable to find the sheds in the mist, dropping his bombs on the railway station instead.

Flight Lieutenant Reggie Marix took Type SS No. 168 to Düsseldorf and had no trouble spotting the Zeppelin hangar.

He dived to 600ft and dropped his bombs – 30 seconds later he watched as the roof fell in and a huge ball of fire rose up 500ft into the air right behind him. Zeppelin Z IX, No. LZ

25, had been towed inside the hangar only a little while earlier and the just under one million cubic feet of hydrogen gas it contained had detonated. The airship, the hangar around it and the workshop next door were completely destroyed by the resulting explosion.

Marix's 'Tabloid' was hit repeatedly by enemy fire from the ground during the attack run including holes through his petrol tank and he ran out of fuel 20 miles from Antwerp. After gliding the aircraft safely down, he borrowed a bicycle and then a car to get back to the airfield.

The RNAS base itself was shelled that night at 8.30pm and some of the aircraft were damaged. Three hours later German soldiers were in the woods on the airfield boundary shooting at the mechanics.

All the aircraft were abandoned as the men swiftly crowded into a pair of cars and drove west at top speed to Ostend on the coast. It is believed that those aircraft not wrecked by enemy artillery fire were later destroyed by the Germans.

Antwerp fell on October 10 and the German advance continued, rolling over British positions at Ghent until Ostend too was taken. Finally, the line held at the Yser river, east of Dunkirk, and a war of attrition began with both sides digging in. ∎

Winston Churchill commissioned the Sopwith Sociable, the only one ever built, for his own personal use. He specified that it should have dual controls so he could be taught how to fly it. The Sociable was later pressed into service with the RNAS, as pictured here, as No. 149.

Chapter 4

ALL AT SEA

Sopwith Schneider, Baby and early seaplanes

Every Sopwith aircraft used during the defence of Antwerp and the subsequent Great Retreat had been destroyed, captured or sent home by the end of 1914.

Types from other firms continued in their place. The Royal Aircraft Factory's B.E.2 had been in use by the Royal Flying Corps from the start and it continued to be received in large numbers by front line units.

Both the RFC and the RNAS operated the Bristol Scout – an adaptable and rugged machine capable of taking off and landing from improvised airfields. And other types such as the Avro 504 and the Martinsyde S.1 picked up the slack.

The Sopwith factory was still operating at maximum capacity however – building floatplanes. The Royal Navy was forming a task force to sail into the Mediterranean,

The rigors of the Great War's early months had taken their toll on the small band of Sopwith machines used for operations on the Western Front but Sopwith floatplanes were about to embark on a perilous new campaign.

around Italy, Greece and up to the Dardanelles straits, bounded on its northern side by the Gallipoli peninsula – part of the hostile Ottoman Empire.

It was a vital sea route connecting Britain and France with their ally Russia and it was cut off when the Ottoman Empire, which is now Turkey, gave up neutrality and sided with the Germans in return for their support in an attack on the Russians in the Caucasus.

In December 1914, as the battle lines were becoming firmly entrenched all along the Western Front, First Lord of the Admiralty

and Sopwith supporter Winston Churchill proposed an attack to open up the Dardanelles route to Russia.

The operation would involve a large number of obsolete warships, including a staggering 18 battleships, which would have been no use against the modern German fleet; an army of occupation and air support from a number of floatplane tenders. Churchill believed that the Ottomans would be a pushover.

However, the straits had been heavily mined and the sides of the passage were

The Sopwith Baby and the versions of it built by subcontractors were the ultimate evolution of the floatplane that won the Schneider Cup in 1914.

A not uncommon sight – a Sopwith Baby that has come to grief is fished out of the sea.

A pair of Sopwith Schneiders joined the Gallipoli campaign in April 1915. One was found to be useless because its propeller was broken and there was no spare; the other was used for reconnaissance, bombing and propaganda leaflet drops. *DH/MG/Brooklands*

overlooked by a series of highly mobile artillery batteries which had an excellent field of fire. It was a strong defensive position.

Nevertheless, the fleet sailed on February 1, 1915, and with it was *HMS Ark Royal*, the first dedicated British seaplane tender.

It carried three Sopwith Type 807 Folder seaplanes, four crated Sopwith Type SS Tabloids, a Short Type 135 and a pair of Wright seaplanes.

While stopping over at Malta en route, one of the Type 807s, No. 808, and the Short were winched out for trials in Valetta harbour. No. 808's engine started without problems and the aircraft was picking up speed when one of its floats hit a wave and broke off, causing the machine to overturn. The ruined airframe was recovered and repairs were begun but it was not a promising start.

On arriving at the entrance to the Dardanelles, the *Ark Royal* was ordered to carry out a reconnaissance mission. This time Type 807 No. 807 was brought out but the sea was rough and its pilot couldn't even get it to take off at first despite making several runs. Even with some of its fuel drained out to lighten it, the aircraft couldn't manage to gain sufficient height to be of any use.

The last Type 807, No. 922, made an attempt but suffered problems with its wireless and had to return without accomplishing anything.

The British fleet was using the Greek island of Tenedos, near the Dardanelles, as a supply base and efforts were made to find a suitably flat area on it where the Tabloids could take off – but these were in vain.

Finally, No. 922 managed a series of successful reconnaissance flights. On March 3, its crew flew to Kephez Point and identified a minefield before counting the number of guns at two forts and radioing back the position of a mobile battery. The next day No. 922's crew reported on Ottoman troop movements. No. 807 was flown to look for Ottoman guns but failed to find them and was hit eight times by rifle fire from the ground. Neither the pilot nor the observer were hurt however.

On March 5, No. 922 came under fire too and six bullets holed its fuselage. One of them hit the pilot, Flight Lieutenant Norman Sholto Douglas, in the leg but he managed to bring the machine back to base.

That same day, No. 808 was taken up to spot for the guns of the battleship *HMS Queen Elizabeth*. While flying 3000ft its propeller

suddenly sheared off and sliced through the top of the starboard wing. The damage was catastrophic and the machine span down into the water. Both crew were injured and No. 808 was a write-off, although its engine was rescued.

No. 807 was subsequently damaged during flight testing and although it was fixed by the end of March it was withdrawn in April.

THE DISASTROUS ATTACK

The main naval assault of the Dardanelles campaign began on March 18. The fleet approached the entrance to the straits at 11.30am and opened fire first on the town of Canakkale and then on the defensive forts.

While attacking the forts, the 17-year-old French battleship *Bouvet* was hit eight times by Ottoman artillery fire. Its forward turret was disabled and one of its masts was shattered. At 1.15pm, the *Bouvet* hit a mine packed with 176lb of explosives, capsized and sank within two minutes. Just 50 of the 710 crew survived. The loss of the *Bouvet* took the Allies completely by surprise and it was presumed that a shell had ignited its magazine. The attack continued.

At 4.16pm, the battleship *HMS Irresistible* hit another mine. The resulting explosion ruptured the hull, causing the starboard engine room to flood. Only three of the men on duty there got out alive. The bulkhead separating the engine rooms then collapsed and the port engine room also flooded, leaving the Irresistible powerless and drifting into the range of the enemy's guns.

Seeing their chance, the Ottoman gunners pounded the British battleship and its gun turrets were put out of action one by one. The crew were rescued by a destroyer and another battleship, *HMS Ocean*, was sent to tow the Irresistible to safety. It too then hit a mine and also had to be abandoned.

HMS Inflexible hit yet another mine which blew a huge hole in its side, flooded the forward torpedo compartment drowning 39

A Blackburn built version of the Sopwith Baby, N1123. Blackburn stuck to the original design whereas another contractor, Fairey, modified it substantially to produce the Hamble Baby.

Another Blackburn built Baby, N1413, on its slipway ready for launch.

men. The operation had been a disaster and the Allied fleet withdrew.

While the navy was making repairs, reinforcements arrived from Britain. A pair of new single-seat Sopwith Schneiders – floatplane versions of the Type SS Tabloid derived from the machine that won the Schneider Cup the previous year – arrived at Tenedos in the hold of the *SS Moorgate* on April 9.

Two Sopwith Type 860s also arrived with the *SS Aragaz* but they could not be assembled due to a lack of space on the *Ark Royal*. Even when they were finally put together on the *SS Penmorrah* store ship, they only flew briefly. One of the Schneiders, No. 1437, was found to have a broken propeller and since there was no spare it was unusable.

The other, No. 1438, was flown on reconnaissance over Smyrna and dropped bombs on targets near the entrance to the harbour. It was also used to drop propaganda pamphlets over the Ottoman front line. Sopwith Type 807 Nos. 807 and 808 were cannibalised to provide spares for No. 922.

After the attempt to force a route through the Dardanelles using naval firepower alone failed, it was decided to land troops on the northern shore who could then capture them instead. Their primary mission was to silence the Ottoman guns so that minesweepers could clear the straits.

Combined British Army and Australian and New Zealand Army Corps (ANZAC) troops was assembled and practice landings were carried out on April 12. The full blown beach assault began on April 25 but it was not to be supported by the navy's Sopwith seaplanes.

They had suffered continuous engine problems and had struggled with the harsh conditions of the Middle East. The Schneiders were single seaters and therefore of less use when detailed notes and observations of enemy positions were required.

The Type 807s, with the exception of No. 922, had proven to be too fragile and underpowered for the tasks required of them. They played little further part in the Gallipoli campaign.

HOME DEFENCE FORCE

Back in Britain, a trio of cross-Channel ferries, *Empress*, *Engadine* and *Riviera*, had been converted into seaplane carriers along with Isle of Man ferry *Ben-my-Chree*. They were equipped with Short floatplanes and Sopwith Schneiders and after delays caused by bad weather they set out into the Channel on May 11, 1915, to hunt for Zeppelin intruders.

The first air raid on the British mainland had been made on the night of January 19-20, the first of 20 in 1915. Zeppelin Nos. L 3 and L 4 dropped 24 50kg high explosive bombs on Great Yarmouth, Sheringham, King's Lynn and rural areas of Norfolk, killing four and injuring 16.

A raid on London planned for February 26 was cancelled due to bad weather – one Zeppelin, No. L 8, crashed near Ghent. A second four Zeppelin raid had been called off due to fog on March 17 and three more airships crashed before the month was out.

Ipswich was bombed on April 29-30 and Southend had been hit on May 9-10. While these attacks were not hugely successful in terms of material damage, they had a huge psychological effect. Most of the casualties were civilians and the airships were soon dubbed 'baby killers'.

Describing an attack later in the year, novelist D H Lawrence wrote: "Last night when we were coming home the guns broke out and there was a noise of bombs. Then we saw the Zeppelin above us, just ahead, amid a gleaming of clouds; high up, like a bright golden finger, quite small, among a fragile incandescence of clouds. And underneath it were splashes of fire as the shells fired from earth burst.

"Then there were flashes near the ground – and the shaking noise. It was like Milton – then there was war in heaven. But it was not angels. It was that small golden Zeppelin, like a long oval world, high up. It seemed as if the cosmic order were gone, as if there had come a new order, a new heavens above us; and as if the world in anger were trying to revoke it. Then the small long-ovate luminary, the new

The distinctive horseshoe fairing of the Sopwith Baby's engine – the main feature that usually distinguished it from the Schneider – can be seen beside this machine's pilot as he releases a carrier pigeon to send a report.

A Sopwith Baby fitted with Le Prieur rockets for anti-Zeppelin duties. The weapons were electrically discharged and extremely difficult to aim with any degree of accuracy. *DH/MG/Brooklands*

world in the heavens, disappeared again. I cannot get over it."

The Zeppelin menace had to be stopped and it was with this in mind that the small fleet set out on May 11. After a largely unproductive day, one of the airships was spotted at 5pm about 70 miles away from the fleet.

Efforts were immediately made to intercept it. A Schneider with wheels fitted to its floats was positioned on the flight deck of *HMS Ben-by-Chree* but its engine backfired and wrecked its starter gear so that the engine could not be restarted.

All three Schneiders from *HMS Engadine* were hoisted out and took off successfully but daylight was fading and only one returned. The second span into the sea and neither pilot nor aircraft were ever recovered. The third

was forced to ditch due to engine problems but both man and machine were rescued.

Another trio of Sopwiths, Type SSs based at Eastchurch for home defence, took off to intercept another Zeppelin reportedly flying over Margate on May 23, but they failed to find the target and were forced to fly home. On June 2, a Schneider carried by the light cruiser *HMS Arethusa* was launched at a third airship but its pilot mistook smoke from the *Arethusa* as a signal to return and the Zeppelin escaped unscathed.

Just over a month later, on July 4, a naval force including *HMS Engadine* and *HMS Riviera* was sent to carry out an aerial reconnaissance mission over the Ems river and Borkum island off the German coast close to the border with the Netherlands. A secondary

mission was to entice one or more Zeppelins into what was hoped would be a trap.

Five two-seater Short seaplanes were sent out for the recce mission but only one, piloted by Lieutenant H Stewart, was able to successfully carry it out. When Stewart returned to the fleet he found that it was being watched by no fewer than four airships.

The trap was sprung. The three brand new factory fresh Sopwith Schneiders on board Engadine, Nos. 3711, 3712 and 3714, were swiftly winched out and started up. Unfortunately, at this point the British became unstuck because one by one the Schneiders' floats broke up in the choppy water before they could get airborne. The Zeppelins drifted serenely away unmolested. This string of failures did very little to endear

A trio of Sopwith Type 807 Folder seaplanes were taken with the British fleet to the Dardanelles for reconnaissance operations. Extremes of heat, rough seas and the inherent fragility of the machines made them difficult and dangerous to operate. *DH/MG/Brooklands*

Rather than stick to the Sopwith drawings, contractor Fairey decided to create its own version of the Baby. The wings were entirely new, the tail was modified and so were the floats. By the time it appeared in 1917, it was outdated but still played an important role by performing anti-submarine duties.

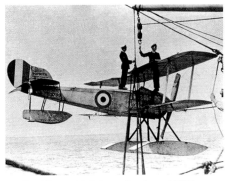

A Schneider, 3788, is brought aboard *HMS Empress*. The vessel conducted anti-submarine and reconnaissance patrols in the Mediterranean in 1916.

Battleship *HMS Irresistible* after it hit a mine and was abandoned by its crew on March 18, 1915 – the day of the disastrous main naval assault on the Dardanelles forts. None of the Sopwith floatplanes with the British fleet was serviceable enough to provide aerial reconnaissance on the day.

Sopwith seaplanes to the Admiralty. According to the official history of the air war's report on the July 4 fiasco: "An exceptional opportunity had been lost. Much had been risked to give the seaplanes their chance. Their repeated failures created a distrust of the Naval Air Service among many responsible naval commanders.

"Not until January of 1916 were any further combined operations against the German coast attempted."

The Schneiders' floats continued to be a serious problem. On July 15, Flight Lieutenant Vincent Nicholl of RNAS Great Yarmouth brought Schneider No. 1567, which had suffered slight damage to one float, in for a landing. On touching down the aircraft rolled over and crashed.

Nicholl later reported: "Machine was completely wrecked in salving. A perfect landing was made and sea was quite calm. It would seem to be a complete waste of money to continue flying these machines until the floats are strengthened."

A total of 37 tons of bombs were dropped on Britain in 1915, killing 181 people and injuring 455 more.

FROM SCHNEIDER TO BABY

From a less than auspicious beginning, over time, the Schneider was modified and improved. From about the beginning of 1916, the Schneider name was dropped and Baby was used instead. Ailerons were fitted instead of wing warping – where cables were used to twist the edges of the wings for turning – and an enlarged tailplane was fitted.

Both of these modifications were retrofitted to some Schneiders already in service. Some early Babies kept the Schneider's distinctive Gnome engine with its hooded cowling but later models had a more powerful 110hp Clerget 9Z engine which required an open-fronted horseshoe shaped cowl – completely changing the look of the aircraft's nose.

A variety of different weapons were fitted to both Schneiders and Babies – with the Baby's official payload consisting of 41lb of grenades and 48lb of Ranken darts as of March 1916. Both of these weapons were designed to be of use against Zeppelins. The darts were streamlined little bombs containing 1lb of explosives and were usually carried in packs of 24. The arsenal of a Baby in January 1917 was a Lewis gun, two sets of Ranken darts or one set of grenade dropping gear. Some were fitted out to carry Le Prieur rockets.

When production switched from Schneider to Baby, the work was contracted out to Blackburn, Fairey and Parnall because Sopwith itself was busy building three new types which will be detailed in subsequent chapters – the 1½ Strutter, the Pup and the

Mechanics at work on a Sopwith Baby. The Baby was not a difficult or complicated machine to maintain and as such survived in service far longer than many other Sopwith types.

A pair of Sopwith Schneider floatplanes. These machines – mounted on the deck of British submarine E-22 – were intended to be used as part of a rapid response force intended to intercept German Zeppelin raiders.

Another view of the Type 807 Folder. This example, No. 807, gave the type its name. It was shot up by enemy ground fire and damaged during flight testing before being cannibalised for parts during the Gallipoli campaign.

Sopwith Baby in flight in 1916.
DH/MG/Brooklands

Fire! A Baby unleashed its load of Le Prieur rockets. *DH/MG/Brooklands*

Triplane. Deliveries of Blackburn's Babies began in September 1916. They were based fairly rigidly on the original Sopwith design with few deviations. Fairey, which built its Babies at its Southampton works on the river Hamble, decided to modify the design.

The Fairey Hamble Baby's wings were of the company's own design and differed from those of their Blackburn or Sopwith siblings in having flaps that ran the full length of the rear spars on both upper and lower wings. The idea was to make it easier to take off.

The Baby was being called upon to carry an ever increasing amount of weight – a Lewis gun and its ammunition, a sea anchor, a carrier pigeon and emergency rations not to mention fuel and oil for two and a half hours' flying. Even with a more powerful engine, this was still a problem.

The new Fairey design resulted in delays and these grew even longer when a new type of float was added. The first Fairey Hamble Babies were not delivered until September of 1917 – a full year after Blackburn's first batch of Sopwith-type Babies. Parnall's first Babies, now based on the Fairey design rather than the original Sopwith one, arrived in mid-December 1917. By now, the war had moved on again. Technology had advanced and single-seat seaplanes were no longer required. Parnall was contracted to produce a

conversion kit for turning Baby seaplanes into landplanes – later to be known as Hamble Baby Converts. The company's final tranche of 74 aircraft were built as landplanes in any case. The Convert kit for retrospective conversion of seaplanes was really just a straight swap – floats were removed from the wide-track struts beneath the fuselage and wheels were attached with small skids.

After successive delays, the war was nearly over and most of the Hamble Baby Converts produced never saw active service. They were delivered straight into storage at Killingholme in Lincolnshire – the county's first aerodrome.

The original Babies, however, were used extensively if not entirely successfully. A mission on March 25, 1916, which involved two Babies, Nos. 8152 and 8153, launching from *HMS Vindex* to attack an airship base at Hoyer in the northernmost state of Germany, Schleswig-Holstein, ended in failure with No. 8153 being captured intact by the Germans.

During an attempt to draw out the German High Seas Fleet on May 4, 1916, 11 Babies were winched out of *Vindex* and *Engadine*.

Before they could get airborne, one capsized in a destroyer's wake, four suffered broken propellers and three suffered engine failure.

Three managed to get aloft. Then one of them clipped the radio aerial of the destroyer *HMS Goshawk* and span into the sea, killing its pilot. Another suffered a belated engine failure and came back down again. The last of the 11, No. 8179, reached the target but its pilot couldn't see it due to mist and was forced to turn around.

Babies were sent up on Zeppelin intercepting missions throughout the remainder of the year but without a single success to show for it. They were also used to drop bombs on German submarines in the Mediterranean and the Channel – though no subs were actually sunk.

When the war ended, many Schneiders and Babies were given or sold to other countries. At the end of 1915 however, while its seaplanes were struggling, Sopwith Aviation began work on three aircraft which would seal the company's reputation as a builder of cutting edge fighter aircraft. ∎

Two of these large Sopwith Type 860 floatplanes were sent to join the fleet in the Dardanelles but there wasn't enough room to assemble them to begin with and even when they were finally put together they were little used.

Chapter 5

Built for BATTLE
Sopwith 1½ Strutter

Sopwith's early aeroplane designs were showing their age by 1916 and with no end to the war in sight, it was time for something new. Dedicated war machines were needed and Sopwith came up with not one but three. The first of these was the 1½ Strutter.

H aving received some disturbing accounts of his machines' failures in the field, Tommy Sopwith decided that urgent action was required. He determined that he needed to hear first hand what pilots on the front line wanted from an aeroplane so he arranged to do just that.

In early June, 1915, he asked to be allowed to visit the British Expeditionary Force in France and permission was duly granted. Sopwith boarded a ship bound for Boulogne and on arrival he drove to the Royal Flying Corps' headquarters at St Omer on June 10.

He then toured a series of aerodromes for the remainder of that day and the following day. He spoke with the pilots and asked them about the mixed bag of British and French aircraft they were using – B.E.2cs, Moranes, Vickers Gunbuses, Avro 504As, Bristol Scouts and Caudrons. He made careful notes and shrewdly observed the performance of these 'rival' machines just as he had done during the military trials at Larkhill nearly three years earlier.

Back at Brooklands, he revealed his findings to test pilot Harry Hawker, works manager Fred Sigrist and the rest of his inner circle and work was begun on making fighting machines that would be an improvement on anything then available to British pilots.

First off the drawing board was the LCT 'Land Clerget Tractor', which first flew on December 12, 1915, followed in early 1916 by the Scout and then the Triplane in February.

The LCT owed part of its structure, particularly the 'W' shape of its central struts – the ones that attached the top wing to the fuselage close to the pilot's cockpit – to a one-off aircraft begun on December 7, 1914, at Sigrist's behest.

This machine utilised the basic framework of the Type 807 and sat to one side of the main production line at Kingston, being worked on slowly. It became known as the 'Sigrist Bus'. Rather than having a single top wing which went right across the aircraft, it had two separate top wings which met in the middle, necessitating the 'W' struts. It also had a fairing over its 80hp Gnome engine similar to that used on the Type SS 'Tabloid'. The Sigrist Bus was used experimentally for several months to investigate the effects of shifting an aircraft's centre of gravity and Harry Hawker set a new British altitude record on June 1 by flying it up to 18,393ft.

The LCT, though largely a new two-seater design, featured the 'W' shaped struts of the Sigrist Bus. To its early pilots, it appeared as though the outer struts of this arrangement ran from the upper wing to the sides of the fuselage near the cockpit only because they had been made too short to reach the lower wing – seeming to be only half a strut. And since the aircraft also had a single set of struts joining top and bottom wing on either side, it

Originally known simply as the LCT or Land Clerget Tractor, the 1½ Strutter got its nickname from the long struts that projected out from the sides of the fuselage to support the upper wing. This is a Mann, Egerton & Co-made example.

A modern day 1½ Strutter replica in flight. The Sopwith two-seater was the first British aircraft to enter service with a synchronised forward-firing machine gun. *TMWolf*

became known as the 1½ Strutter.

A single-seat bomber version of the LCT was also designed and the Admiralty ordered both – starting with an order for 150. The two-seater was designated Type 9400S or 9400L when fitted with a larger fuel tank for long range operations. The bomber became Type 9700. At the time of the 1½ Strutter's introduction, the War Office was still under the spell of the Royal Aircraft Factory and was slow to order it – preferring to crank out hundreds more horribly vulnerable B.E.2cs, ds and es.

The Admiralty had bought almost all of Sopwith's overall aeroplane production output up to this point but that was to change dramatically with the 1½ Strutter. Belatedly realising what a potent machine it was, the War Office put in its own order for what it referred to as the 'Sopwith two-seater'.

In the light of what came later, the 1½ Strutter may seem like just another delicate two seater observation aircraft but at the time it rivalled the capabilities of the very best single seater scouts – fighters – available.

It was also the first British production aircraft on the Western Front to feature a forward firing machine gun which could shoot through the propeller without shooting it off thanks to synchronisation gear. In addition, it had a Lewis gun fitted to a ring-mounting which was operated by the observer. It was the world's first true two seat fighter.

The 1½ Strutter had an adequate 110hp Clerget engine and newly designed independently sprung front wheels. Less favourably, it had its fuel tank mounted between the pilot and the observer which not only put both at risk in the event of a fire but also created a gulf between them which made communication at altitude more difficult. Other novelties included air brakes – handwheel operated panels on the trailing edge of the lower wings near the fuselage – and a large adjustable tailplane. Despite these features, it lacked manoeuvrability when compared with later machines.

In the bomber version, the rear cockpit was not fitted – in its place was equipment for carrying four 65lb bombs internally. These were stored horizontally and four bomb bay

In spite of its inherently fragile construction, the Sopwith 1½ Strutter had a reputation for being a tough and hard-wearing aeroplane. It was seemingly about to soak up damage and survive rough landings with relatively little damage – earning it the respect of its crews.

doors were fitted which opened automatically as soon as the mechanism to drop the bombs was engaged. They were then pulled shut by rubber bungee cords.

The first 50 machines off the production line were fighters and of the remainder, 31 were ordered to be built as bombers. Eleven of these were specially fitted out for carrying French 50kg 'Gros-Andreau' anilite bombs.

These nasty weapons were narrow and fitted with guide vanes externally. Inside were two receptacles of roughly equal size separated by a thin wall or 'cap'. The rearward one was sealed and filled with pressurised nitrogen peroxide plus a detonator. The forward one at the bomb's nose had a hole known as the 'eye' and through it passed a percussion pin which was operated by a release key.

This front section remained empty except for the percussion pin until takeoff, when it was filled with petrol. When the bomb was dropped, the release key twisted the pin and this punctured the cap mixing the two liquids to form an explosive which was either touched off by the detonator or, failing that, impact with the ground.

The problem was that the nitrogen peroxide often leaked and gave off an extremely poisonous gas that could cause loss of consciousness followed by damage to the stomach and intestines. This wasn't such a problem on the ground since the leaky bombs could be isolated but at altitude it could be fatal to the Type 9700's lone crewman.

Later on in its British production career, the aircraft was fitted with a more powerful 130hp

In flight, the 1½ Strutter presented an extremely clean and uncluttered profile.

Clerget engine. In addition to the bomber Strutters, a number of single-seat Home Defence versions were also built which had the forward cockpit faired over and which were flown from the rear cockpit instead.

Initially, the pilot was separated from his Vickers gun by a long stretch of fuselage, then the Vickers was removed entirely. One or sometimes two Lewis guns were mounted on the top gun instead.

OVER THE SOMME

The first production model Type 9400s were delivered in the spring of 1916 and the RNAS's 5 Wing at Dunkirk had a complete flight of them by the end of April. 5 Wing was set up as a long-range bombing outfit and for this purpose it operated Bréguet Vs and Caudron G.IVs. The 1½ Strutters were initially intended as bomber escorts, being the two-seater 'fighter' version, but later they were used as bombers themselves with bomb rails fitted beneath their lower wings.

It was a pair of 1½ Strutters serving with 5 Wing that became the first Sopwith aircraft involved in a dogfight when, during a patrol near Ostend at 14,000ft on July 9, 1916, their pilots spotted a small enemy formation flying below at 10,000ft.

The Sopwith pilots dived down to attack but after a short engagement the forward firing gun on one aircraft jammed and the observer's Lewis gun on the other did too.

Ahead of the massive Somme offensive the commander of the RFC, Major-General Hugh Trenchard, had been keen to get the new 1½ Strutters into front line service. The first RFC unit to receive the 1½ Strutter was 70 Squadron. It was a newly formed unit, sent to France on May 24, 1916, but by July 1, the first day of the Battle of the Somme, it had only received four Type 9400s and these had had to be diverted from RNAS depots since production could not keep pace with demand.

While most British 1½ Strutters were uniformly painted in PC10, a sort of brownish olive drab, the French frequently decorated theirs with bright colour schemes and symbols.

Even so, these four took off at 6am for a reconnaissance mission over Cambrai, beyond the battlefield to the north-east. Twenty-five minutes later all hell was let loose on the Somme. RFC pilot Cecil Lewis, who was flying above the battle's opening artillery barrage, later wrote: "It was the greatest bombardment of the war, the greatest in the history of the world.

"It was now a continuous vibration, as if Wotan, in some paroxysm of rage, were using the hollow world as a drum and under his beat the crust of it was shaking. Nothing could live under that rain of splintering steel."

The pilots of 70 Squadron flew over the closing stages of the barrage as they returned to base, landing at 7.20am. Ten minutes later, the big guns abruptly ceased firing. Mere minutes after that, the German soldiers who had been hiding in their deep dug-outs emerged to see wave after wave of British soldiers marching towards them in lines. They manned their machine guns and opened fire.

This great tragedy in British military history goes entirely unrecorded in 70 Squadron's official history which simply states: "Aeroplanes of 70 Squadron which left to reconnoitre Cambrai at 6am were back on their aerodrome an hour and 20 minutes later. They had met with no opposition and reported no unusual movements."

The 1½ Strutter was extremely highly regarded when it was first introduced because it could conduct long-distance patrols and reconnaissance while looking after itself in a fight should the need arise.

They were also useful as escorts to other long-ranged aircraft which lacked their own defensive armament. In fact, they were so highly valued that pilots went to great lengths to prevent their capture.

On August 7, 1916, Second Lieutenant Cecil William Blain, 19, from Hooton, Cheshire, was forced down in 1½ Strutter A380 over German territory near Walincourt, south of Cambrai. Realising that his advanced new aircraft was about to be captured, instead of landing safely he deliberately steered the machine into some trees and wrecked it.

Blain was taken prisoner but escaped and survived the war – only to die while test piloting Sopwith Camel C1588 at Martlesham Heath on January 22, 1919. The aircraft's port wing cracked at 450ft during level flight and it

This aircraft, A1089, was used for pilot training at the Central Flying School at Upavon. Even after its withdrawal from front line use, the 1½ Strutter remained in service as a training machine until the end of the war.

side-slipped into a crash from which there could be no escape.

At first, pilots spoke favourably of the 1½ Strutter but technological advances, not the least of which were made by Sopwith itself, soon put its abilities in the shade.

One pilot, William Sholto Douglas, who later became commander in chief of Fighter Command during the Second World War, wrote: "We found that our precious aircraft were much too slow when pitted against the new Albatros and Halberstadt scouts.

"The Sopwith 1½ Strutter was not a particularly easy aircraft to maintain, and there were a number of modifications that we had to make before the new machines could be used.

"After some hair-raising experiences we found that it was necessary for us, if we were to engage the enemy on anything approaching equal terms, to fly underneath his formations so as to lure him into attacking us; and then we would trust to the good shooting of our observers to pick off the Huns as they came diving down."

Eventually, the 1½ Strutter was operated by nine complete RFC squadrons, Nos. 37, 39, 43 (bomber), 44, 45 (bomber), 46, 70 (bomber), 78 and 143. While Sopwith itself constructed 146 1½ Strutters, an army of subcontractors produced many more.

The greatest among them was Lincoln-based Ruston, Proctor & Co, which turned out 350. The overall total built in Britain was around 1200.

FRENCH STRUTTERS

While the Sopwith 1½ Strutter was built in relatively large quantities in Britain, the French built and operated it on a truly gigantic scale. When the 1½ Strutter was seen in action over the Western Front, the French were impressed despite being deeply embarrassed that the British should have created a machine so manifestly superior to

Restored French-built Sopwith 1½ Strutter 1B2. The aeroplane now flies from the La-Ferté-Alais airfield. The French built nearly three times as many 1½ Strutters as the British. *Memorial Flight Association*

anything that their own industry could manage at the time.

The French authorities asked for details of the 1½ Strutter from Sopwith, arranged the delivery of some fully built examples from the RNAS and bought the rights to build it themselves under licence.

Tommy Sopwith swiftly set up an office for the Sopwith Aviation Company in Paris to coordinate the distribution of construction drawings to the seven French firms that were to build the machine – Amiot, Bessoneau, Darracq, Hanriot, Loiré et Oliver, REP and Sarazin Frères. Meanwhile, the French Army took delivery of several ex-RNAS 1½ Strutters and flight tested them.

The French proved to be difficult customers – the staff at the Sopwith Paris office had to deal with firms wanting to introduce a spate of modifications, which they duly made and then claimed their versions were superior to the original.

This may well have been true, primarily because the French tended to keep the best and most advanced engine designs for their own use before allowing the British build them under licence. Therefore, the French 1½ Strutters were various fitted with the 135hp Clerget 9Bb, the 135hp Le Rhone 9Jby or the 145hp Clerget 9Bc.

Three different versions were built, compared to the British two. They were known as the SOP 1A2, SOP 1B1 and SOP 1B2. The 1A2 stood for Type 1, artillery (as in spotting for), two-seater. The 1B1 stood for Type 1, bombardment, single-seater, and the 1B2 was a new two-seater bomber version exclusive to the French.

All these changes and variations from the original template meant that by the time French production of the 1½ Strutter began in early to mid-1917 the aircraft was already obsolete as a fighter. It was as a bomber, however, that the French found the aircraft to be of most use and they replaced their existing types with Sopwiths throughout the remainder of 1917.

A1914 was captured intact by the Germans and flown in their colours.

Naval 1½ Strutters were flown from the turrets of large warships – in this case *HMAS Australia*, an Indefatigable-class battlecruiser.

The seven French manufacturers churned 1½ Strutters out in huge numbers. So huge, in fact, that it may never be known precisely how many the French made. Estimates vary between 4200 and 4500 and 60 squadrons were still operating the type when the war ended in 1918.

The French flew their 1½ Strutters over the Western Front and in Italy and 514 examples were bought by the Americans in spring 1918. The British had suffered heavy losses through combat and crashes and when the Admiralty decided it needed 1½ Strutters for shipboard duties in 1918 it ended up buying some French-built machines to make up the necessary numbers.

SHIP STRUTTER

Late in the war, 1½ Strutters took on a new role with the Royal Navy – spotting for naval artillery. A modified version, the Ship Strutter

was developed for launch from capital ships.

These aircraft had their Vickers guns and synchronisation gear removed. Wireless sets and Aldis signalling lamps were then fitted. One was first flown from a battle cruiser, the *HMAS Australia*, on April 4, 1918.

The vessel had a wooden launch platform fitted over its Q turret atop which the aircraft was positioned along with 'quick release' equipment – effectively a safety line. When the Ship Strutter was to be launched, the ship had to speed up and angle itself at about 30° to the wind, with the turret rotated to face directly into the wind. Men held on to the lower wings, clamps were removed from the aircraft's control surfaces and the quick release line was attached. The tail was kept elevated at 2ft on a special trolley. The pilot then started his engine and gradually built up the revs. At maximum power, he had to wave his hand at

which point the men let go of the wings and stood clear. At another signal, the quick release line was given a sharp tug, disengaging it. The Strutter then hopefully took off – using every inch of the 30ft of decking available to do so.

The aircraft would then spot for the vessel's big guns. Battleships and battle cruisers began to carry two aircraft each – a two-seat reconnaissance aircraft on a forward turret platform and a single-seat fighter on a rear turret. By the war's end, the Grand Fleet had more than 100 aircraft launchable from turret platforms. Nearly 40 of these were 1½ Strutters.

A number of 1½ Strutters were also flown from aircraft carriers – HMS Furious carried 14. These had either the usual wheeled undercarriage or a set of specially designed.

After the war, around 170 1½ Strutters remained in service with the RAF, including those carried by naval vessels.

But despite the numbers produced on both sides of the English Channel, the 1½ Strutter was not destined to be remembered as Sopwith's finest hour. The next machine to leave the firm's drawing boards at Kingston has a claim to more enduring fame – the Pup. ■

Sopwith 1½ Strutter A1924 was operated in France by the Royal Flying Corps' 70 Squadron in mid-1916 before the machine was wrecked in October of that year.

This 1½ Strutter replica located at the Military Aviation Museum, Virginia Beach, California, sports a French colour scheme. *Kurt Fanus*

The Germans used cut grass to camouflage this French Sopwith 1B1 after it was forced down on their side of the lines. The idea was to prevent it from being spotted and destroyed by other Allied aircraft.

Strutter N5093 probably pictured at Brooklands during testing.

THE SOPWITH 1½ STRUTTER ACE

The highest scoring Sopwith 1½ Strutter pilot by far was Geoffrey Hornblower Cock of Shrewsbury, Shropshire, who joined the 28th Battalion of The Artists Rifles Officers Training Corps in December 1915 aged 19.

He transferred to a pilot training unit, 25 Squadron of the Royal Flying Corps, in June 1916, joined 45 Squadron in September and it moved to France on October 14, 1916.

Cock's first two kills were made within minutes of one another at around 10.30am on April 6, 1917, while flying Sopwith 1½ Strutter A1075 near Lille. He first destroyed an Albatros D.III before hitting another until it fell from the sky 'out of control'.

His next victories were made in a different 1½ Strutter, A8260, on May 7. This time it was Siemens-Schuckert D.I – a German copy of the French Nieuport 17 – which he sent down out of control at 6.30pm.

A pair of D.IIIs followed on May 9 at 4.50pm and 5pm and he shot down still more on May 20, 27 and 28. On June 16 he downed an Abatros D.V and more D.IIIs followed on July 6, 7 and 13.

In total, Cock shot down 13 German aircraft during 97 sorties before being shot down himself over Warneton on July 22, 1917, by Hauptmann Wilhelm Reinhard of Jasta 11. Moments earlier he had shot up another Albatros D.III and set it on fire to claim his 13th and final kill.

At this time he was the last survivor of the 45 Squadron pilots who had gone to France nine months earlier. He was a prisoner of war until December 1918.

Four days after being shot down Cock, by now a temporary second lieutenant, was awarded the Military Cross. His citation read: "For conspicuous gallantry and devotion to duty. On many occasions he showed great courage and determination in attacking and destroying hostile aircraft, and in dispersing hostile troops from a low altitude. His skills as a formation leader has set a fine example to the other pilots of his squadron."

SOPWITH 1½ STRUTTER IN ACTION

An extract from Into the Blue by Norman Macmillan, published by Jarrolds Publishing:

On May 7, one of our two-seater Sopwiths hung above the lines on a single machine defensive patrol. The machine had been patrolling for an hour and a half and the pilot and observer were both somewhat bored.

They had still half an hour to stay on the lines. Suddenly they spotted the white Archie bursts of British anti-aircraft shells. The old Sopwith turned slowly, as was her nature, towards the white puffs. She climbed wearily upwards.

Near Dickeybusch the pilot and observer spotted the enemy, two Huns approaching our lines, just above the shell bursts.

The Sopwith drew nearer. Her fixed front gun was useless. The Huns were too high. The pilot flew underneath the Huns to enable his observer-gunner to open fire with the rear gun, which could fire upwards. He trusted to the Archie gunners to cease firing.

It may have been that our Archie gunners considered themselves superior to Sopwith One-and-a-half Strutters in action against the enemy. In any case they did not cease fire, and their shells burst below the Huns and right on the level of the old two-seater. Unheeding, the Sopwith carried on with the job in hand.

The observer sighted on one of the Huns 200ft above him on his left. As the first few rounds rattled out above his head from the upturned muzzle of the Lewis gun the pilot held his bus steady to enable the observer to shoot straight.

After six bursts of fire the Lewis gun jammed. While the observer was engaged in clearing the jam, he felt the old bus wobble. He had just time to see the Hun fall out of control when their own machine turned over sideways.

The pilot felt the plane shudder and almost at the same instant a shell burst white overhead. The plane went out of control and he heard the observer scream: "God! Look at our tail."

The pilot looked over his shoulder. The tail plane was crumpled like a half-closed concertina, where the British shell had smashed it in its passage. A second shell hit their machine as it turned over. It passed clean through the fuselage halfway between the observer and the rudder.

It carried away what little control the first shell had left unharmed and burst a couple of hundred feet above them.

The pilot pulled at his elevator control, but nothing happened. The nose of the machine dropped. She gathered more and more speed. The pilot shut off his engine. The observer buried his head in his cockpit. The pilot could do no more. Shot down by their own artillery they were falling earthward, unhurt, in a wrecked machine.

Gradually the attitude of the plane changed. The uncontrolled machine raised her nose

higher and still higher. The earth disappeared. She hung on her back, upside down. The two men in her held on for dear life. They almost fell out. They shuddered at the thought of that 9000ft fall to earth.

The bus dropped her nose. The earth came into view again. She dived and flattened out. Neither of her occupants had looped before. It was their first loop. The pilot could do nothing.

He was impotent, a mere pawn in the game of destiny, his life and his observer's cradled in the cockpit of chance.

She looped again of her own accord. The two clung on while the nose rose above the horizon and steered an erratic course across blue sky and cloud in a dizzy circle. They held on more grimly still while she hung upon her back, both suspended upside down 8000ft above the earth.

A bang behind them sent a tremor down their spines. They thought the fuselage had broken and that in the next instant they would hurtle downward in the final plunge to earth. And in that instant they found time to curse the Archie gunner who had not ceased fire.

But the miraculous happened. The fuselage had not failed. The crash was caused by the observer's extra drums of ammunition falling from their boxes, and, as the bus came jerkily out of the loop, they rolled up to the tail end of the fuselage.

The drums weighted and balanced the aeroplane, for the tail of an aeroplane in normal flight carries a downward load. The wild plunge and loop changed to a dive, zoom and stall, gentle by comparison.

For 8000ft they stalled downwards. In the pilot's somewhat incoherent story he said that the observer was unconscious; at another that he cursed and swore; again, that he prayed. The pilot himself sat in his seat temporarily bereft of coherent thought. There was nothing to be done. In a matter of minutes he would either be dead or alive. And there was nothing he could do.

Would that last dive carry them to earth like a stone? Would they be dashed to pieces unable to prevent the crash? Or would the final stall occur so low that they might almost make a landing and crash lightly?

Into the Blue author Captain Norman Macmillan.

It is terrible to have one's life tossed thus into the lap of chance. The pilot's brain was numbed by the awfulness of his own impotence. Their suspense was nearly over. The ground was very close. The pilot saw the gunners running away from his falling plane. He watched the ground with eyes unnaturally dilated. Here was the ending.

At 30ft the plane flattened out and zoomed. It hung in the stall for a moment at 60ft, then turned slowly over. Its nose went down... the earth rushed up. She headed straight for a disused gun-pit. The dive carried her nose right into it while her outspread wings struck the ground on either side.

The wings broke back, but held at the roots. The nose of the plane, buried in the gun-pit, rested gently on the bottom. The two men got out. Physically they were unhurt, but mentally they were both wrecks.

No man can go through a time like that unscathed, and although they put up a gallant effort to fly again with the squadron their nerves were too badly strained and they returned to England. The Hun that fell before them to the observer's gun dropped in the enemy lines. Its fall was watched by several people who saw the combat, but its fate was never known. Whether it, too, had the luck of the Sopwith we shall never know.

Above: RNAS Sopwith 1½ Strutter in flight. The type served with both the RNAS and the RFC.

Above right: The sheer distance between the pilot and observer aboard a 1½ Strutter could make communication difficult, particularly above the general din of open cockpits.

Right: At least two 1½ Strutters were adapted as 'Comics' for Home Defence duties with 78 (HD) Squadron. One of them, B762, is pictured at Martlesham Heath in 1917. Its forward cockpit was faired over and the pilot's controls were transferred to the rear cockpit instead.

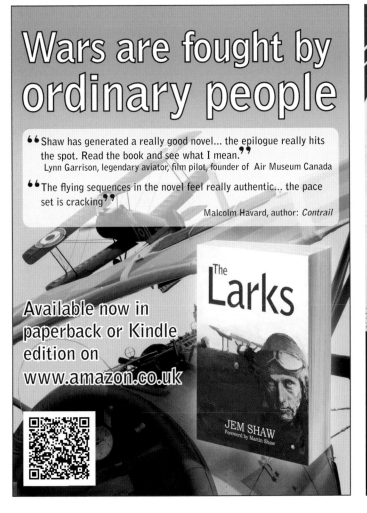

Chapter 6

LEARNING THE ROPES
Pilots, training and crashes

From gentleman aviator to young veteran of the trenches, the pilots of the Royal Flying Corps and later the Royal Air Force faced dangers and endured hardships that often had little to do with enemy action. The arctic cold of flying at altitude, the inherent unreliability of early aeroplanes and the fear of being burned alive meant a transfer to the RFC wasn't exactly a cushy option.

Aerial warfare was in its infancy when the First World War began in 1914 – just six years after the first powered flight in Britain. The aircraft pilots flew, Sopwith machines included, were flimsy, unreliable and open to the elements.

The first military aviators were gentlemen flyers, volunteers who had learned to fly at one of the schools based at Brooklands and elsewhere at their own expense. The cost of around £75, or £7300 in today's money, meant flyers tended to be well off and often well connected.

Officialdom was against them however. The War Office largely regarded the Royal Flying Corps as a unit of artillery spotters and map makers and training pilots for these tasks was not a high priority. Just 200 pilots were being trained at any one time even by 1915.

By 1917 however, they were being recruited and trained on a much greater scale – and with an average age of 20. Potential pilots, many of whom had transferred from front line infantry units, were given a rigorous medical examination to assess their ability to endure the rigors of high altitude flying. The candidate had to hold his breath for 45 seconds and then sit in a chair mounted on a turntable which was then rotated 10 times in 20 seconds. The medical failure rate was an acceptable 12%.

Assuming a pass, the pilot was then sent to a barracks where he underwent physical training and basic drill before being moved on to study at one of the two Schools of Aeronautics – one based in Reading and the other in Oxford. Here he was given a thorough and wide-ranging education in everything from map reading to the mechanics of aero engines, electricity, magnetism, codes and even meteorology, since understanding the weather was crucial to successful flying.

The final stage of training took place at the Central Flying School at Upavon in Wiltshire. Cadets took to the air in slow and steady machines which, in the early part

Sopwith Pup B5357 was one of numerous machines crashed during flight training with 23rd Training Wing, South Carlton, Lincolnshire. *Phil Curme*

An Avro 504K and Pup B5256 had an unfortunate coming together – with the former machine coming off worst at South Carlton. *Phil Curme*

Pups that crashed during pilot training were not necessarily wrecked beyond repair. *Phil Curme*

An American examines the wreckage of Sopwith Camel B7301, also at South Carlton. *Phil Curme*

Balloonists who went up slung beneath a large bag of gas to observe enemy movements were usually attached to a parachute. The men who flew in aeroplanes enjoyed no such luxury. There has never been a definitive answer as to why this was the case. Broadly, there was simply no support for the idea at the highest levels of the RFC or the RNAS.

of the war, meant Maurice Farman MF.11 Shorthorns and MF.7 Longhorns. Later in the war, more advanced types were used, such as the highly successful two-seater Avro 504k – which was produced in huge numbers for this purpose, having been retired from a front line combat career fairly early on.

Once flight training had been completed, the pilot could then finally be posted to serve with a squadron. Getting to this stage was an achievement in itself. In 1917 an official memorandum estimated that of the 6000 pilots being trained, about 1200 would not survive to complete the course since pilots only had a 10% chance of surviving a crash – and it was frighteningly easy to crash with inexperienced instructors and unreliable aircraft.

A staggering 8000 would-be pilots died while training during the course of the war.

Flying an early aircraft under any circumstances placed the pilot's body under immense stress. Just sitting behind a Clerget engine, for example, was as noisy as sitting next to a road drill and it gave off constant fumes and the smell of burnt castor oil since there was no exhaust pipe. It was reported by some pilots that the constant exposure to castor oil – also a medicinal laxative – had other even less pleasant side effects.

Above an altitude of about 10,000ft it became very cold and difficult to breathe. At 20,000ft the temperature was about –43ºC. Fortunately, sitting behind the engine meant some of its heat radiated into the cockpit to provide a measure of warmth against the bitter chill. This was not the case in 'pusher'

types with the engine to the rear however.

Prolonged exposure to extremely low temperatures affected the pilots' mental as well as their physical wellbeing and many reported feelings of detachment and depression. This situation was not helped by the oxygen starvation which also accompanied high altitude flying.

The petrol tank feeding the engine was usually positioned behind the pilot and it didn't take much to ignite it – turning the whole aircraft into a ball of flames from which there could be no escape. Some pilots kept a service revolver in the cockpit to give themselves a quicker end in the event of their machine catching fire.

No form of parachute was ever issued to pilots or observers of aeroplanes even though the crews of observation balloons had them

The Maurice Farman Longhorn was used extensively as a training mount for British pilots. Its name is derived from the long curving skids that curl up at the front.

and used them effectively on numerous occasions when attacked by enemy aircraft.

Pilots' lives were made no easier by their weaponry either. The main weapon of choice for Sopwith machines throughout the war was the Vickers. Belt-fed, it could fire up to 600 rounds per minute without having to be reloaded but few front line aircraft could carry more than about 700 rounds due to their weight and they therefore had to be used sparingly.

While there are numerous examples of Vickers guns being fired for extended periods without jamming, conditions on the ground differed greatly from those in the air. When subjected to very low temperatures, the Vickers tended to jam with alarming frequency. Rounds being loaded too far or not quite far enough into the belt feed was also a prime culprit for guns jamming in the middle of a dogfight.

In some cases, the Vickers guns were found to have been manufactured to incorrect tolerances – which meant their working parts fitted together too tightly. When the guns became hot and the metal expanded, they jammed. Mechanics gradually learned to use an abrasive to make them fit together less tightly and a new type of oil with a lower freezing point was available from the spring of 1917. This significantly reduced the number of jams experienced.

The other type of machine gun frequently fitted to Sopwith machines was the Lewis. They proved to be more reliable than the Vickers but even with a double capacity drum they had to be reloaded after every 97 rounds. Changing the drum on a Lewis gun was tricky – particularly if you were in the middle of a fight with enemy aircraft – since it required two hands. The gun itself weighed 27lb too, which made it difficult to shift while simultaneously flying an aeroplane one-handed.

Late in the war, the standard 0.303 Mark VII rifle cartridge fired from the Vickers machine gun was being used in tremendous quantities – beyond anything that Britain's existing factories could manage alone. Therefore, the work was outsourced to numerous new factories both at home and abroad.

In some cases, the quality of cartridges being manufactured at these facilities left a lot

A mock-up demonstrating the principle of synchronising or 'interrupter' gear designed to prevent a pilot shooting his own propeller off while firing through it. *49 Sqn Assn*

Royal Flying Corps aircrew are taught the basics of firing a machine gun. Learning how to clear a blockage was as important as knowing how to shoot straight.

to be desired. The strength of the cordite charge they contained could vary significantly and sometimes the percussion caps of these cartridges would simply fail to ignite it. Sometimes cartridges were not completely round and would not fit easily into the gun they were intended for and pilots were obliged to carry a wooden mallet in their cockpit to help them remove jammed casings.

Sometimes cases, though round, were too thin and split into pieces before they could be successfully ejected from the gun. The next round would then be forced in on top of the fragments and no amount of mallet work could clear the resulting mess – only armourers on the ground with specialist tools could extract it.

Pilots who had experienced this problem in the middle of a dogfight, if they survived would often turn to individually pre-selecting their ammunition before their next flight.

FIGHTING TACTICS

Under sudden attack from a previously unseen enemy, presuming they were not killed outright by the first salvo, the pilots of late-war single-seat fighters could often save themselves by immediately applying some rudder, moving the joystick and throttling into a steep diving turn.

Those flying slow and highly stable two-seat observation planes had no such opportunity and had to rely on the fast reflexes of their observer, assuming they survived the first salvo, to swing their gun round and fight off the attacker.

On the other hand, the best way to attack a high-flying two-seater was from behind and below, in their blind spot. One tactic was to give the observer a target to shoot at – a fighter flying a reasonably safe distance away –

while a second approached it below and moved in for the kill.

Lone RFC pilots attacking two-seaters were advised to approach and attack from below and then overshoot the target slightly and turn away, still below, so that the observer's gun would be blocked by the lower wing of his own aircraft as the pilot turned and tried to bring it to bear. A turn would then bring the RFC pilot's machine back behind and beneath the enemy for another go.

The best attacking distance was about 100ft. Given the opportunity, the optimum position for an attack was from behind the target with the sun behind you. This took time to set up and towards the end of the war, observers

experimented with using mirrors to dazzle attackers at the critical moment.

Learning how to spot an enemy aircraft – often appearing as no more than a tiny speck moments before an attack – was a skill that the top pilots picked up early on. There were many accounts of novices who, during attacks on enemy formations, were at a loss to understand what all the fuss was about and what their more experienced comrades were firing at.

Clouds could be both a vital aid and a deadly hindrance. Lost in a bank of dense cloud, perhaps hiding from an attacker, it was very easy to become disorientated and lose all sense of direction. Under these circumstances,

An RAF training poster from 1918 warns pilots to beware of the 'Hun in the sun'. In reality, pilots were almost as likely to be killed in an accident or due to mechanical failure.

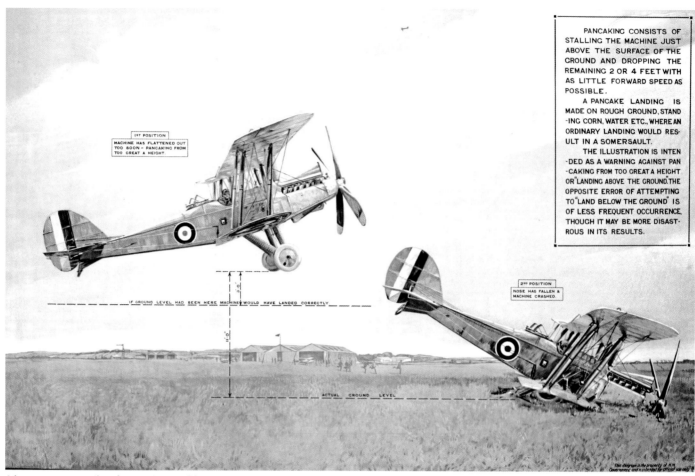

A lesson to young pilots from a First World War instructional poster about 'pancaking'. Aircraft of the day were supremely unforgiving in the hands of a novice. Relatively minor mistakes could result in serious injury or death.

collisions with other aircraft or the ground were common. Conversely, a cloud could provide useful cover when approaching an enemy who had not yet detected your presence.

The aircraft themselves were a hindrance to effective dogfighting. Overstressing your machine's airframe by making a sudden steep dive or pulling a loop that was just a little too tight could have fatal consequences. Engine failures were common and pilots were warned never to attempt a turn with a dying engine – even if the airfield was close at hand. The advice was: "In case of engine failure, don't turn back – put her nose down at once and make some sort of landing ahead."

Similarly, it was frighteningly easy to stall your aeroplane's engine while attempting to land, resulting in a 'pancake' where the machine dropped to the ground with very little forward speed. This was fine from three or four feet but any higher and the machine could be wrecked. In fact, 'pancaking' was advised as the best way to land on rough ground or a body of water since landing in the usual way could easily result in the aeroplane's wheels hitting an obstruction, causing it to flip over onto its back.

FLYING IN FEAR

Any successful fighter pilot of the First World War had seen his own worst nightmare played out right in front of him – an aeroplane shot down in flames and a swirl of black smoke.

If he was very successful, he saw this scene again and again. Combat took place at relatively low speeds and close proximity so pilots often had a ringside seat when an aircraft was shot down and its pilot killed.

When the crew of a burning machine realised the full horror of their situation, they often reacted in ways that unnerved those who witnessed their death – some tried to beat out the flames with their gloved hands, others got to their feet in the cockpit while screaming and swearing, still others simply jumped into the air 10,000ft up with their

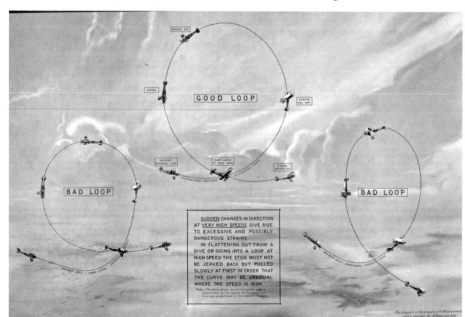

Young pilots joining the Royal Flying Corps and later the RAF were often initially dazzled by the mere idea of flying and struggled to grasp the disciplines needed for flying both safely and effectively. Early aeroplanes had to be flown within their structural limits, as this contemporary poster points out.

A class of would-be RFC pilots are shown a training model of a single seat scout. About one in five pilots was killed during training.

Many of the RFC's pilots learned how to fly in a Maurice Farman MF.11 Shorthorn or an MF.7 Longhorn. This is a Shorthorn.

AN UNFORESEEN DANGER

The aircraft flown throughout the war were relatively fragile and their structure could come apart due to overzealous manoeuvring, critical wires or structural sections being severed in combat or just being left out in the damp for too long.

There were warning signs to watch out for – weakened wings might begin to flap around before coming apart or there might be severe vibrations. Every now and again though, an aeroplane would completely and instantly disintegrate. It could be flying in formation one minute and become a cloud of flying splinters and falling debris the next.

Australian pilot Arthur Henry 'Harry' Cobby saw this happen: "There was no black smoke, no flame and no explosion; just hundreds of tiny pieces and three large objects where seconds before there had been an aeroplane. The three large objects were the engine, the fuel tank and the pilot."

Another pilot who had recently witnessed the same bizarre occurrence was later flying a patrol when he noticed a small black dot in the air ahead of him. It grew with frightening speed and the pilot dived his machine just in time to see a high calibre artillery shell pass low overhead.

The fuses of artillery shells were typically set to detonate after hitting something solid – and the wood and canvas structure of an aeroplane failed to qualify. Therefore, the shell would simply pass through, annihilating the flying machine in the process.

On April 7, 1918, a shell is believed to have hit the engine block of an S.E.5 flown by Captain Guy Borthwick Moore, a 1 Squadron ace with 10 'kills', and detonated. The resulting explosion turned Moore's machine into a huge cloud of tiny particles which then gently fell back to earth. Eyewitnesses, the pilots who had been flying alongside, said there were no recognisable sections of aircraft left and nothing of Moore's body was ever found.

arms spread and their clothing wreathed in the fires of burning gasoline.

Many carried a service revolver in the cockpit which was ostensibly for self-defence if they happened to come down behind the German front lines. In reality, the six-shot weapon could be used to put an end to the horrendous suffering caused by being burned to death. Experienced pilots had nicknames for petrol – the Orange Death, Witches Water, Hell-brew or the Infernal Liquid.

A few pilots, those who kept a cool head and had nerves of steel, attempted to extinguish their burning machine by putting it into a steep dive or land it despite its condition. While this worked occasionally, it was nevertheless a desperate last resort.

Even when there was no fire, serious damage to the aircraft or its engine could be equally fatal – the pilot having no means of escape.

In his book Sagittarius Rising, RFC pilot Cecil Lewis wrote of a fellow flyer: "Roberts was a crack pilot, and if human skill could have got that machine out, he would have done it. His elevators and ailerons were still intact, and by shutting off his engine he almost managed to avert disaster – but not quite.

> *"He could not stop the machine spinning; but he could stop it going into a vertical diving spin."*

"He could not stop the machine spinning; but he could stop it going into a vertical diving spin. He tried every combination of elevator and bank. No good. The machine went on slowly spinning, round and round

and round, all the way down from 8000ft to the ground. It took about five minutes. He and his observer were sitting there, waiting for death, for that time.

"The machine fell just this side of the lines. They say a man in the trenches heard shouts, as it might have been for help, come from the machine just before it struck the ground and smashed to a pile of wreckage.

"The observer was killed, for the fuselage broke in half; but Roberts escaped. He was badly smashed up, but breathing. They got him on to a stretcher and sent him down to hospital. He had been out all through the Somme battle without leave, his nerves were right on the edge, and we heard, with what truth I never knew, that this fearful experience put him out of his mind.

"As far as we were concerned he was gone – the dead or wounded never came back to us – and in the swiftly changing pattern of the days we forgot him." ■

Chapter 7

The Fokker
SCOURGE
Early German air superiority

The rapid development of Sopwith's 1½ Strutter, Pup and Triplane was necessitated by the introduction of a German aeroplane fitted with revolutionary technology in the summer of 1915. The Fokker E.I was a simple but deadly machine that swept the RFC's aircraft from the skies. In their slow, stable observation platforms, Britain's pilots were being "murdered rather than killed", spurring Sopwith into action.

During the earliest stages of the war in the air, pilots and observers had fired on enemy machines with pistols and rifles, but within months consideration was being given to more effective armament.

The first aeroplanes to be successfully fitted with weapons were British and French –

among them the Vickers FB5 'Gun Bus' pusher, which had a .303 Vickers machine gun mounted in the nose, and the French Morane-Saulnier L and N.

The latter both had a propeller at the front and a machine gun mounted behind it but no synchronisation gear. Instead, the propeller blades were fitted with bullet deflecting metal

wedges to stop them being shot off – with varying degrees of success.

The Germans were very concerned about these developments and attempted to combat the Allies' armed machines by fitting machine guns to two-seaters and using large twin-engined aircraft where having an engine on each wing meant there was nothing in the way

It looked like a throwback to the flimsy machines that were being flown before the Great War began but its armament was where its genius lay. For the first time, a fighter could fire effectively through its propeller without shooting the blades off. The example pictured here is a replica built in the US in 1981.

Inventive French airman Roland Garros fitted his Morane Saulnier L with metal wedges on the back of its propeller blades so he could fire his machine gun directly through them without any form of synchronising gear. Using this system he became the first man to shoot down an enemy machine while firing directly ahead through a propeller.

Roland Garros in his Morane Saulnier L with propeller-mounted bullet-deflecting wedges clearly visible. The capture of Garros's aeroplane prompted the German authorities to seek their own means of firing safely through a moving propeller – resulting in the Fokker Eindecker and the infamous Fokker Scourge.

of the nose-mounted gun. Neither solution was very satisfactory but then came a breakthrough in April 1915.

Dutch aircraft manufacturer Anthony Fokker's engineers had been working for months on a mechanical system to synchronise the rotation of a propeller with the trigger action of a machine gun and it was almost ready when a French Morane-Saulnier L fitted with propeller wedges was captured.

It had been flown by Roland Garros, the first man to shoot down another aeroplane using a machine gun that fired through a propeller. Garros, who had shot down three German machines using his Type L, suffered a blockage in his fuel system and was forced to land behind enemy lines. He tried to burn his machine but the machine gun and propeller survived.

The German authorities, realising what they had, immediately asked a number of aircraft manufacturers to copy it. Fokker then produced his firm's synchronisation gear – known as the Stangensteuerung or 'push rod controller'. It was fitted to the most suitable Fokker type at the time, the M.5K, to become the prototype for a new machine, the E.I or 'Eindecker'.

Fokker demonstrated the E.I to German fighter pilots during May and June 1915 and it was soon being issued to squadrons in ones and twos as an escort for their reconnaissance machines. Kurt Wintgens was the first to score a victory in the Eindecker – turning the tables on the Allies by forcing down Morane-Saulnier Ls on July 1 and July 4. Neither of these was counted as a 'kill' since the machines had not been unequivocally destroyed but on July 15 he blew a third Type L out of the sky.

By the end of the month there were 15 Eindeckers in service. On August 1, at 5am, B.E.2c aeroplanes of the RFC's 2 Squadron bombed the base of Feldflieger Abeilung (Field Flying Company) 62's base. This woke

up the unit's pilots including Oswald Boelcke and Max Immelmann. Both ran to their machines and took off in pursuit of the British raiders. Boelcke's gun jammed and he had to turn back but Immelmann caught up with the attackers.

He selected a target, which was unarmed, and after 10 minutes of manoeuvring succeeded in riddling it with bullets, hitting the pilot in the arm and forcing him down. This was the beginning of the Fokker Scourge.

Thereafter, Eindecker pilots began to shoot down British and French machines with alarming regularity. The total number of Allied machines shot down between the start of August and the end of the year was just 28 but there was a growing perception that the aeroplanes being flown by the French air force and the RFC were uniformly inferior to this menacing new enemy weapon.

The first month of 1916 saw another 13 Allied machines shot down by Eindeckers, most of them French, a further 20 followed in February. Unknown to the Allies, most of these were actually shot down by a handful of experienced German aces but the psychological effect was devastating.

Some became convinced that the Eindecker was unstoppable and morale among Allied airmen – which was on a knife edge in any case, given the other difficulties they had to contend with – dipped dramatically.

The B.E.2c, which was being produced in huge numbers and sent to the front to replace losses, was an extremely stable aeroplane which could practically fly itself given the right conditions. This made it perfect for taking aerial photographs or drawing maps as a reconnaissance platform – its intended purpose – but very slow and difficult to manoeuvre since it had a natural tendency to want to fly in a straight and level line.

As the casualties mounted, the British began to fly in larger formations and B.E.2cs that had previously been flown without an observer to save weight for more fuel or a bomb load now had a full crew. Although the Eindecker was, in reality, a difficult and fragile machine to fly, British pilots felt acutely vulnerable in their B.E.2cs and desperately hoped for new aeroplanes that would give

The Royal Aircraft Factory B.E.2c was easy meat for the Fokker Eindecker. It was slow and extremely stable – which made it ideal as an observer's platform but useless in air-to-air combat.

The fate of many Fokker E.IIIs – particularly once the Allies discovered that they were hardly the all-powerful machines they had once seemed to be.

German pilot Kurt Wintgens began the 'Fokker Scourge' by becoming the first Eindecker pilot to destroy an Allied machine.

them a new edge over the Germans. For their part, the Germans became paranoid that their own 'edge' would be revealed if an Eindecker happened to be captured, so patrols behind the Allies' lines were forbidden.

This meant British pilots were sent on 'offensive patrols' over enemy territory to look for them – a policy that did nothing to ease pilots' sense of foreboding.

BEATING THE EINDECKER

Ahead of the Battle of Verdun, the fear generated by the Eindecker had given the Germans air superiority. As a result, German preparations for their attack on February 21, codenamed Unternehmen Gericht or 'Operation Judgement', were largely carried out without any overflights from French

reconnaissance machines. The battle proved to be one of the costliest of the war for both sides with up to half a million casualties each; and as it progressed, the French introduced a machine that would break the Germans' aerial blockade – the Nieuport 11.

While it still lacked synchronisation gear, it was simply better than the Eindecker in every other respect. It could do 97mph to the Fokker's 81mph, its maximum range was 205 miles to 123 and it took 15 minutes to reach 10,000ft compared to the Fokker's leisurely 20 minutes to just 6500ft. The machine gun aiming problem was overcome by mounting its single Hotchkiss or Lewis gun in a fixed forward firing position on the top wing.

Where the Eindeckers were being deployed in dribs and drabs, officially as escorts for

reconnaissance machines, the Nieuport 11 was sent into battle en masse in dedicated fighter squadrons known as escadrilles de chasse. The Fokker and its pilots, even the aces, simply could not compete and the French had succeeded in winning back air superiority by the end of the Battle of Verdun in December 1916.

The British change in tactics of flying in larger groups also paid off, as had the introduction of the F.E.2b pusher to the RFC's ranks. On its own, the F.E.2b was a more even

Building the fearsome Fokker Eindecker. The most common model was the E.III – although its reputation far outstripped its actual combat effectiveness.

The 'father of air fighting tactics' Oswald Boelcke was among the first to fly the Fokker Eindecker.

Max Immelmann, another of the small cadre of German pilots responsible for the 'Fokker Scourge', was also Germany's first fighter ace.

MP Noel Pemberton Billing claimed that the Royal Aircraft Factory-built machines of the RFC were seen by their pilots as 'Fokker fodder'. He championed the cause of private manufacturers such as Sopwith. And himself.

match for the Eindecker, being slower and less manoeuvrable than the Nieuport 11, but in formations where it outnumbered its German opponents it was usually the clear winner. The Airco DH.2 began to arrive in numbers in February 1916, another pusher that trumped the Eindecker on performance, and the RFC also began to use the Nieuport 11 itself.

In April 1916, an Eindecker E.III landed at a British aerodrome by mistake and it was soon discovered, through test flights, that it was far less effective than many had previously believed. Suddenly fears of the Fokker Scourge evaporated.

That same month, the Sopwith 1½ Strutter entered service – a machine that was vastly superior to the Eindecker. It could fly at 100mph – 13mph faster than the Eindecker – its service ceiling was about 15,000ft compared to 11,900ft and it could stay airborne for four hours, compared to just an hour and a half.

The Germans were forced to accept that they were once again the underdogs and new aeroplane types from Fokker and Halberstadt were rushed into production to combat the Nieuport, Airco and Sopwith types.

Tactics changed too and in the face of larger Allied flying formations, the fighter pilots from several German reconnaissance units banded together to form Kampfeinsitzer Kommando units – the beginning of a move towards the Jagdstaffeln that was already in full swing by the middle of 1916.

The Eindeckers themselves had all been retired from the front line by September 1916. In fact, Immelmann, Wintgens and Boelcke were all dead by the end of October.

Allied air supremacy did not last long however, as the Jagdstaffeln began to receive new Albatros fighters in August 1916. These machines upped the ante once again and forced the Allies on to the back foot – a situation which culminated in 'Bloody April'

in 1917 when the British lost 245 aeroplanes in a single month, with 211 airmen dead or missing and another 108 taken prisoner.

Away from the battlefields of France, the 'Fokker Scourge' had also had a dramatic effect in Britain's corridors of power – which would in turn have a knock-on effect for the Sopwith Aviation Company.

Aviation journalist Charles Grey Grey, or C G Grey as he was more commonly known,

> ## "Hundreds, nay thousands of machines have been ordered which had been referred to by our pilots as 'Fokker fodder'"

founder of *The Aeroplane* magazine, had long disliked the Government's Royal Aircraft Factory and in particular its superintendent Mervyn O'Gorman.

He despised O'Gorman and regarded his ability to leapfrog the 'proper authorities' as a serious problem for Britain's aviation industry. The advent of the Fokker Scourge served his purposes very well by demonstrating that the factory's products were far from the scientifically proven machines O'Gorman claimed they were.

He found an ally in the radical MP Noel Pemberton Billing, founder of what would become the Supermarine Aviation Works. While he attacked the policy of allowing the factory to design most of the RFC's aircraft through the pages of *The Aeroplane*, Billing told anyone who would listen that Britain's private aircraft manufacturers had been stifled by the favouritism shown towards the

factory's products by the RFC. He grabbed national headlines by claiming a situation had arisen where: "Hundreds, nay thousands of machines have been ordered which had been referred to by our pilots as 'Fokker fodder'. I would suggest that quite a number of our gallant officers in the Royal Flying Corps have been murdered rather than killed."

The phrase 'Fokker fodder' in particular seemed to stick in the public consciousness and gave the impression that the Royal Aircraft Factory's machines, while demonstrably inferior to those in German service, were criminally so.

A parliamentary inquiry was ordered and O'Gorman, though cleared of any direct blame, was forced to leave when his contract expired in October 1916 and was not renewed.

Royal Aircraft Factory-designed machines were still churned out in significant numbers but pilots hated them – particularly the R.E.8, which had been intended as a direct replacement for the B.E.2. The only exception was the S.E.5a which helped to regain Allied air superiority over the Western Front in 1917 alongside types such as the Sopwith Pup, Triplane and Camel. ■

FLOWN BY DEAD MEN

There are a number of documented instances that serve to illustrate the B.E.2c's remarkable and notorious stability. In his book Captain Roy Brown – A True Story of the Great War 1914-1918, Alan Bennett writes: "There had been occasions upon which a B.E.2c had been seen flying steadily along in a strange direction, ignoring everything around it. A curious pilot had flown alongside and discovered that both crew members were dead. In two documented cases, B.E.2c 'flown' by a dead crew had made a good landing after running out of fuel – one in a field and the other on the beach near Dunkirk."

Chapter 8

The gentleman's STEED

Sopwith Pup/Scout/Type 9901

Light and simple with a small engine and a single machine gun, the Sopwith Pup wasn't much to look at on paper, but in the air it proved to be precisely what British pilots wanted; a fast, no-nonsense machine that handled well and could outperform any of its German adversaries at high altitude.

Three aeroplane types had been worked on simultaneously by Sopwith Aviation towards the end of 1915, and the second to emerge, after the 1½ Strutter, was the Scout. It was based on a 'runabout' designed and constructed at the behest of Harry Hawker – the S.L.T.Bp – and its internal structure was very closely related to that of the earlier Tabloid.

Its length from the sternpost to the engine bulkhead of its fuselage, and its fuselage depth, were identical. Wing chord – the distance from front to back – was also the same and there were numerous other similarities.

Where the types differed most significantly was in power-to-weight ratio. Empty, the Tabloid weighed 1220lb, compared with the Scout's 787lb – making it 35.5% lighter. Even with the Tabloid's more powerful 100hp engine, it was still hauling around 12.2lb per hp, compared with the 80hp Scout's 9.8lb per hp.

Combined with everything Sopwith's designers and engineers had learned about aerodynamics and aircraft construction since the Tabloid, the difference was spectacular. The Scout had a top speed of 111mph, compared with the Tabloid's 87mph, and a ceiling of 17,500ft compared with just 7000ft.

Its lightness could make the Scout a handful when taxiing on the ground in strong winds, but this was regarded as a small price to pay for its performance in the air. Armament was a single fixed forward-firing Vickers' machine gun, and the Scout's engine was a Le Rhône.

The first prototype Scout built was given the number 3691 and declared ready for testing on February 9, 1916 – while the 'Fokker Scourge' was at its peak.

Unlike other Sopwith types, after the first six prototypes had been constructed, when the RNAS awarded its first production contract for

One of Harry Hawker's earliest 'runabouts', really a development testbed, the S.L.T.Bp became the basis for the Sopwith Pup.

One of the last batch of 20 Pups built by Sopwith, N6473 came to grief while serving with the Royal Navy's Training Establishment at Cranwell, Lincs, probably in October or November 1917.

Pups had a single Vickers gun. They seldom carried a second firearm due to the extra weight. *Paul Le Roy*

A Standard Motor Company-built Pup – A635 flew with the RFC.

A sight that no German aviator wanted to see – a Sopwith Pup on the attack. *Paul Le Roy*

the type in April 1916, it went to William Beardmore & Co because Sopwith's production facilities were already operating at maximum capacity building the 1½ Strutter.

While drawings were being prepared and facilities made ready, testing of No. 3691 in May by the RNAS demonstrated that the Scout was a first-class fighting machine. It was around this time that an RFC officer, Brigadier-General Sefton Brancker, is said to have seen an early Scout sitting next to a 1½ Strutter and said: "Good God! Your 1½ Strutter has had a pup!"

The name quickly stuck and before long, even though it was always known officially as the Sopwith Scout, the Sopwith Pup was being lauded as the machine that would succeed the Nieuport 11 and Airco DH.2 as the next generation of British fighter.

With the Royal Aircraft Factory having been disgraced by the fallout from the 'Fokker Scourge', its virtual monopoly on supplying the RFC fell away and the War Office placed its own order for Pups. The RNAS's machines were made by Sopwith itself, where production capacity was soon found, and by William Beardmore & Co, while the RFC's orders were fulfilled by the Standard Motor Company and Whitehead Aircraft.

The first Pups began to see front-line service in September 1916 with the RNAS and the type's first victory was chalked up by Australian pilot Stanley Goble of 'A' Naval Squadron, 1 Naval Wing, on September 24. He took on a pair of German machines in his Pup, the prototype No. 3691, and brought one of them down, according to his report, "on fire in a spiral nose dive".

The following day another 1 Naval Wing pilot, Edward Rochfort Grange, also scored a victory in a Pup, this time N5182. He had

been flying over the sea about five miles from Ostend when he encountered a large seaplane, a Sablatnig SF 2, and shot it down, killing both of its crew members.

With the Battle of the Somme still ranging on the Western Front, nearly three months after it had begun, and with the RFC taking losses from the new German Albatros D.I machines, its commander Hugh Trenchard made an appeal for reinforcements from the RNAS.

This resulted in the formation of 8 Naval Squadron from volunteers who were members of 1, 4 and 5 Naval Wings. 'Naval 8' was officially formed on October 26 at

Saint Pol-sur-Mer, before being sent south to Vert Galand Farm in the Somme region. Its first missions were flown on November 3 and a week later Pup pilot Stanley Valentine Trapp forced an enemy scout to land, while fellow Canadian Daniel Galbraith shot another down 'out of control'.

Galbraith and Goble, who had also signed up for 8 Naval Squadron, each shot down an LVG two-seater on November 16 and on November 23 Galbraith scored his sixth and final victory when he attacked a formation of six LVGs and shot one of them down. Three of the others were forced to land.

The squadron continued to rack up

Sopwith aeroplanes built during the Great War often received compliments for the quality of the workmanship that went into them. This replica upholds the traditions of the company. *Paul Le Roy*

This Pup was one of 850 built by the Standard Motor Company, which produced more Pups than any other firm. B1704 was one of a batch of 150 destined for the RFC.

N5180 was the very first production Pup and was manufactured by the Sopwith Aviation Company itself.

victories through into 1917 and on January 4, Grange and two others, Robert Alexander Little and Allan Switzer Todd, attacked a formation of seven Albatros D.IIs from above. Grange managed to shoot down three of them, but Todd was attacked by another three all at once. Little tried to rescue him, but all he got was a good view of Todd twisting to the left and his left wings coming off.

As Little and the three Albatros machines flew off in separate directions, he looked down and saw that a crowd had gathered around Todd's machine, an Albatros lay on its back nearby and two more had crash-landed in the nearby field. Todd's killer, Manfred von Richthofen, sliced the section of fabric that bore the number of Todd's Pup, N5187, off the machine and took it as a trophy.

The German, who had so far made 16 kills, including Todd, his first Sopwith pilot, later reported: "About 4.15pm, just starting out, we saw above us at 4000m altitude four aeroplanes, unmolested by our artillery.

"Only when they were approaching did we notice they were English. One of the English aeroplanes attacked us, and we saw immediately that the enemy aeroplane was superior to ours. Only because we were three against one did we detect the enemy's weak points.

"The aircraft itself always behaved in a most gentlemanly way"

"I managed to get behind him and shot him down. The aeroplane broke apart while falling."

It was the first of only two Pups shot down by the infamous Red Baron – the second being B1795 flown by Algernon

ABOVE: The Pup was powered by a relatively small engine – an 80hp Le Rhône – but it was so light its performance was still exceptional. *Paul Le Roy*

This Pup replica is painted in the markings of RNAS Pup N6205 'Betty', flown by Joseph Stewart Temple Fall. He used N6205 to shoot down a trio of Albatros D.IIIs in late April to early May 1917. *Paul Le Roy*

Sopwith Pup replica painted to appear as a Squadron 66 machine – B2162 – with upper wing-mounted Lewis gun. *Paul Le Roy*

Frederick Bird of 46 Squadron, who was taken prisoner after being downed at 7.35am on September 3, 1917.

Naval 8 continued to successfully fly its Pups against the enemy until February 1, when it was re-equipped with the Sopwith Triplane and the Pups were handed over to 3 Naval Squadron. One of its pilots, Edmund Pierce, said: "At Vert Galand, we took over old Sopwith Pups from 8 Naval Squadron, and they certainly had a bashing before we got them."

The second, third, fourth and fifth highest-scoring Pup pilots all belong to 3 Naval Squadron, and claimed most of their kills during the summer and autumn of 1917.

PUPS WITH THE RFC
Following in their RNAS counterparts' footsteps, the first RFC unit to be equipped with the Pup was 54 Squadron, which arrived in France on Christmas Eve 1916.

One of its pilots, Robert Foster, wrote: "From the flying point of view, the Sopwith Pup was certainly the finest aircraft of its day – no vices, beautiful to handle, and with only 80hp in its Le Rhône engine of outstanding performance.

"We attained 18,000ft with regularity, and could get even higher. In operations our best chances came from climbing above the maximum height obtainable by the German fighters and then hoping to make a surprise attack.

"The Germans were always superior in level speed and in the dive, but the Pup was much more manoeuvrable and we could turn inside any German fighter of the day. The winter of 1916/17 was bitter in Northern France, and at 18,000ft everything froze – the engine throttle, the gun, and the pilot.

"With open cockpits, no oxygen, indifferent flying clothes, a number of us were frost-bitten, an experience which one

found extremely painful. The aircraft itself always behaved in a most gentlemanly way, but needed careful handling. A dive of 160mph was fast enough, and at 180mph the wings were definitely flapping, and a gentle recovery was essential, since to lose a wing when one had no parachute offered no future.

"The Pup's one disadvantage was its extreme lightness. When operating in strong winds, our squadron's practice was to call out all available personnel when a patrol was landing back.

"The men would be spread out in two lines on the airfield between which the aircraft would land, and have their wing-tips seized before a gust could blow them over."

Foster himself crashed in strong winds after several attempts at landing when a man caught one wingtip, but another missed the other. Foster's machine rolled over on to its back. Later, his squadron

The wreckage of 3 (Naval) Squadron Sopwith-built Pup N6186. It was shot down near Écourt-St-Quentin on May 1, 1917. The pilot, A S Mather, was taken prisoner.

commander told him: "I knew you would make a balls of it. But why waste the squadron's time making 13 shots to land? Why not crash the first time?"

The highest scoring of the war's 28 Pups aces was the RFC's Maurice Douglas Guest Scott from Exeter in Devon. He started the war as a soldier with the 3rd Loyal North Lancashires before being transferred to the RFC in February 1916. He was initially posted to 18 Squadron where he scored his first victory, shooting up and then capturing an Albatros C.I as an observer sitting behind the nose-mounted machine gun of a Vickers' F.B.5 'gun bus'.

He then trained as a pilot and was posted to 54 Squadron in 1917. On April 5, he shot down a German observation balloon while flying a Pup and the following month he destroyed two more Albatros C-types. During the summer he was reassigned to 46 Squadron where, during September, he shot down seven enemy machines – including two in one day on September 30.

A promotion to flight commander followed and Scott was relieved from duty and sent to join the Home Establishment on October 8. Having joined 91 Squadron, based at Tangmere, West Sussex, he was out flying Sopwith Pup C267 on March 16, over Shoreham, when, after a loop, the machine rolled before diving into the ground. Scott survived the initial crash, but died of his injuries the following day without regaining consciousness.

He had suffered shock, a fracture of his left thigh and severe lacerations to the front of his scalp. C267 was examined, but no obvious mechanical failures could be found. Scott was awarded the Military Cross on March 18 and the local coroner recorded a verdict of death by misadventure.

Another RFC pilot and one of Britain's top aces of the war, James Thomas Byford McCudden, in his book Flying Fury, wrote: "On May 1, 1917, I had taken charge of another machine for fighting instruction, this time a Sopwith Scout, vulgarly termed a 'Pup'."

After spending a few days with the machine, he wrote, "I was just feeling at home on the Sopwith 'Pup', and it was a remarkably fine machine for general all-

The Sopwith Pup's clean and simple fuselage made it a classic. *Paul Le Roy*

round flying. It was so extremely light and well surfaced that after a little practice one could almost land it on a tennis court."

McCudden spent a wonderful summer tootling around in his Pup, even chasing a formation of twin-engined German bombers out over the Channel in it, before returning to his regular steed – and the one in which nearly all of his 57 kills were made – the S.E.5a.

During the course of the war, the Pup was widely used by the RFC, serving with 18 squadrons. It also flew with RNAS squadrons 1N, 3N, 8N, 9N, 11N and 13N, and Australian Flying Corps training squadrons 5, 6 and 8.

DESIGNED TO BE DITCHED

As the summer of 1917 passed, the Pups of both the RNAS and RFC were being perilously outclassed by German types such as the Albatros D.V, and the survivors had been withdrawn by the end of the year.

It may have been struggling to keep

up on the front line, but the Pup's ability to fly and manoeuvre at high altitude made it an ideal Home Defence fighter. Two Pup squadrons were moved to England to intercept high-flying Gotha G.IV bombers after a raid on London on May 25, 1917, saw 95 people killed and another 195 injured.

To improve the performance of these interceptors still further, most were modified with 100hp Gnome Monosoupape engines in long chord cowlings that had four cooling intakes on their upper rim. Several also had their firepower improved with the fitment of a fixed Lewis gun over the upper wing centre section in addition to their single forward-firing Vickers' machine gun.

Another role that made use of the Pup's unique qualities was that of the carrier-borne aeroplane. By the beginning of 1917

N5186, seen here with Le Prieur rockets for taking on Zeppelins, served with several RNAS units – first 8 Squadron at Dunkirk, then 3 Squadron and finally 4 Squadron, where it crashed.

it was more than apparent that many of the Navy's floatplanes were simply too fragile to be effective shipborne fighters and a replacement of some sort was needed.

One suggestion was to fly Pups from carriers without converting them to seaplanes – this meant that the pilot, assuming he was unable to reach land, was obliged to ditch in the sea once his mission was complete or when his fuel ran out. Naval officer Frederick Joseph 'Rutland of Jutland' Rutland was a strong advocate of this idea – believing that Pups were inherently safer to ditch than seaplanes were to land on water.

Rutland himself flew an anti-Zeppelin patrol from the deck of *HMS Manxman* on April 29, 1917, but after ditching his Pup remained afloat for only 20 minutes before being pulled under by the weight of its engine. It had even been fitted with an airbag inside its rear fuselage for added buoyancy, but this seemed to make little difference.

Tests were carried out with an improved version of the airbag, the Mark I Emergency Floatation Bag, on June 23, and it was found that a Pup could be made to remain afloat for up to six hours. However, the biggest problem was that unmodified Pups, even with the airbag, tended to flip over when their landing gear hit the water.

Experiments were therefore carried out using landing gear that could be jettisoned after take-off, but in practice it was found that Pups tended to flip on to their backs

Whitehead-built Pup B2192 received an outlandish paint scheme while serving with the School of Special Flying at Gosport in Hampshire between August and September 1917. It was flown by instructors Captain Ernest L Foot and Captain Harold H Balfour. Flying ace William Barker also flew it on one occasion.

when ditching even without their landing gear. The best solution was found to be hydrovanes, which stabilised the Pup as it entered the water.

With these trials under way, on June 28, Rutland flew a fully armed Pup from a 19ft 3in platform fixed over the forward-firing 6in gun of the *HMS Yarmouth* – a light cruiser.

The length of the platform meant the vessel had to be steaming into the wind for Rutland to get enough lift for a takeoff but he managed it nonetheless and in August it was decided that one ship in each cruiser squadron should carry its own flying platform.

On August 2, Pup pilot Edwin Harris Dunning flew from the deck of aircraft carrier

The Sopwith Pup was 'light as a feather' which some pilots loved but others disliked. *Paul Le Roy*

Magnificent Pup replica 'B2162' in New Zealand. *Paul Le Roy*

HMS Furious and then managed to land it again while it was steaming along at 26 knots – men on the deck almost being able to pull his aircraft down out of the air using rope toggles attached to the wings and fuselage. On August 7, he repeated the feat but on the second attempt of the day his machine slipped off the side of the deck and he drowned after being knocked unconscious.

Two weeks later, on the morning of August 21, Second Lieutenant Bernard A Smart flew a Pup from the Yarmouth's platform in pursuit of a Zeppelin, designated L23 that had been spotted. He climbed to 7000ft above the airship and dived down on to it, guns blazing. After breaking off his attack, he saw that L23 was burning and beginning to sink down towards the ocean.

There was no way for Smart to return so he ditched, but was picked up safely. It was the first time that an aircraft had taken off from a moving ship to engage an enemy aircraft. Smart's Pup sank and no survivors were recovered from the L23.

Shipboard Pups, as well as Home Defence Pups, were sometimes fitted with Le Prieur rockets for anti-Zeppelin missions. These stick-stabilised weapons consisted of a cardboard tube filled with 200g of gunpowder with a conical wooden tip attached using doped paper or linen tape. This had a slot cut in it, into which was inserted a triangular knife blade to form a 'spear point'. A 4.9ft stick was taped to the base of the rocket for guidance and to ensure it sat snugly in its steel launching tube.

A rack of four tubes was fitted to the aircraft's outer struts on each wing, giving a total of eight rockets, and they were ignited electrically by the pilot using a switch in his cockpit. This would launch all the rockets consecutively – ideally at a range of 350-500ft while diving at a 45 degree angle. The steeper the dive, the more accurate the rockets, although clearly this increased the risk of the aeroplane suffering structural damage.

One of the firms that manufactured the

Pup, engineering and shipbuilding organisation William Beardmore & Co, was responsible for creating one of only two major variants of the design to reach active service – the W.B.III. Beardmore had already fulfilled a naval order for Pups when it was asked to create a 'foldable Pup' to take up less space onboard vessels.

This required a complete redesign of the Sopwith original, including the wings losing their stagger so they could be folded back, and the undercarriage being arranged so that it could be tucked up into the lower fuselage. Floatation gear and wingtip skids were added, the control system was altered and the fuselage was slightly lengthened. A total of 100 were built.

Production of the Pup overall reached around 1850 although the precise number may never be known since some were delivered as spares and others were constructed from several crash-damaged machines.

The other major variant of the Pup design was the Sopwith Triplane. ∎

A German soldier stands over the body of the RFC's Lieutenant R S Asher beside the wreck of his Sopwith Pup A7321, which was shot down in September 1917.

Pictured with an access panel removed on the side of its fuselage, Pup B6086 was built by the Standard Motor Company and delivered to the RFC for training rather than front-line service.

The German air force valued aeroplanes such as the Pup and pressed them into service whenever it happened to capture a serviceable example – like this one.

SOPWITH PUP IN ACTION

An extract from Sopwith Scout 7309 by Gordon Taylor, published by Cassell:

Looking through my logbook, it could appear that most of these operations were routine. Actually, however, every minute of every flight was different. Once over the lines we were in the jungle, and we lived like predators in the jungle night.

By now, on the northern front, all our illusions were gone. It was different from Vert Galand Farm, where we had come riding in with banners on our lances; a new purpose shining before us, refusing to believe in the limitations of our mounts. Now that phase had passed and those of us who survived to fly in the north did so with a cold-blooded appreciation of the facts.

The war would be long and death was easy. On both June 4 and 5 we escorted the bombers to Rumbeke. The AA was very active but we saw no Huns.

We could only imagine that the Germans had not yet moved their elite fighter force up north to meet the coming air attacks associated with the ground offensive. It is possible that they did not know of the Allied plans to launch an offensive in the north.

If they didn't, they were soon to learn about it, for on the morning of the sixth a terrific barrage was put down on Messines Ridge by the British artillery.

A flight was on the early morning patrol and we flew relatively low that day, led again by Jock Andrews who had returned from leave. Looking down from 4000ft the shelling of Messines was a terrible sight. Over a large area the ground, already shattered by the explosion of 19 huge mines, was bouncing up like the surface of water in a heavy storm. It seemed impossible that anybody could stay alive in such devastation, yet afterwards the German troops still put up a gallant opposition to the Allied infantry attack.

Our job was to prevent the German observation aircraft from flying over the battle area, and this kept us busy for most of the patrol. We first located two-seaters up near Ypres and immediately attacked them. I was able to get into a good position, but my gun stopped firing after the first few rounds and the Hun escaped.

After a certain amount of trouble I was able to rectify the stoppage and soon afterwards, approaching the line on the German side, we sighted two more observation Huns. Andrews took one, and I the other.

I got off about a hundred rounds into him before he dived steeply away to the east. We re-formed and continued searching the hazy air for enemy aircraft. Andrews turned and signalled to me to take over the patrol.

His machine slid away down west, and in a few moments had disappeared (we afterwards found that he had a jammed gun and then his engine started to pack up, but he scraped back over the lines). I sighted another Hun two-seater, sneaking in to have a look at the war. I

went straight for him alone because every second of his observation was important and he had to be driven off immediately and if possible destroyed.

As soon as he saw me he turned away, but the rear gunner was accurate and got me in his fire. I swung off to divert him and dived to take him from behind and below. He was quick to realise the danger and went down all out for the earth. I rammed my throttle right on and screamed the little Le Rhône madly in a frantic attempt to get the Hun; but it was futile. He drew away.

Frustrated and angry, I followed him right to the earth, madly trying somehow to catch him. He flattened out low over the ground and flew away east leaving me right on the deck over Hunland. I flew down a road and saw a car moving slowly westwards. I could see what looked like two officers in the back, and a driver in front. I swept round and dived on the car, opening fire as it came into my sights.

It rushed in on the nose of my aircraft, suddenly passing under me, and I hauled away up in a climbing turn. Looking down, I saw that the car was in a ditch and two men in uniform were running across the field, away from it. I couldn't see the third. At least I could chalk up this car as crashed!

I flew on, low, and suddenly came on a camouflaged Hun battery. There was a panic as my machine flew over. I turned and came back in, firing into the site. Then it was gone. A village came up – Zonnebeke, I think.

There were troops in the street. I dived on them immediately, saw them running for cover. Then my gun stopped firing. I had shot away all my ammunition. I held her down flat to the ground, and hared back over the lines. I was near the end of my fuel, so I held on west and flew back to Estrée Blanche. Andrews and three others were back, but Charlie Marsh did not return.

The ground strafing had stirred my imagination, so I took a second opportunity to go off on a private war. I located another Hun battery east of Ploegsteert Wood and shot it up. Then two cars, which stopped under trees when fired upon. I couldn't locate them accurately then, so went off in search of other game.

It was eerie, flying low over Hunland. It seemed a sinister, alien place; not like our world. I chased away over some fields, saw another car; got into position and opened up. My gun fired about 10 rounds, and stopped. I could not clear the stoppage. So I turned and headed back for the lines.

As the torn, brown earth came in below I got in the crossfire of two machine guns, weaved about, but could not shake them off for some seconds.

Then flat on the ground again, following the contours of the earth; hurrying over the trenches to safety, like pulling your leg out of shark-infested water. At last I was back. I hauled up higher off the ground, and made my way quietly back to the aerodrome.

'Sopwith Scout 7309 author Gordon Taylor, centre, with his Pup and ground crew.

Chapter 9

Good things come in THREES
Sopwith Triplane

The third of Sopwith's late 1915 fighter trio saw the body of a Sopwith Pup married to an unusual triple set of narrow wings. It also had a 130hp engine and the ability to climb at an astonishing rate. Produced in only small numbers, the Triplane nevertheless had a big impact on the war in the air…

The idea of building an aircraft with three sets of wings was not new when the Sopwith team started work on the Triplane but it had been abandoned by even the most minor manufacturers for several years after a rash of early efforts.

The first powered triplane to fly had been built in 1907 by Danish inventor Jacob Ellehammer and the following year six further triplane one-offs followed – most of them French and most of them failing to even become airborne.

In 1909, three more were made, an Italian machine that crashed after making only a short hop, a French machine that wouldn't fly and the first in a series built by Alliott Verdon 'Avro' Roe. The latter became the first all-British machine to fly, being powered by a JAP V-twin engine rather than a French one.

While almost everyone else gave up on triplanes, Roe persevered, having patented his design. The Roe Triplane II followed the first in 1910, two examples being built, and Roe even sold a small number of his third 'tripe', the Roe III.

His final triplane, the Roe IV, was first flown in September 1910 and was used for pilot training at Brooklands until August 1911, when it was scrapped – this time frame coinciding with Tommy Sopwith's early months as a pioneer of aviation but before the arrival of Harry Hawker.

There were single Belgian and Russian triplanes built in 1911, neither being very promising designs, but none were built in 1912, 1913 or 1914.

Towards the end of 1915, as Sopwith was working on its next generation of fighters,

Thin wires on Triplanes produced by contractor Clayton & Shuttleworth may have given the type a bad reputation for structural weakness. *Paul Le Roy*

A line-up of Sopwith Triplanes belonging to 1 (Naval) Squadron.

Sopwith Triplane N5438 had a fairly short career in service, flying with 1 (Naval) Squadron between May and June 1917. It was flown by Canadian ace Cyril Askew Eyre, though he scored all six of his victories in other machines. Eyre was finally killed on July 7, probably in Triplane N6291.

Nieuport's Gustave Delage fitted an extra wing to a Nieuport 10 biplane – although the centre wing was oddly positioned much further back than the other two.

In addition, a huge Moraine-Saulnier twin engine bomber, the TRK, was built as a triplane in 1915 but it is uncertain whether it ever flew. Meanwhile, Armstrong-Whitworth started work on a highly unconventional and ungainly fighter known as the F.K.6 in 1915 but it wasn't finished until the following year.

It therefore seems that the most likely

inspiration for Sopwith's beautifully clean and simple Triplane was the Roe IV. This had thin wings, giving the pilot an excellent view all round while retaining sufficient lift to give it a reasonable performance for the time.

When the first Sopwith Triplane was passed for testing by the company's experimental department on May 28, 1916, the prototype Pup was still the only one in existence. The two aircraft, N500 and No. 3691 respectively, were the same in almost every respect except for their wings. Where the Pup had a conventional biplane structure with upper and lower wings that were 5ft 1½in wide, front to back, the Triplane had wings just 3ft 3in front to back.

A criticism of the Pup from its inception had been restricted upwards visibility due to the size of its wings, and the Triplane effectively solved this problem. The cost, however, was an extra 200lb in weight due to the supports and material required for the extra set of wings. Therefore, rather than having the Pup's 80hp Le Rhone, N500 was fitted with a 110hp Clerget engine off the 1½ Strutter production line to give it the

additional oomph required to overcome its weight disadvantage.

Being essentially a rewinged Pup, the Triplane also suffered from a firepower disadvantage in having only a single machine gun, where most German types of the period had begun mounting two.

It could, however, outclimb anything the Germans had in service at that time and delighted pilots, even those who had flown the Pup, with its performance.

As with the Pup, both the RFC and the RNAS placed orders for the Triplane. Between July 1916 and January 1917, the Admiralty gave Sopwith two contracts for a total of 95 Triplanes and two more to Clayton and Shuttleworth of Lincoln for another 46. Another, for 25, went to Oakley of London. The War Office ordered another 106 from Clayton and Shuttleworth but this was cancelled in February 1917.

Oakley, which had never built aircraft before, only ended up making three of them due to a design change requiring the aeroplanes to be built with two machine guns instead of the originally specified one.

N6306 was shot down while being flown on patrol over Zonnebeke, West Flanders, in June 1917. The Triplane's pilot, A B Holcroft of 10 (Naval) Squadron, was wounded in the crash but survived and became a prisoner of war.

By the time Oakley had managed to make the change by the middle of 1917, the Triplane, now variously nicknamed the Tripe or Tripehound, was obsolete and the order was cancelled, though the three built by that point were accepted.

THE TRIPLANE IN ACTION

In mid-June, 1916, N500 was sent to be tested alongside Pup No. 3691 at Furnes in Belgium. Within 15 minutes of landing, it was sent up to intercept an enemy machine that had been sighted. Australian RNAS pilot Roderic Stanley Dallas took N500 up on July 1 and encountered a pair of large German biplanes north of La Panne at 12,000ft. He fired 40 rounds into the first, saw his rounds hit and watched as the machine nosedived towards the sea.

The second enemy aeroplane then attacked Dallas. His gun jammed and he was forced to return to base.

Three months later, on September 30, Dallas used N500 to shoot down another German machine, an Albatros D-type single seater this time. It was still the only Triplane in service.

After much further testing, the first production Triplanes were finally delivered in February 1917. These had a Clerget 130hp engine in place of the 110hp model and a smaller, variable incidence tailplane for improved turning and handling.

The Triplane initially entered service with 1 and 8 Naval Squadrons and they were joined by a third Triplane unit, 10 Naval Squadron, in May. The pilots of all three found it to be an exceptional machine.

Opinion was divided, however, as to whether the Triplane was better than the Pup. RFC pilot Oliver Stewart, in The Clouds Remember, wrote: "It would be difficult to analyse the feature in this machine that made it so attractive to fly.

"It seemed light and elegant yet wiry. And there was the visual effect of the triplane arrangement which made the pilot feel that he had unlimited quantities of lift available. The response to the controls was not of that lightning quickness exemplified by the Sopwith Camel, but it was by no means sluggish.

The Sopwith Triplane was agile and had a high rate of climb. Its performance both impressed and terrified the Germans, so much so that they copied the triplane structure with the Fokker Dr.1. *Paul Le Roy*

"At first it was thought that the triplane could not be looped and flick-rolled with safety, but later it was made to do all the aerobatics of its time, and it did them well.

"Captain Vernon Brown was an exponent of aerobatics with the Sopwith Triplane, and he successfully demonstrated that the aeroplane was capable of the whole gamut of aerobatics, and that although it did not appear to do the manoeuvres with the suddenness of the biplanes, it did them with infinite grace.

"The Triplane spun rather slowly, and its flick-roll was also rather slow compared with other machines of the time; but what it lacked in quickness it made up in the smoothness and grace of its movements. A

Triplane looping looked like no other machine and gave the loops an individual quality. Irreverent pilots said it looked, when doing aerobatics, like an intoxicated flight of stairs."

Another RFC pilot, Cecil Lewis, wrote in Sagittarius Rising: "One day the Sopwith Triplane arrived at Martlesham for tests.

"Of all machines, the Triplane remains in my memory as the best – for the actual pleasure of flying – that I ever took up. It was so beautifully balanced, so well-mannered, so feather-light on the stick and so comfortable and warm.

"It had what was then a novel feature, an adjustable tailplane to trim the machine fore and aft. Set correctly, with the throttle about

Another Triplane that flew with 1 (Naval) Squadron was N5364.

The origin of the species? The Roe series of triplanes, constructed by Alliott Verdon Roe, may have influenced Tommy Sopwith when he was learning to pilot aeroplanes.

This New Zealand-based replica Triplane is painted in the colours of Canadian ace Raymond Collishaw's machine 'Black Maria'. *Paul Le Roy*

three-quarters open, the Tripe would loop, hands off, indefinitely. Not for this, but for its docility, the lack of all effort needed to fly it and yet its instantaneous response to the lightest touch, it remains my favourite.

"Other machines were faster, stronger, had better climb or vision, but none was so friendly as the Tripe. After it, I never wanted to fly anything but a scout again, and on active service I never did."

The first squadron action seen by the Triplane took place during 'Bloody April' – as the RFC and RNAS flew in support of British forces during the Battle of Arras. 1 Naval Squadron moved from Dunkirk to Chipilly, near Albert, towards the end of February – placing it close to the British front line. 8 Naval Squadron moved first to the Somme area in March and then to St-Eloi near Arras.

Both Triplane units quickly began to make an impact on the Germans. Dallas alone shot down eight enemy machines in April, as did Naval 8's Robert Alexander 'Bob' Little, an Australian.

At around noon on April 24, Little set off from Naval 8's base at Vert Galand in search of a two-seater that had been spotted in the area. He found it flying at 12,000ft above Auchel aerodrome – a DFW C.V built under licence by Aviatik. Diving down, he saw that a pair of Nieuport 17s from 40 Squadron RFC were also attacking it.

He later reported: "He turned north and I followed, firing whenever the opportunity presented itself. I noticed that the observer was not returning my fire so I closed in on him. He was losing height all the time, and when a mile east of Bethune I observed my tracers going into his fuselage.

"I was firing from a range of 10 to 15 yards. He then nosedived and I dived after him. He landed in a field and I was unable to get my engine to start after the dive and had to land alongside the hostile machine. I ran into a ditch and overturned.

"I got out of the machine and went across to the Germans and took them prisoner. The pilot told me he knew he would never get back when he saw me coming to attack him."

Little took his captives, Hans Huppertz and Friedrich Neumüller, to lunch at Naval 8's base, and his fellow pilot Edward Crundall said: "The three of them went to lunch and soon they were the best of pals, exchanging souvenirs and relating their various experiences.

"The Germans spoke good English, and both of them had been awarded the Iron Cross. They were very surprised when large plates of meat were served to them because, in Germany, they said, meat was very scarce."

Little went on to become the highest scoring Australian ace of the war with 47 victories but was killed while attacking Gotha bombers during a night raid.

When the war ended, Neumüller tried to contact Little but, when he heard that he had died, sent a note to his widow instead: "Because he was so amiable to me on the darkest day of my soldier's life, I will never forget him. He was in every respect a knightly adversary of the air."

TRIPLANE TO THE END

At the end of the month, on April 29, both Triplane squadrons, Naval 10 having yet to convert to the type, took on the skilled pilots of Germany's Jagdstaffel 'Jasta' 11 – commanded by 24-year-old Manfred von Richthofen, who flew a bright red Albatros D.III.

A flight of six Naval 8 Triplanes took on von Richthofen first. He wrote later: "We flew on, climbing to higher altitude, for above us some of the 'Anti-Richthofen

N5912 is one of only two surviving original Sopwith Triplanes. *RAF Museum*

One of three designs developed by Sopwith during late 1915/early 1916, the Triplane's synchronised machine gun was still a novelty when the first prototype rolled off the production line but by the time examples reached service, the Germans were already mounting machine guns in pairs.

Club' had gathered together. Again, we were easy to recognise, the sun from the west illuminating the aircraft and letting their beautiful red colour be seen from far away.

"We closed up tightly, for each of us knew we were dealing with 'brothers' who pursued the same trade we did. Unfortunately, they were higher than we were, so we had to wait for their attack. The famous Triplanes and SPADs were new machines, but it is not as much a matter of the crate as it is who sits in it – the 'brothers' were wary and had no spunk."

The Triplanes attacked but their formation quickly broke up and Albert Edward Cuzner, a Canadian, found himself in the sights of the Red Baron. Von Richthofen wrote: "The aeroplane I had singled out caught fire and, after a short time, burned in the air and fell north of Henin Liétard." It was the German ace's 52nd victory.

While the pilots of 1 and 8 Naval Squadrons were battling Germany's finest, 10 Naval Squadron was swapping its Pups for Triplanes. The unit's commander was Bertram Bell and it consisted of three flights of five Triplanes each.

The leader of 'C' Flight was Raymond Collishaw, who had arrived on April 26. Two days later, on April 28, he flew three missions in Triplane N5490. The first was an offensive patrol to Ostend-Bruges and Collishaw came across a German two-seater flying at 12,000ft. After firing 40 rounds at it, his single Vickers gun jammed and he was forced to break off the attack to clear it.

With the blockage gone, he followed the two-seater as it dived to 6000ft, the German observer slumped dead or dying across his gun to the rear as the pilot tried to shake Collishaw off. After another burst, Collishaw's gun jammed again and he was forced to let the enemy machine go.

The second mission of the day was to cover a British seaplane that had landed on the Channel just off Nieuport. Rescuers were en route by ship but in the meantime four German fighters appeared and made a beeline for it.

Collishaw, circling overhead, latched on to one of the fighters and fired into it until it broke up in mid-air, the remains dropping onto the beach below. The other three Germans, even though they outnumbered the solitary Triplane, were so unnerved they turned and fled for home.

Collishaw, having found his bearings in Naval 10, was deeply critical of what he saw as some of the other pilots' ineptitude or even cowardice in some cases. He believed that when the squadron was formed, other units had been asked to contribute pilots towards it and some had used this as an excuse to offload their worst personnel. He wrote: "The situation was quite intolerable and I complained bitterly to the commanding officer. As a result there was a general clearing out and the undesirables were replaced by experienced pilots from 3 Wing which was disbanding."

Collishaw shot down another German machine on April 30 and got two more in May but all that changed when Naval 10 fell under the command of the RFC later that month and was moved to a new airfield, Droglandt, which was just 14 miles behind the British front line at Ypres.

Now Collishaw commanded 'B' Flight. The Triplanes of 'A' Flight had their engine cowlings and the panels behind them painted red, those of 'C' were blue and the machines of 'B' were black. On this basis, Collishaw decided to give the five aircraft of his flight black-themed names – his own

Other companies and pioneers tried to produce aeroplanes with a Triplane configuration but none but Sopwith succeeded in producing such a simple yet effective design. *Paul Le Roy*

machine was Black Maria and the others were Black Roger, Black Death, Black Sheep and Black Prince.

The names were painted in stencilled 3in high white letters on the side of each machine's fuselage.

Between June and July, Collishaw shot down 30 enemy machines. Ellis Reid, pilot of Black Roger, made all 19 of his kills during those two months. John Sharman of Black Death got seven, Gerry Nash of Black Sheep got five and William Melville 'Alex' Alexander of Black Prince scored eight.

Rather than flying all together, the 'Black Flight' usually flew in twos or threes and the sight of their black machines quickly began to strike fear into the hearts of their adversaries.

Their remarkable string of successes came at a cost. Black Sheep was shot down on June 25. Nash was wounded in the leg but still managed to destroy his machine after landing behind enemy lines. He was taken prisoner by the Germans. Black Death suffered structural failure on July 22, resulting in Sharman's death. He had been diving on an enemy machine at high speed when the steel cables holding his wings together snapped and they folded back. Reid failed to return from a patrol on July 28 and was believed to have been killed by anti-aircraft fire hitting Black Roger.

Collishaw's last two Triplane kills, on July 27, were made with N533, one of six experimental

A scene never seen during the war – the Sopwith Triplane had been retired from front line service before the arrival of the German Fokker Dr.1. Here replicas of both types are flown together during an air show in New Zealand.

Triplanes fitted with a pair of synchronised Vickers guns rather than just one, but the type was nearing its end. Naval 4 had converted from its Pups to another new Sopwith type in June – the Camel – and the Triplane squadrons were to follow in August. ∎

WHAT HAPPENS IF YOU GIVE A TRIPEHOUND A BAD NAME

Almost a century later, doubt still lingers over why the Sopwith Triplane was never produced in larger quantities. Only around 150 were produced and the RFC's orders for more were cancelled – resulting in the RNAS being the only service to use it for front line operations.

MP and Supermarine founder Noel Pemberton Billing even asked about it in the House of Commons on March 20, 1917. He asked the Under-Secretary of State for War "whether the order for the Sopwith Triplane scout has been altered or cancelled; and, if it has been cancelled, will he say when this machine was offered to the authorities; when the order was placed; what number were ordered and what deliveries have taken place, and if this order has been cancelled for what reason?"

The Minister, Major John Baird, declined to answer any of Billing's questions and said that to do so would "give to Germany information which would enable them to know how long it takes us to produce new machines".

The answer might lie with the experiences of 10 Naval Squadron before its deployment to the Western Front in May 1917. Raymond Collishaw wrote: "During our time at Furnes, and even before I arrived on the squadron, there had been several accidents resulting from structural failure of the Triplane in the air.

"The notion had taken form in the heads of some of the pilots that the Triplane, despite its virtues, could not be trusted and was likely to fold up without warning."

At this stage there were no alternative machines for the pilots of Naval 10 to fly and Collishaw himself had seen no evidence of structural weakness in the Triplanes he had flown. He therefore took a Triplane up in the air and put it through a series of aerobatic manoeuvres to prove that it was sound.

It later transpired that some of the machines built by Clayton and Shuttleworth had been fitted with bracing wires that were thinner and weaker than those used by Sopwith itself in building the Triplane. The error was swiftly corrected but the damage was done. The extra machines ordered from Claytons were cancelled and production was taken no further.

Triplane pilots had an excellent view past the triple set of narrow wings. *Paul Le Roy*

The real 'Black Maria' – ace Raymond Collishaw's aeroplane.

SOPWITH TRIPLANE IN ACTION

An extract from Air Command by Raymond Collishaw, published by William Kimber:

The idea was to send out a patrol of F.E.2ds far behind the enemy lines. These, it was hoped, would attract the attention of the Germans and fighters would be sent up after them. They would then lure the unsuspecting Germans westwards to a point where large numbers of our own fighters would be waiting.

The F.E.s would then turn and fight and overwhelming formations of fighters would come down on the Germans and massacre them. So much for the vaunted chivalry of the knightly war in the air.

One thing that I learned very early in my air force career was the astounding number of things that can go wrong in any sort of military plan that involves more than one person and even then it cannot always be depended on.

In this instance, however, things went off very well indeed for us. In accordance with instructions, a patrol of eight F.E.2ds of 20 Squadron – the same unit that had shot down von Richthofen earlier in the month – left its aerodrome at 6.15pm. One of them had to land because of engine trouble but the others carried on towards Menin, about 20 miles behind the German lines.

On arrival there, flying at 12,000ft, they were greeted by several formations of Albatros fighters, about two dozen machines in all. Half the Germans worked round to the west, to cut off a retreat by the F.E.s, while the remainder attacked the 20 Squadron machines from the rear.

Normally the F.E.s would have formed into their usual defensive circle but their job was to decoy the hostile fighters back towards their own lines. Therefore, the F.E.s maintained formation and turned to the north-west, fighting off the Albatroses as they did so.

The rendezvous point was over Polygon Wood and by the time the F.E.s arrived there, still furiously fighting off their attackers, a sizable number of additional German machines had joined in.

Waiting for them were no fewer than 59 Allied fighters, most of them RFC machines with some French aircraft and, of course, our 12 Triplanes. We were all patrolling in layered formations, waiting for the enemy to arrive, and when they did we went down at them.

It was a very brisk affair indeed. I cannot give details concerning our other squadrons that were engaged but our scraps extended all the way from 16,000ft down to 4000ft. Some of the enemy fighters, exercising caution, had stayed up well above the F.E.s and we ran into a formation of six Albatroses at about our own height.

Nick Carter led 'A' Flight in an assault on them and getting close in behind one fired 15 rounds which he reported as going right into the pilot. The Albatros turned over on its

Air Command author and top scoring naval fighter ace Raymond Collishaw.

back and went down. The remaining German fighters dived down to between 8000ft and 9000ft and we all followed them.

They were joined by seven other Germans and a more or less private dogfight of our own ensued, one of numerous such scraps that were going on all around, above and below us. I dived on a formation of three Albatros D-Vs, picking out one of them and opening fire.

Tracers from both my guns went straight into the pilot's cockpit. The pilot, I am sure, was hit, but so was something else, for the wings folded and the Albatros went straight down, shedding pieces as it fell.

Off to one side I saw another German fighter go down, this one under the fire from a Spad, and then half a dozen of the enemy came down on my flight from high above. They split up as they came down on us and two of them singled out Ellis Reid, who turned away to the eastward to avoid them.

He managed to avoid their attack by flying underneath them and then pulled up above one of them. Diving down, he fired on it and the Albatros broke up in the air and went down.

Ellis by then was some distance away from the main scrap and as he turned back to rejoin us he was again attacked by a pair of Albatroses, one flying above the other. Feinting a counterattack on one of them, he drove it off, then going down and opening fire.

He got away several accurate bursts at the pilot and the German machine side-slipped out of a turn that it was in and went down. Shortly afterwards he was attacked again, this time by a single enemy fighter. The two manoeuvred for some time, getting down as low as 4000ft before Ellis was able to get on the German's tail and fire. The enemy fighter went down in a steep nosedive and smashed into the ground. Meantime, while Ellis had been having these

private engagements, the rest of us had been busy. I turned on to one of the enemy fighters that was on the tail of a Triplane and worked very close in before opening fire.

My tracers went right into the pilot and I am certain that he was killed. His machine went down spinning but I was unable to follow its fall. Alex drove down another but again I do not know whether it crashed or recovered.

It was at this stage in the fight that we lost Gerald Roach. I did not see it happen but Alex explained it to me after our return to Droglandt. Alex saw a German fighter swing in behind Roach from slightly above and it was apparent that Roach had no idea at all that anyone was behind him.

Alex made a climbing turn, firing his gun from extreme range in an effort to drive away the German machine, but the enemy pilot refused to be deterred and, getting right behind Roach, opened fire. Roach went down, likely never having known what hit him. The fight carried on furiously for about an hour and then, as was usually the case, suddenly ceased and none of the enemy was in sight.

Sopwith Triplane replica bearing the markings of Collishaw's machine. *Paul Le Roy*

Sopwith Pup & 1½ Strutter over the Sopwith sheds at Brooklands

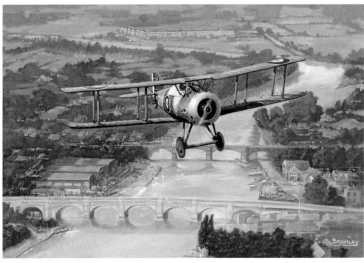
Sopwith Snipe over Kingston with the Ham factory behind

Designed and Built in Kingston - 100 years of world class aircraft

The Sopwith Aviation Company and its successors H.G Hawker Engineering, Hawker Aircraft, Hawker Siddeley Aviation and BAe designed and built aircraft in Kingston upon Thames from 1912 to 1992

You can find much more about Kingston's aviation heritage under **Short histories** and **Documentary slideshow** on the Kingston Aviation Centenary Project website

www.kingstonaviation.org

If you are interested in the thousands of people who worked in Kingston's aviation industry we are building **Photo Galleries** on the website and adding **Oral History** recordings by ex-employees

Hawker P1127, Sea Harrier & Harrier II over the Richmond Road factory at Ham in North Kingston
Paintings copyright Mark Bromley

If you worked in Kingston's Aviation industry we would be pleased to hear from you, especially if you have any photographs we can scan for our website or any material to donate to the Sopwith/Hawker archive at the Brooklands Museum

Ex-employee's can also join the Hawker Association who publish newsletters and hold monthly meetings in Kingston

Find out how to contact us on our websites

www.kingstonaviation.org

www.hawkerassociation.org.uk

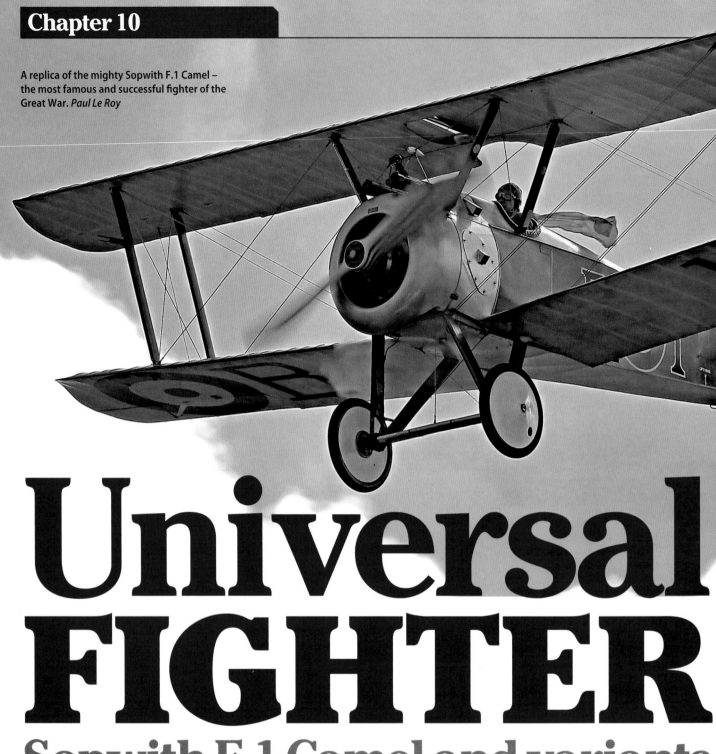

A replica of the mighty Sopwith F.1 Camel – the most famous and successful fighter of the Great War. *Paul Le Roy*

Universal FIGHTER

Sopwith F.1 Camel and variants

One aircraft is associated with the Sopwith name, perhaps even with the Great War itself, more than any other – the Camel. It destroyed more enemy aircraft than any other Allied type, some 3000, and it saw off some of Germany's best pilots. It fought on all fronts and in all conditions. It was truly a universal fighter…

As the third year of the Great War, 1916, drew to a close it was clear that trio of Sopwith types developed at the end of 1915 – the 1½ Strutter, the Pup and the Triplane – were already being overmatched by German Albatros types with their twin forward-firing guns. A radical solution was needed and quickly –

The Sopwith team pooled their ideas and the results were set down on paper by chief designer Herbert Smith. It is no exaggeration to say that the whole aeroplane was built around its twin synchronised Vickers machine guns yet the F.1, as Sopwith named it, had something else too.

Unlike the Pup and Triplane, it was not a direct descendent of the Tabloid. Structurally, it was a new design. All the largest and heaviest parts of the aeroplane, the guns and ammunition, the fuel tank, the engine and the pilot, were concentrated within a very short space of fuselage.

The first engine tried was a rotary 110hp Clerget 9Z and behind that a hump-like fairing was fitted, covered the back end of the guns. This gave the pilot some shelter from the icy slipstream in flight but reduced forward visibility.

As a result of this design, the F.1 had an unusually set-forward centre of gravity and consequently tricky handling. It also had remarkable manoeuvrability – thanks in part to torque from the engine, which turned

The Camel was the first British aeroplane to feature two forward-firing synchronised machine guns.
Paul Le Roy

Camel B9268 was built by Boulton & Paul for the RFC.

clockwise as seen from the cockpit.

Taking off was difficult and many Camel accidents occurred when the pilot was attempting to gain altitude immediately after leaving the ground. During take-off, the engine had to be fed a rich mixture of petrol and air but as height increased there was less need for this.

There was a fuel mix fine adjustment lever in the cockpit, and if this was accidentally left in the take-off position, the engine would begin to splutter and if no correction was made it would stall. A spin would then ensue and this typically occurred at such a low altitude that there was no chance of recovering it. The Camel would spin into the ground and the pilot would, most likely, suffer fatal injuries.

Assuming that the pilot made the appropriate correction to the fuel mix lever and managed to get airborne, a right turn would cause the aeroplane's nose to drop alarmingly but the machine would then make the turn with incredible speed.

When turning left, however, the nose rose up and the aeroplane turned only ponderously. Pilots who later flew the type often turned right even when they wanted to go left because it was simply quicker to go around that way until you were pointed in the right direction.

The first prototype F.1 was declared ready for flight testing by the Sopwith Experimental Department on December 22, 1916. When the second was ready, it had a more powerful

130hp Clerget 9B engine and a slightly flattened 'hump'. The third prototype had a further revision to its hump and it was this version that entered production.

It took less than a month for the RNAS to realise this 'Camel's' potential and the first order, for 50, was made in January 1917. A second RNAS order for another 50 from Sopwith later in the month was cancelled. The third prototype, however, was tested by the RFC, which was also showing an interest. Another Camel was given to the French authorities for testing.

Extensive tests on various prototypes were carried out at Martlesham Heath and one example, N517 – which may have been the second prototype – was sent to France, where it was tested by RNAS squadrons 6, 10, 9, 11 and 12, in that order, before a pilot crashed it on June 29.

With Sopwith operating at full capacity, an order for 250 Camels was given to Lincoln-based subcontractor Ruston Proctor & Co on March 2, 1917. More and more orders were now placed, with machines from particular batches being split between the RNAS and the RFC, rather than complete runs going to one service or the other.

The first production Camels began to arrive with 4 (Naval) Squadron throughout May and June 1917 – replacing the unit's Sopwith Pups. Most of these aeroplanes had the 130hp Clerget 9B engine but 11 had the AR.1 engine designed by W O Bentley, which developed 150hp and dramatically improved the Camel's performance.

Flight Commander Alexander MacDonald Shook was the first pilot to shoot down an enemy machine using a Camel when he attacked an Albatros D.III fighter near Ostend. Just 10 minutes later he got a second German machine – a C-type.

His fellow Naval 4 pilots also began to rack up victories using their Camels and towards the end of the month 6 Naval Squadron also began to receive the type as replacements for its Nieuport 17bis machines.

Now still more RNAS units were taking the Camel. First 3 (Naval) Squadron, then 8, then 9 in July. 11 (Naval) Squadron also then began to receive them.

Due to a shortage of pilots, Naval 6 and 11 were disbanded in August and their pilots and Camels redistributed to Naval 9 and 10.

The RFC received its first Camel on May 25, 1917 – N6332 was transferred from the RNAS and delivered to the aircraft depot at Candas north of Amiens on the Somme front. It was

While it was designed as a pure fighter, the Camel could be fitted with bombs, as shown here, and pressed into service for ground attack missions.

flying with 70 Squadron by June 13, where the type was to replace 1½ Strutters. A second Strutter unit, 45 Squadron, received its first Camel on July 25 and a third unit, 43 Squadron, also began to receive them.

"Trollope in Camel C8270 downed seven enemy machines in one day"

Delays hit the delivery of the RFC's first Camels however, since 24 machines were held back for Home Defence duties after a series of raids on Britain by German bombers. In September, more Camels arrived and 3 Squadron received them, as did 28 Squadron.

Next a number of RFC units flying Pups had them replaced by Camels, including 46, 54, 65 and 66 Squadrons. New squadrons were formed specifically to fly the Camel too – such as 71 (Australian) Squadron and 73 Squadron. Nearly all of the RFC's machines were Clerget powered.

Home Defence squadrons too received many more deliveries of Camels, although many of these machines were powered by 110hp Le Rhone engines – which was considered superior to the Clerget.

By now the Camel was becoming almost a universal standard type in British service. Pilots in France, Italy and elsewhere were accumulating an increasing number of victories using it and its capabilities and limitations were becoming readily apparent.

It was found that the Camel was at its most manoeuvrable between 9000ft and 12,000ft – above that altitude its rapid turning ability became a hindrance since it bled off too much speed. Therefore, Camels units were typically assigned patrols at that altitude while S.E.5a units would patrol higher up.

Pilots seldom flew on their own any more –

On the ground and at low speeds the Camel could be a handful. Its tricky handling could make it a dangerous machine for an amateur to fly. *Paul Le Roy*

A row of Camels belonging to 45 Squadron.

This brightly painted Camel was flown by 27-victory ace Captain Clifford MacKay McEwen of 28 Squadron. He named it Florence.

formation flying became the norm – and formation leaders usually scored more victories than anyone else since they fired the critical opening shots during an attack.

Once the element of surprise had been lost and a dogfight developed, it became much more difficult to shoot down an enemy machine. The Camel was by no means invulnerable either, and while it was extremely agile, scores of Camel pilots were shot down by the enemy.

Losses were exacerbated by the pressing need for RFC and RNAS squadrons to attack ground targets on the Western Front, particularly during the huge German offensive that began on March 21, 1918 – the Spring Offensive. Having been designed to combat enemy aeroplanes at altitude, the Camel was highly vulnerable to fire from enemy troops on the ground and losses soon mounted alarmingly.

There were also more instances of air-to-air combat during the German attack and some Camel pilots managed to achieve stunning

The 2F.1 Ship's Camel differed from the F.1 in several respects – most noticeably in its armament. It had only one fixed Vickers but did have a Lewis gun mounted on its upper wing.

successes. Three days after the assault began, Captain John Lightfoot Trollope of 43 Squadron, flying Camel C8270 managed to shoot down seven enemy machines in one day – three at around 11am and the remainder at about 3.20pm.

On April 12, 1918, Captain Henry Winslow Woollett nearly matched Trollope's achievement by shooting down six in one day while flying Camel D6402 – three at about 10.30am and the rest at around 5pm. Most of these were Albatros D.V single seat fighters rather than more vulnerable two-seaters.

TWO-SEAT TRAINERS AND NIGHT FIGHTERS

Early on in the Camel's career it was already being delivered in such significant numbers that there was an urgent need to train pilots on its use. Six machines made by Sopwith itself were delivered to the Central Flying School at Upavon and the RNAS sent some of its Camels to the training facilities at Eastchurch and Manston.

Camels tended not to last too long during training since the type's difficult handling, particularly at low speeds, plus the fuel mix issue, resulted in many inexperienced pilots crashing them.

Instructors too found the Camel tricky and they were responsible for a number of serious accidents. Therefore, a two-seat trainer conversion for single-seat Camels was

developed. The first of these was produced by the personnel of the 23rd Training Wing at South Carlton in Lincolnshire using Camel B3801 – a standard F.1 – in early 1918. More soon followed.

Converting a single-seat Camel to a two-seater required extensive internal modifications. The machines guns and their associated components were removed, the pilot's seat was moved forwards a little way, the gravity tank and 30 gallon pressure tank were taken out and another seat fitted in their place accompanied by full dual controls.

The oil tank under the aeroplane's front decking was replaced with a combined fuel and oil tank – the vastly reduced fuel load shrinking the amount of time the Camel could spend in the air to just 20 minutes in some cases. Most two-seat Camels had separate cockpits but at least one, B5575, had no partition between the instructor and the trainee.

The precise number of conversions is unknown but at least eight RAF training stations are known to have used them – Chattis Hill, Cranwell, Eastchurch, Joyce Green, Minchinhampton, Montrose, Redcar and Upavon.

As was the case with instructors' Pups, many unmodified Camels used at training schools were finished in bright and colourful paint schemes – the like of which would never have been allowed at the front.

Meanwhile, the 24 Camels that had been

A censor has scratched off the numbers of these Camels of 32 Squadron at Humieres Aerodrome on April 6, 1918.

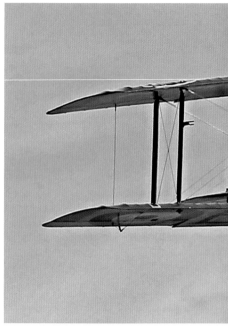

Shorter in the fuselage than the Pup by 6¾in but with an 18in greater wingspan, the Camel embodied many of the lessons the Sopwith company had learned from early combat experience in its machines. *Paul Le Roy*

held back for home defence duties, which had been passed to 39 Home Defence Squadron at Hainault Farm near Ilford in Essex were soon joined by more to combat the threat of German Gotha bombers attacking London.

A unit specifically set up for home defence using Camels, 44 Squadron, was established at Hainault Farm with many experienced pilots among its personnel in July 1917. In addition, 65 Squadron was moved to Wye in Kent for home defence and began to receive its first Camels in August 1917.

During that same month, the Germans switched from daylight raids to night bombing – which made them more difficult to successfully intercept. As a result, 44 Squadron began to retrain and re-equip so that its Camels could be used safely at night. The aircraft were fitted with brackets for Holt's flares, illumination for cockpit instruments and wingtip navigation lights.

One major problem with flying the Sopwith Camel at night proved to be the glare produced when its twin Vickers machine guns

were fired right in front of the pilot's eyes – resulting in temporary blindness. In addition, explosive/incendiary 'RTS' (which stood for Richard Threlfall and Sons – the inventors) bullets were being introduced for home defence squadrons.

These rounds were highly effective but also extremely sensitive. They did not necessarily fire at the same speed as ordinary .303 rifle bullets either, so they could not be guaranteed to pass through a spinning propeller even when it was fitted with synchronisation gear.

As a result of these problems, a new version of the Camel was created – known as the Comic. This had the Vickers guns removed entirely and replaced with a pair of Lewis guns mounted on the upper wing, a position from which their RTS bullets would clear the propeller completely. In order to make the guns easier to reach, the Camel's cockpit was

The Camel's unique abilities stemmed from the way it concentrated all its major loads into a small section of fuselage – the engine, guns, pilot and fuel tanks are all right up front. *Paul Le Roy*

moved further to the rear – where the main fuel tanks had been.

Where the cockpit had been, a B.E.2e main fuel tank was fitted which could hold about 18 gallons. This was about half of the Camel's usual fuel load. The Camel's 'hump' was also removed and a headrest was fitted behind the cockpit. With its smaller tank and altered centre of gravity, the Camel Comic's performance actually outstripped that of the regular F.1. While straight line speed remained the same, the Comic's rate of climb was improved along with its performance at altitude. It could reportedly turn well at up to 20,000ft. It is believed that the first Comics entered service in either November or December 1917 with 44 Squadron. They were usually fitted with Le Rhone 110hp engines rather than the 130hp Clerget. Despite the benefits of the Comic conversion, only a small number were made – most home defence Camels were simply fitted with Holt flares and lamps.

> ## "Night fighting Camels shot down Gotha bombers over Britain"

Successes in shooting down Gothas over Britain resulted in night-fighting Camels also being used in France by the recently formed RAF. A dedicated unit, 151 Squadron, was formed from flights of 44, 78 and 112 Squadrons on June 12, 1918. It flew to France on June 16 and was based at Fontaine-sur-Maye near the Somme front.

All of its Camels were F.1s fitted with night-fighting gear, rather than Comics. Although it was in active service for only five months, 151 Squadron achieved numerous successes in combat – 26 in all. A second night-fighting Camel unit, 152 Squadron, was formed in October 1918 but it was too late to see action.

2F.1 SHIP'S CAMEL

Alongside the two-seat and 'Comic' conversions, another major sub-type of the Camel was the dedicated naval version – the 2F.1. During the last week of November 1916, Sopwith was allocated a pair of serial numbers, N4 and N5, for two machines described as 'Baby (Improved) Seaplanes' and given the type FS.1.

The F.1 Camel's design was being finalised at this point and the FS.1 floatplane N4 looked very similar albeit with a pair of pontoon floats, a tail float, a fuselage that could be split in half for easier storage, a narrower wingspan, longer ailerons, only a single Vickers gun and a Lewis gun mounted upside down on the centre section of the upper wing.

Holt's flares

Night fighter Camels were fitted with long vertical brackets for Holt's flares that hung down from the aeroplanes' wingtips. The flares themselves were 4in long by 2in diameter cartridges made by the Yorkshire Steel Company of London, having been invented by RFC pilot Captain F V Holt.

Each cartridge had two wires attached to a binding post on the bracket. Cables then connected the binding post to an activation button in the cockpit. When the button was pressed, usually at about 300ft, the cartridge was ignited electrically.

The magnesium cartridge, held well away from the fabric covered wooden wing by the bracket, would then burn for about a minute – giving enough time to check position and height. More than one flare was usually carried for safety purposes.

Glare from the burning flare was a serious problem however – its flat white light reflected off the backs of propeller blades and wings and cast misleading shadows on to the ground. Initially a metal shield was fitted around the flare brackets but this created additional problems and the shield idea was ditched. In the end, pilots took to having the backs of their propeller blades covered in lamp black and their lower wings too.

In spite of these problems, Holt's flares did work and remained in service until shortly before the Second World War.

The 'hump' over the Camel's guns provided the pilot with some limited protection from the elements. *Paul Le Roy*

Trials were carried out involving Camels being flown from the underside of British airship HMA R23.

One of the most unusual Camel variants was the home defence 'Comic'. The Vickers guns were removed and the cockpit was moved further to the rear. Armament was a pair of Lewis guns. *DH/MG/Brooklands*

It was powered by the Camel's 130hp Clerget 9B rotary engine.

N5 was built with a wheeled undercarriage, which could be detached by the pilot in preparation for ditching in the sea, but otherwise embodied all the differences that had separated N4 from an F.1. N4 was sent to the RNAS Type Test Flight at Grain in Kent for testing on March 24, 1917, but was destroyed in a crash three days later. N5 first flew at Hendon on March 3 but crashed at Martlesham Heath on the same day as N4.

Unlike N4, N5 was rebuilt and fitted with a mounting rail that allowed the Lewis gun to be reloaded and fired upwards. Provision was also made for the use of Le Prieur rockets. A wind-driven generator was also set into the port side of the fuselage to power a wireless radio set. Plans were made to convert N5 into a floatplane but were not carried out.

Sopwith received an order for 50 more examples of the N5 machine on September 8, 1917, and it was given the new type number 2F.1 as well as being referred to as the Ship's

Camel. Further orders were subcontracted to Clayton & Shuttleworth, Hooper & Co and Beardmore, which used Arrol-Johnston as its own subcontractor for the work.

Around 230 2F.1s were built, with all the production models being powered by the Bentley BR.1 150hp engine. Elevator control wires, which previously had run through the interior of the fuselage, were moved to external runs so that floatation bags could be installed.

Deliveries to the RNAS began in October 1917. Some went to shore stations but most were rolled out across the fleet to replace Pups and Beardmore W.B.IIIs on gun turret platforms and ramps. In all, 22 cruisers and 25 battleships/battlecruisers embarked 2F.1s.

2F.1s were first used in anger on June 1, 1918, when German seaplanes attacked the 2nd Light Cruiser Squadron near the Heligoland Bight. *HMAS Melbourne* and *HMAS Sydney* launched their 2F.1s – N6756 and N6783 respectively.

After 82 minutes, the pilot of the former, Flight Lieutenant L B Gibson had lost sight of the enemy and ditched alongside *HMS Centaur*. The other pilot, Flt Lt A C Sharwood, claimed to shoot one of the enemy machines down but this was done out of sight of the fleet and after he had ditched near some British destroyers his claim was disallowed.

HMS Galatea launched its 2F.1 on June 17 and the pilot, low on fuel after having unsuccessfully taken on the enemy, had to make a forced landing in Denmark. *HMS Furious* launched N6810 on June 19 but this met with a similar lack of success.

> ## "I dived with full engine to 50ft and zigzagged to avoid enemy fire"

THE TONDERN RAID

It might have seemed as though the 2F.1 force was doomed to repeat the failures of Sopwith's earliest naval machines but a single daring mission cemented the type's place in history – the Tondern Raid.

For the first time ever, plans were drawn up to fly strike aircraft from a carrier vessel against a target on land. The vessel was *HMS Furious* and the target was the German airship base at Tondern near the border with Denmark. The mission had involved eight 2F.1s but one pilot was forced to drop out and there was no time to train a replacement – leaving seven. *Furious* left Rosyth on July 17,

Once a Ship's Camel had been flown off its host vessel there was no way for it to land back on board. The pilot could either find somewhere else to land or ditch his machine near friendly vessels and hope to be picked up. 2F.1s were fitted with floatation bags in their fuselage to keep them on the surface for as long as possible.

A Camel of 44 Home Defence Squadron RFC Hainault Farm. Note the bracket on the end of the right wing designed to hold a Holt flare.

1918, with a large escort of battleships and cruisers and sailed towards the target. Bad weather resulted in a 24 hour delay but the raid began on July 19 at 3.21am. One pilot, Captain T K Thyne, suffered engine trouble and had to turn around but the remaining six pressed on.

The first flight of three Ship's Camels arrived over the target at 4.35am and three airship sheds were attacked. The largest, which housed Zeppelins L54 and L60 was destroyed. One of the 2F.1s, flown by Lieutenant William F Dickson, made it back to the fleet and was picked up by *HMS Violent*. The others made forced landings in Denmark, the pilots being taken prisoner shortly afterwards.

The second flight arrived 10 minutes later and the flight commander, Lieutenant Bernard Arthur Smart, later recalled: "At 0445 hours, I saw Tondern some 10 miles to the south-west and steered west. Shortly after, fairly heavy anti-aircraft fire opened on us. I was unable to see the sheds for some minutes, but eventually three AA batteries close together attracted my attention, and near them I discovered the sheds, two large ones and one smaller, one of the larger having the roof partially destroyed and emitting large volumes of dense black smoke.

"When in position I gave the signal and dived on the remaining large shed, releasing my bombs at 800 to 1000ft. The first fell short, but the second hit the centre of the shed, sending up a quantity of smoke or dust.

"Whether this burst into flames later I am unable to state, as the whole surroundings were thick with mechanics or soldiers armed with rifles and machine-guns, which gave so disconcerting a fire that I dived with full engine to 50ft and skimmed over the ground in a zigzag course to avoid it, and by the time I got clear I was unable to see the sheds on account of the thick screen of smoke from the first shed."

Smart found his way back to *HMS Furious* and ditched nearby at 6.30am. He was forced to sit on the tail of his sinking aeroplane for 15 minutes in 15ft waves before it finally sank completely and he fell into the sea and lost his life preserver. He was picked up minutes later having swallowed a lot of sea water.

Another second flight pilot, Lieutenant Samuel Dawson, made a forced landing in Denmark and was taken prisoner. The flight's last pilot, Walter Albert Yeulett, crashed into the sea. His body and the wreck of his Ship's Camel were later washed ashore. Dickson and Smart were awarded DSOs (Smart's being a bar to his earlier DSO) by the King. The three captured men were awarded DFCs and Yeulett received one posthumously.

As well as being flown from turrets and dedicated aircraft carriers, Ship's Camels also flew from lighters towed by destroyers. The first flight test from a ship-towed platform took place on May 30, 1918. Lieutenant Colonel C R 'Sammy' Samson flew 2F.1 N6623 with skids fitted instead of wheels down a set of grooves on the deck of a lighter being towed at 32 knots by *HMS Truculent*.

Unfortunately, the skids jumped out of the grooves, the Camel fell off the deck rather than flew and was then run over by the lighter. Samson's machine was destroyed but he survived. The idea was not abandoned however. On August 11, 1918, the Harwich Light Cruiser Force attempted to lure out some Zeppelins. One of its flying boats

The seven Sopwith 2F.1 Ship's Camels involved in the first ever strike against ground targets by carrier-borne aircraft line up on the deck of *HMS Furious* ahead of the Tondern Raid.

The 2F.1 Ship's Camel was designed with a fuselage that could be split in half to save space on board a ship. *DH/MG/Brooklands*

spotted one approaching at 8.25am, L53, and Lieutenant S D Culley's 2F.1 was launched from a lighter being towed by the *HMS Redoubt*. He initially lost sight of the airship in clouds but after climbing to 19,000ft, near the Camel's ceiling, he suddenly sighted it 300ft above his machine. He pulled back on the stick and fired into it.

After seven rounds, one of the two fixed Lewis guns on his upper wing jammed but the second kept firing. L53 abruptly burst into flames and then broke into two pieces and fell burning into the sea. It was the last German airship to be destroyed during the war.

Experiments were also carried out with launching 2F.1s from British airships. A number of Camels were launched from HMA R23. Tests of the rig required to carry an underslung Camel took place in July 1918 and by October 3, R23 had flown for three hours with a Camel attached.

An unmanned F.1 Camel, D8250, was launched on November 3, 1918. Its rudder was locked in a neutral position and its elevators were set at 2º down. The aeroplane detached successfully and drifted down before overturning when it hit the ground. Three days later, a manned test took place with Lieutenant R E Keys at the controls.

He said: "My engine was started before leaving the ground and I kept it running at 500rpm. The rigid airship attained the height of 3000ft during which time the aeroplane was quite rigid and satisfactory.

"The saddle fitting over the end of the fuselage was then removed. I gave the signal to be released and on being released the machine dropped about 10ft and picked up her glide and was immediately under control. The machine showed no tendency whatever to get out of control. The speed of the rigid airship was 30mph." Further tests were planned in the early 1920s but no further flights from airships took place.

During the course of the Great War, the Camel was credited with shooting down 1294 enemy aircraft – more than any other single type operated by any nation. The most successful single aeroplane in the history of the RAF was a Camel, B6313, flown by William George Barker. He used it to shoot down 46 enemy machines.

The Camel was operated by 58 British squadrons, by the US, Canada, Australia, Belgium, Estonia, Georgia, Greece, Latvia, the Netherlands, Poland, Russia and Sweden. Just under 5500 Camels are believed to have been built though the exact number will never be known for reasons outlined in chapter 22. ∎

Sopwith Cam

An extract from No Parachute – A Classic Account of War in the Air in WWI by Arthur Gould Lee:

Gould Lee's squadron was ordered to support a surprise attack using tanks on Wednesday, November 21, 1917. The day was misty and rainy but the pilots were still able to guide their Camels towards their targets just behind the German Hindenburg Line defences. Gould Lee writes:

We passed over a succession of unoccupied camps and horse lines, then, as we approached the Lines, saw large assemblies of cavalry waiting and reserves of infantry moving up in scattered columns.

There were four of us, Charles Courtneidge the flight commander, myself, Dusgate and Hanafy, but at this point Dusgate's engine conked, and he turned away and crashed in what had been our front line less than an hour previously.

A few seconds later we passed over the deep wide trenches of the dreaded Hindenburg Line, with its vast belts of barbed wire, through which the first waves of tanks had crushed hundreds of lanes.

From then on the mist was made denser by the smoke-screen laid in front of the advancing tanks from zero hour onwards, which still hung around.

We pass over the rear wave of the advance, reserve and supply tanks, field artillery, support troops and so on, then quickly catch up the first wave. Everything flashes by like a dream, and as we rush forward at over 90mph, 20ft up, I get split-second glimpses that remain vividly in the memory.

I see the ragged line of grey diamond shaped monsters, 30 to 50 yards apart, stretching into the mist on either flank, rolling unevenly forwards, their tracks churning round, their exhausts throwing out blue-grey smoke. I see, behind each tank, a trudging group of infantry, casually smoking, looking up at us.

Other knots of infantry stroll along a little in rear, between the tanks. To a flank, I see a disabled tank, flames leaping up, the troops standing helplessly around. A chance enemy shell bursts between two tanks, knocks down a small bunch of soldiery like ninepins.

The ground slopes upwards, trapping us under the clouds, so that our wheels almost touch the grass. I have to rise to clear a tank ahead, skim over it, down in front. It seems to be standing still. Then we've passed them, we're ahead of the advance and approaching the Boche.

Smoke shells burst ahead, a flash of red flame and masses of belching cloud, which we speed through – nauseous smelling stuff that stings the eyes. In patches, where smoke

The Camel was a tough machine. This aeroplane was involved in a mid-air collision in 1918 but the pilot was able to land it safely.

merges with mist and cloud, we fly blind.

Now we reach the rear of the Hindenburg defence system, two lots of trenches, with troops in field grey waiting in them, their forward view blocked by a pall of smoke. We issue out of the screen so low and so fast that they have no time to fire and as we skim just over their heads, I see them staring up at us in incredulous amazement.

Then they're behind. More smoke-shells burst ahead, and suddenly, unexpectedly, we're at the wood, at the Y-junction of our road and two others.

All this time we've managed to keep in loose formation, but now we break up and climb, in order to dive and bomb. At once, we're in the clouds and have to drop.

The 5.9s below are firing, producing more smoke. Charles and Hanafy have vanished, engulfed in cloud and smoke, and so there we are, the three of us, whirling blindly around at 50-100ft, all but colliding, being shot at from below, and trying to place bombs accurately.

Even at this frantic moment, my mind switches to my beautifully dead-on practice bombing on our bullet-free smoke-free aerodrome, but I don't have time to laugh.

The night before, Charles had indicated which of the seven groups of guns each of us was to tackle, but in this blind confusion there wasn't a hope of picking and choosing. The main thing was to get rid of the darned bombs before a bullet hit them.

In a sharp turn I saw a bunch of guns right in line for attack, so dived at 45° and released all four bombs. As I swung aside I saw them burst, a group of white-grey puffs centred with red flames. One fell between two guns, the rest a few yards away.

Splinters suddenly splash in my face – a bullet through a centre-section strut. This makes me go hot, and I dive at another group of guns, giving them 100 rounds, see a machine gun blazing at me, swing on to that, one short burst and he stops firing.

As I climb up, a Camel whizzes past me out of the mist, missing me by a yard. It makes me sweat with fright. This is too dangerous, and I lift into the cloud to 300ft, stay there half a minute, come down.

Lateau Wood is behind me. There isn't much room below, I nearly hit a high tree, swerve violently, skim through tree-tops with the mist clinging to the branches, then suddenly no trees, an open road. I fly along it, trying to get my breath. My heart is racing, and it isn't through being at 20,000ft.

A long column of artillery limbers – just what I need to recover my balance. I zoom, then switchback along the column, spraying short bursts in each little dive. I glance back – it is a shambles, half of them in the ditches. I'm sorry for the horses, though.

I'd no idea where I was, nor which way I was going. The compass was spinning madly.

A Classic Account of War in the Air in WWI

NO PARACHUTE

ARTHUR GOULD LEE

Suddenly the clouds lifted a little, I rose to 300 odd, and could see 300-400 yards. I didn't recognise the ground. There were no trenches, but ahead were encampments and military set-ups.

The tents looked odd. And the soldiery – field greys! Then suddenly – rak-ak-ak-ak! And tracer! I swung the Camel violently round. Two V-strutters were coming up behind me, guns flashing, a third behind them. Then beyond I saw a line of canvas hangars, a large field. A Hun aerodrome!

I was in no frame of mind for heroic air combat at 300ft, but to save my skin, swung sharply round again, put a burst into the first Hun as he whizzed past me, did another tight

turn, put another burst at the second Hun – then my guns jammed. There was only one thing to do and I did it – climb up into the clouds.

After the War, Arthur Stanley Gould Lee, from Boston, Lincolnshire, remained in the RAF and rose to the rank of air vice-marshal before retiring in 1946. He wrote several books before his death on May 21, 1975.

■ No Parachute by Arthur Gould Lee, published by Grub Street Publishing, is available from all good booksellers and online at www.grubstreet.co.uk

Chapter 11

DEATH
of the Red Baron

The Great War's most famous duel

The most famous man to fly an aeroplane during the Great War was German ace Manfred von Richthofen. Nearly a century after his death, and when most other aces have been forgotten, the Red Baron remains a household name. His final battle, flying his distinctive scarlet Fokker DR.I triplane against British Sopwith Camels, has become one of the war's most iconic moments.

He was a national hero and Germany's highest-scoring ace, but by the beginning of 1918 Manfred von Richthofen had grown weary of war.

Born into Prussian nobility, von Richthofen had been a cavalryman before he transferred to the German air service in 1915, aged 23. At first he was arrogant and treated the war like a hunt and British airmen as his prey.

For each aeroplane he shot down he ordered a silver cup and had it engraved with the date of the victory and the type of machine he'd destroyed. He also collected trophies from his foes' machines too – usually the British military serial number cut from the canvas side of the wrecked machine.

These were mounted on the wall of his trophy room alongside other trinkets such as captured pistols, and even a light fitting made from a British aero engine. His greatest early triumph came on November 23, 1916, while flying an Albatros D.II when he shot down and killed British ace and Victoria Cross recipient Lanoe Hawker.

On January 4, 1917, at 4.15pm, he shot down his first Sopwith – Pup number N5193, piloted by 30-year-old Flight Lieutenant Allan S Todd. It was his 16th victory. Todd's body was later found in the wreckage of his machine and the serial number was carefully removed for the baron's collection – though whether he removed it himself is unknown. It was this 'kill'

One of several modern replicas of the Red Baron's distinctive Fokker DR.I. Most depict it as bright red, but in reality the paint finish was very far from perfect and almost certainly much darker in tone. *Oliver Thiele*

that earned von Richthofen the prize he most coveted, the Pour le Mérite or 'Blue Max' medal.

Within weeks, he had assumed command of Jagdstaffel or 'Jasta' 11, a fighter squadron, and had his personal aeroplane, a new Albatros D.III, painted red for the first time. Thereafter, he usually flew red-painted machines, though they were seldom entirely red, nor even a particularly bright red.

In March 1917, he destroyed 10 British machines and the following month, known to the RFC as 'Bloody April', another 21, bringing his overall total to 52. After his 50th victory, he was invited back to Germany to meet the Kaiser, who congratulated him in person. He also met the Empress, went hunting on his family's estate and began work on his autobiography.

By the middle of 1917, the Germans were struggling to match the Allies for the sheer number of aeroplanes they could put in the air. Therefore, it was decided that a smaller number of large formations should be established so that air superiority could be achieved in localised areas as needed.

On June 24, Jastas 4, 6, 10 and 11 were combined to form Jagdgeschwader 1 and von Richthofen, now flying an Albatros D.V, was appointed as its commanding officer. This large, mobile formation of brightly painted fighters quickly became known to Allied pilots as the 'Flying Circus' .

Despite commanding such a large unit, von Richthofen continued to lead from the front and his tally of victories began to rise once more. Then, on July 6, 1917, during a battle with F.E.2d fighters of 20 Squadron RFC, von Richthofen suffered a bullet wound to the head that splintered his skull.

He became disorientated before losing consciousness completely and barely came round in time to prevent his aircraft from crashing. Instead, he was able to bring it down for a rough landing before being hauled from the cockpit and taken to hospital. Several rounds of surgery were needed to remove fragments of shattered bone from his head.

Despite being warned against it, von

During his early career as a fighter pilot, Manfred von Richthofen saw himself as a hunter and the British as his prey.

Canadian Arthur Roy Brown was 24 when he fought the Red Baron's 'Flying Circus' over the Somme on April 21, 1918.

Richthofen returned to active service on July 25, achieving four more victories from August 16 to September 3. The last of these was a by now seriously outdated Sopwith Pup, B1795 of 46 Squadron, flown by Lieutenant Algernon Frederick Bird. Bird surrendered to von Richthofen in the air, landed and was taken prisoner. Anthony Fokker, founder of the aircraft company that bore his name, visited the downed Pup with von Richthofen, the ace having been flying the former's new prototype triplane Fokker F.I at the time.

A grinning Fokker put on Bird's heavy flying coat for publicity photographs and sat on the Pup's tail, while von Richthofen stood uneasily by, the bandage around his head wound still visible beneath the rim of his cap. By now the Baron was suffering from headaches and sickness. His temperament changed and his appetite for showmanship and 'the hunt' had evaporated.

He finally decided that he needed a break and took convalescent leave from September 5 to October 23. Returning in November, he added two more victories to bring his total up to 63 before taking

another break from the front line. Back in Germany, he visited striking munitions factory workers and saw first hand how people were now being affected by food and coal shortages.

The national mood was one of increasing dissatisfaction and unrest. At home in Silesia, at the end of January 1918, von Richthofen's mother and sister urged him to be careful when he returned to the front, and he later said that embracing his mother had filled him with a grim foreboding.

By now, von Richthofen's heavily censored autobiography, Der Rote Kampfflieger 'The Red Fighter Pilot' had been published, but he dismissed it, saying that it was "too insolent" and that he was "no longer that kind of person".

As the buildup to Germany's Spring Offensive began – an all-or-nothing big push – Manfred von Richthofen gritted his teeth and climbed into the cockpit of a deadly new aeroplane, the Fokker DR.I triplane.

He had already been approached about stepping down and returning home as his nation's greatest hero, but he was determined to see the war through to the bitter end.

There would be no more silver cups and trophies.

Von Richthofen's first victory of the year came on March 12 when the crew of a Bristol F.2b two-seat fighter, like Bird, surrendered to him in the air and were taken prisoner after landing. The following day he got his first Sopwith Camel, B2523 of 73 Squadron, piloted by Lieutenant Elmer Ernest Heath. He disabled the Camel, but then allowed Heath to land safely without attacking further.

Thereafter, von Richthofen launched into another killing spree with aircraft after aircraft falling to his guns. Having started on March 12 on 63 victories, in just 18 days it was 74. Six more machines fell in April, taking his total to 80 on April 20.

Manfred von Richthofen was flying this Fokker DR.I, serial 127/17, when he made his 71st, 74th and 76th kills. The first and last of these were both Sopwith Camels.

Wilfrid 'Wop' May, 22, was a rookie with 209 Squadron when its members fought the 'Flying Circus' on April 21, 1918. He'd been told to stay out of the fight, but couldn't resist joining in. Von Richthofen singled him out as his latest victim, but the battle did not turn out the way the ace intended.

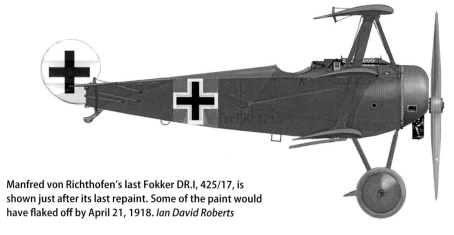

Manfred von Richthofen's last Fokker DR.I, 425/17, is shown just after its last repaint. Some of the paint would have flaked off by April 21, 1918. *Ian David Roberts*

SOPWITH V FOKKER

Another pilot had been getting back into the action after a winter break at home, meanwhile. Flight Lieutenant Arthur Roy Brown had enjoyed a break in his native Canada and the US after serving with 9 (Naval) Squadron of the RNAS during 1917.

He returned to the unit in France at the end of January and was pleased to discover that during his absence it had been re-equipped with the latest version of the Sopwith Camel – the one with the 150hp Bentley BR.1 engine and new hydraulic actuating gear for its guns.

He took one up, B3781, on January 30, 1918, at 10.45am for a practice and then went on an uneventful patrol in the same machine the following morning.

On February 2 he was promoted to acting flight commander – the RNAS equivalent to captain. Things were looking up. They were looking even rosier when, after only a few days at the front, Naval 9 was sent back to England for a rest, leaving its aircraft behind to be reallocated to other units.

When the time came to return to France, Naval 9 was allocated 12 new BR.1 Camels and Brown got B7270. He flew it to Middle Aerodrome in France on March 20 and tested its guns the following day at 3.10pm. One hour and 50 minutes later he was back in the air again – the Spring Offensive had begun, and the Germans had forced Naval 9 to retreat by pounding their base with 5in artillery shells.

The next day, Brown achieved his seventh victory by shooting down a German two-seater in flames north-east of Houthulst Forest. During a patrol on March 23, Brown's machine guns malfunctioned and wouldn't stop firing. B7270's synchroniser gear failed too and one of his propeller blades was hit by bullets and nearly shattered. After landing, he wrapped it in several yards of adhesive tape from an orderly station.

On April 1, Naval 9 became the newly formed RAF's 209 Squadron. Flight Commander Brown became Captain Brown and one of his unit's first new members was

Wilfrid Reid 'Wop' May. Brown claimed his eighth kill on April 12 – a Fokker DR.I triplane – shared with another pilot from his flight, Lt Francis Mellersh. The following day he unknowingly ate a contaminated rabbit for lunch; that night was violently sick and was admitted to hospital with food poisoning.

By April 19, he was still recovering, but not wishing to let his colleagues down he returned to duty, surviving on a diet of milk and brandy. The next day he took May, the rookie, on patrol over the front line and May fired his guns in combat for the first time. It was at 6.43pm that evening that von Richthofen scored his 80th victory – over Second Lieutenant David Greswolde 'Tommy' Lewis in Camel B7393.

The Baron's bullets set Lewis's machine on fire and the flames burned away the canvas from the tail of his machine. He made for the ground and the airstream kept the flames off him a little, though he was still badly burned. Von Richthofen watched to see him land and climb from the cockpit before flying away.

The next day, April 21, Brown in Camel B7270, Mellersh in B6257 and May in D3326, set off on patrol at 9.30am. After an hour and a half in the air, he spotted a large formation of between 15 and 20 Albatros D.V and Fokker DR.Is and dived in to attack it with his wingmen. Pulling out of his dive, Brown found two enemy fighters on his tail and veered away. Having shaken them off, he then saw that rookie May was being pursued and fired on by a red triplane.

May said later: "I noticed it was a red triplane, but if I had realised it was von Richthofen, I would have probably passed out on the spot. I kept on dodging and spinning, I imagine from about 12,000ft, until I ran out of sky and had to hedge hop over the ground.

"Von Richthofen was firing at me continually, and the only thing that saved me was my poor flying. I didn't know what I was doing myself, and I do not suppose that von Richthofen could figure out what I was going to do.

The Fokker DR.I was built in small numbers, like the Sopwith Triplane. Just 320 were made, and the type was notorious for suffering structural failure – though not through poor workmanship. An inherent design flaw meant the upper wing carried a much higher lift coefficient than the lower wing.

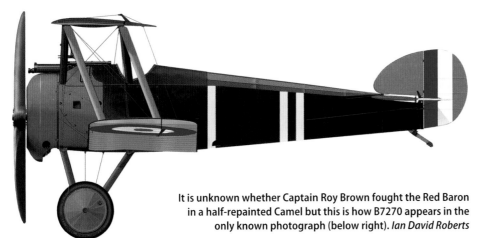

It is unknown whether Captain Roy Brown fought the Red Baron in a half-repainted Camel but this is how B7270 appears in the only known photograph (below right). *Ian David Roberts*

British pilots inspect the Red Baron's guns after the recovery of his wrecked Fokker DR.I.

Captain Brown's Sopwith Camel, B7270, had a 150hp Bentley BR.1 engine, but in this photo it had not been painted with a fuselage roundel.

"We came over the German lines and troops fired at us as we went over – this was also the case coming over the British lines. I got on the Somme river and started up the valley at a very low altitude. Von Richthofen was very close on my tail. I went around a curve in the river just near Corbie, but von Richthofen beat me to it and came over the hill.

"At that point I was a sitting duck, as I was too low down between the banks to make a turn away from him. I felt that he had me cold, and I was in such a state of mind at this time that I had to restrain myself from pushing my stick forward into the river as I knew that I had had it."

Accounts from observers suggest that von Richthofen, who was a good enough shot to have killed May, was trying to shoot his wings and force him down. After flying down the Somme canal, May turned and flew into the village of Vaux-sur-Somme and down a street towards a church.

Von Richthofen broke off his attack and turned right – now with Roy Brown following him. Just west of the church, Brown opened fire. The Fokker turned right again and now flew over a heavily defended part of the Somme. Troops on the ground also began to open fire on the red aeroplane.

A single bullet entered the Fokker from the right-hand side and hit von Richthofen in the ribs before exiting his body via his upper left chest. May later reported that the triplane had crashed on the side of a hill. In fact, von Richthofen managed to retain a measure of control over his machine and brought it down in a field north of the village.

It was a rough landing and the Fokker's wheels broke off before it finally skidded to a halt in a cloud of dust. British soldiers raced to the stricken machine and found von Richthofen still alive, though covered in blood. One, Gunner Ernest Twycross, later claimed to have been beside him when he mumbled one word "kaput" and died. The Red Baron was only 25.

Brown believed that he had shot down the triplane, although he did not know who the pilot was and did not see it crash because he then went to the aid of Mellersh, whose Camel was being attacked by another pair of DR.Is. May denied having seen Brown attack von Richthofen.

The April 21, 1918, war diary entries of two units in the area on the ground – the 11th Australian Infantry Brigade and the 14th Australian Field Artillery Brigade – both state that one of their machine gunners brought down the red DR.I. In the former, Sergeant Cedric Bassett Popkin was given the credit, while in the latter it was Gunner Robert Buie.

The downed aeroplane was salvaged by a team from AFC 3 Squadron led by Lt Walter Warneford, and von Richthofen's body was recovered and autopsied that night. The angle of the entry wound suggested that Popkin had been the only one in a position to have fired the fatal shot – but this has never been, and is unlikely ever to be, conclusively proven.

Von Richthofen's Fokker DR.I had already been plundered for souvenirs by the time Warneford's men reached it – some sections of fabric had been taken by British soldiers – but it was largely intact. Photographs were taken of British airmen examining the Red Baron's guns and Roy Brown himself got von Richthofen's seat, which he donated to the Royal Canadian Military Institute in Toronto in 1920. The institute also has a piece of fabric from the aircraft signed by Brown and the members of his squadron.

The DR.I's engine ended up at the Imperial War Museum in London and its control column was donated to the Australian War Memorial in Canberra.

Von Richthofen himself was given a full military funeral by members of AFC 3 Squadron and buried in the cemetery at Bertangles, near Amiens, on April 22, 1918.

His corpse was moved to a military cemetery at Fricourt in the 1920s, but in 1925 von Richthofen's youngest brother Bolko had it disinterred and taken back to Germany, where he was given a state funeral, before being reburied at the Invalidenfriedhof Cemetery in Berlin with other heroes of Germany.

After spending the Cold War in the Soviet zone of Berlin, von Richthofen's remains were dug up again and moved to a grave at the Südfriedhof, in Wiesbaden, where is he is now situated next to Bolko, his sister Elisabeth and her husband.

Roy Brown, who was officially credited with shooting down von Richthofen by the RAF, was taken off the front line just nine days later suffering from nervous exhaustion and the flu. After serving as an instructor in June he was involved in a back crash while taking off in a Sopwith Camel in July and spent the rest of the war in hospital.

Back in Canada, he left the RAF and worked as an accountant before founding a small airline and editing an aviation magazine. He died of a heart attack in 1944 aged 50. ∎

After the pilot of Sopwith Pup B1795 surrendered to him in mid-air, von Richthofen and Anthony Fokker went to examine the aeroplane and posed for pictures on its tail. Fokker even wore the British pilot's coat.

Chapter 12

ENGINE TROUBLE
The problem with powerplants

Aero engine technology was in its infancy when the Great War began and some of the Sopwith Aviation Company's finest aircraft were dogged by mechanical unreliability due to their third party-supplied powerplants. It was a problem that just wouldn't go away...

The vast majority of Sopwith aircraft produced were fitted with rotary engines – where the whole engine span around with the propeller.

Most of these engines were lubricated with castor oil using a total loss system, where the oil was sprayed around the rapidly rotating cylinders and then shed from the aircraft, and cooled by air passing over the engine from the front.

Rotaries were lightweight and compact, being relatively 'flat', and typically produced a higher power to weight ratio than car-type engines which had their cylinders in a line or in a 'V' formation.

The shape, position and action of the rotary engine also tended to enhance the manoeuvrability of the aeroplane to which it was fitted.

Later Sopwith machines used a variety of other engines. For example, the Dolphin used a V8 Hispano-Suiza ('Spanish-Swiss') and the Dragon used the ABC Dragonfly radial – where the cylinders were arranged like those of a rotary but the engine remained still while the propeller rotated.

None of these types was without serious mechanical drawbacks. Engine failure was what every pilot dreaded. It was a frequent occurrence in these pioneering machines and it often proved fatal.

CLERGET ROTARIES

Engines from the Clerget 9 family of nine-cylinder rotaries were fitted to more Sopwith machines than any other type. They powered most Babies, 1½ Strutters, Triplanes and Camels.

Although the Clerget 9 was designed by the French company Clerget-Blin et Cie, it was produced under licence in Britain by Gwynnes of London and Ruston, Proctor & Co of Lincoln.

During the war, Gwynnes made 1750 of them while Ruston, Proctor & Co made 1900. Another 2045 Clergets were delivered to British manufacturers by French contractors.

The most common '9' was the Clerget 9B which was used to power the Camel. It was a tough engine but it suffered from a cooling problem. The airflow over the front of the engine didn't reach the rear sufficiently so the cylinders tended to distort at the back due to overheating.

An 'obdurator' ring was fitted which expanded to account for the distortion but these didn't last very long. Due to the precision engineering and balancing required to produce a Clerget it was also extremely expensive, costing £907.50 in 1915 – the equivalent of £79,000 in today's money. The rest of a Sopwith Camel airframe only cost £874 (£76,085 today).

Most of the Clerget rotary engines used by British manufacturers, including Sopwith, were made in Britain under licence. This is the Clerget engine test shop at Ruston, Proctor & Co in Lincoln.

The 9B was also heavy on its fuel and oil consumption. It used 12 gallons (54.5 litres) of fuel per hour and 14 pints of oil – although this was positively frugal compared to later engines.

BENTLEY BR.1 ROTARY

Engineer Walter Owen 'W O' Bentley – who would later find fame and fortune with his car company – came up with a solution to ease the Clerget's cooling problem. He had offered his ideas about aluminium pistons to the Admiralty at the onset of war and was soon made a lieutenant in the Royal Naval Volunteer Reserve.

Bentley was assigned to work as naval liaison officer at Gwynnes, persuading the company to adopt aluminium pistons for its Clergets. Aluminium is a better conductor of heat and therefore was a better distributor of the cooling effects of airflow. The stroke was also increased by 12mm. This resulted in the Clerget 9Bf, which produced an additional 10hp over the 9B's 130hp.

Bentley then moved on to Humber of Coventry where he built the AR.1 'Admiralty Rotary 1' which was renamed BR.1 'Bentley Rotary 1' in his honour in July 1917. This was essentially a further refined version of the 9Bf which upped the horsepower again to 150hp.

The Admiralty naturally used most BR.1s for its own machines. Camels produced for the RNAS by Clayton & Shuttleworth in Lincoln used it almost exclusively.

HISPANO-SUIZA 8B

Designed by Hispano-Suiza in neutral Spain but produced in France by Brasier, the water-cooled '8' had its eight cylinders in a 'V' formation. The 8A produced 150hp but

The most commonly fitted Sopwith Camel engine was the Clerget 9B.

it was the 200hp 8B that was chosen to power the Sopwith Dolphin. It had a cast aluminium block, steel linings for its cylinders and aluminium pistons which made it light and improved cooling.

It also had reduction gearing between the engine and the propeller which was a serious weakness. Brasier used insufficiently hardened metal for the gears which resulted in a nasty tendency for them to shear off without warning. Lubrication was also a problem.

The solution for the reduction gearing was simply to remove it and drive the propeller directly from the engine. Dolphins with this modification were known as Dolphins IIIs. The lubrication issue was never fully resolved.

BENTLEY BR.2 ROTARY

The Sopwith Snipe was built specifically with the Bentley BR.2 in mind as a powerplant. The engine produced a whopping 230hp and 50% more torque than the BR.1, though it was also 70lb heavier. It was manufactured with incredible precision for the time, with the crankcase and cylinders being milled from solid blocks of metal. There was extensive use of aluminium and the cylinder walls were lined with steel.

Manufacturers of the BR.2 included Crossley Motors of Manchester, Daimler, Gwynnes, Humber and Ruston, Proctor & Co, and a total of 2567 had been made by December 1918.

The BR.2 lacked many of the vices of previous rotaries, such as cooling issues, but at a price – it used 20 gallons of fuel per hour and 16 pints of oil. It was also used in the Sopwith Salamander and, costing just £874, it was hoped that the BR.2 would become the standard military fighter engine for years to come.

ABC Motors founder and chief designer Granville Bradshaw talked a good engine but in practice his ABC Dragonfly was a disaster.

Engineer Walter Owen 'W O' Bentley modified the Clerget design to produce two of the best rotary engines of the war – the BR.1 and the powerful BR.2, which powered the Snipe.

ABC DRAGONFLY

A competitor to the BR.2, the radial nine-cylinder Dragonfly promised big things. It was rated at 340hp and at 600lb it had a better power to weight ratio than the BR.2 (which weighed 490lb). Designed by maverick talent and ABC Motors founder Granville Bradshaw, it was apparently simple to build and had copper plated cooling fins which, Bradshaw said, were highly effective.

On the basis of its claimed performance, large orders were placed for the Dragonfly – 11,848 units from 17 contractors. In addition Sopwith, which had a close association with ABC, drew up plans to use it in a Snipe-type fuselage, which resulted in the Sopwith Dragon. Further Sopwith types designed with the Dragonfly in mind included the Bulldog, Snark, Snapper and Cobham.

The trouble was the Dragonfly did not deliver on Bradshaw's promises. The copper plating proved to be useless and the cylinder heads reportedly glowed a dull red when the engine was running at full power. Overheating was so severe, in fact, that propellers were even charred in flight. In addition, the level of power produced was more like 300hp, which made it roughly as effective as a BR.2, and fuel consumption was appalling at about 24 gallons (100 litres) per hour.

The Dragonfly had also unwittingly been designed to run at the torsional resonance frequency of its own crankshaft, which resulted in severe vibration. Service life of a Dragonfly engine was around 30-35 hours and each unit cost £1072. Serious efforts were made to fix its problems but only minor improvements resulted.

In spite of the large orders made, just 13 ABC Dragonflies had been delivered by October 31, 1918. Another 10 trickled in by the end of the year. Eventually, all the orders were cancelled. ∎

Numerous problems with the Hispano-Suiza 8B fitted to the Sopwith Dolphin seriously damaged the type's reputation. The reduction gearing was a particularly weak point.

The bulky ABC Dragonfly engine as fitted to the Sopwith Dragon.

Chapter 13

If it looks right, it is right. If not…
THE DOLPHIN

As the war progressed, air-to-air combat increasingly took place at high altitude. Whoever could fly the highest held the advantage so Sopwith set to work on a fighter designed for battles high above the clouds. The Dolphin was highly capable but became a victim of its own unusual design.

The RAF Museum's Sopwith Dolphin shows how heavily armed the type was with both Lewis guns fitted. In practice pilots often had these removed in the field. This recently completed composite aeroplane uses many original components including the rear fuselage of C3988, the cowlings, radiator, fuel tank, header tank, wheels, struts and fin from D5329, the tailplane from C4033 and the elevators from D3725. *RAF Museum*

The interior of the Dolphin's cockpit was cramped, with its two machine guns mounted very close to the pilot. The long tubular Aldis gun sight mounted through the centre of the tiny windscreen is prominently displayed in this view.

The Dolphin as it often appeared during frontline service – with its Lewis guns removed.

The Hun in the sun was a menace that every RFC and RNAS pilot flying and fighting on the Western Front encountered sooner or later.

The need to gain sufficient altitude to fly down on your enemy with speed, surprise and blinding sunlight on your side was matched only by the need to be able to spot enemies before they could do it to you.

With this in mind, Sopwith's chief designer Herbert Smith began work in early 1917 on a radical successor to the Camel that could reach almost unheard of altitudes and which also afforded its pilot unparalleled upwards and sideways visibility.

The resulting biplane had a 'tall' fuselage that effectively filled the space between the upper and lower wings. There was no centre section between the upper wings, just an open square frame of supports.

The tall fuselage therefore had the striking effect of placing the top of the pilot's head between and slightly above the upper wings. Eye level was just above them, allowing the pilot to look in any direction above or to the side with an unobstructed view.

> ## "It is extremely promising with an excellent view"

This was in marked contrast to the Camel, which gave its pilots a particularly poor field of vision with the guns ahead of the pilot and the wing above serving to narrow the view considerably.

Obtaining this effect meant that the aircraft's top wings were set further back than those at the bottom – a highly unusual arrangement at the time which was only otherwise seen on the already deeply unpopular Airco D.H.5.

The engine was the same geared 200hp Hispano-Suiza that powered the S.E.5a and the SPAD S.XIII which were both about to become extremely successful aircraft.

Smith's new design was worked on as a private Sopwith venture and was given the company type number 5F.1. Four prototypes were built and by the time the first had been built and flown, in May, it was already being referred to as the 'Dolphin' – the reason for which was not recorded at the time and is now unlikely to ever be discovered.

That first Sopwith Dolphin had a Hispano-Suiza engine with a single deep flat radiator under the propeller and a tail fin and rudder

D3615 was built as part of a batch of 200 Dolphins destined for the Royal Flying Corps.

Aeroplanes used by flying instructors tended to be the few in British service with anything approaching a gaudy paint job. This Dolphin, which has a face painted on its nose, was based at No. 2 Fighting School at Marske, between Redcar and Saltburn in Yorkshire.

Every Dolphin pilot feared that this would happen to them. If the machine 'flipped', as pictured here, the pilot risked head injuries and could find it extremely difficult to get out of the cockpit.

that were very similar to those of a Camel. A test flight on May 22, 1917, was witnessed by the director of air services at the Admiralty Commodore Godfrey Paine.

He wrote: "I was down at Sopwith's today and saw the trials of the new single-seater 200 Hispano (French) fighter. This machine is extremely promising, and possesses some very good features, chiefly as regards excellent view.

"A Camel was in the air at the same time and was absolutely outclassed as regards speed and climb by this new machine. Owing to the upward view being so exceptionally good, the pilot was able to keep below the Camel, whose pilot was powerless to do anything; in fact, he did not know where the machine was."

Less than a month later, the Dolphin was sent to the Aeroplane Experimental Unit at Martlesham Heath for official trials. Its examiners found it was nose heavy and tested it with 20lb of lead ballast in the tail. They also

unsurprisingly found that it offered unsurpassed visibility and was very manoeuvrable.

On the downside, the engine tended to spurt oil out over the pilot during flight, the aircraft's radiator was found to be inefficient, its carburettor was difficult to reach for maintenance and its magnetos were temperamental. Examiner Captain Henry Tizard also wrote: "There is no protection for

the pilot in the event of the machine turning over on landing.

"It is suggested that it might be advisable to fit two curved steel tubes, one on each side of the fuselage, to hold the machine off the ground when on its back. This should not add much to the weight and head resistance."

Tizard flew the Dolphin to France on June 13 and was greeted by an inaccurate burst of

British anti-aircraft fire since the gunners on the ground did not recognise its unusual shape. The following day, the prototype was flown by Captain William Avery 'Billy' Bishop – a Canadian ace who usually flew the Nieuport 23 and who already had 25 'kills' to his name (he ended the war with 72, making him the British Empire's top ace).

Bishop's report to his commanding officer said: "The view was exceptionally good, the pilot being able to see everything in front and behind him as well as below him in front. He also has a good view above behind." In terms of handling, guns and speed: "The machine is extraordinarily quick in turns and very handy. The guns are in a position where the pilot can easily work at them, i.e. when correcting jams etc. With the engine only giving 2000 revolutions the speed at 2000ft was 106 knots = 122mph."

"*This would be an unpleasant machine in which to turn over on the ground*"

It seemed a foregone conclusion that the Dolphin would be required on the front line as soon as possible and it was no surprise when Sopwith received an order for 500 of them – the firm's largest single order to date – on June 29, 1917.

Not long afterwards, Hooper & Co of London was contracted to build another 200 and a further 200 were ordered from Darracq Motor Engineering Co, also of London.

A second prototype was produced which had the frontal radiator removed and replaced with smaller triangular wing-mounted units on either side of the aircraft. The nose was completely redesigned, with the cowling ahead of the pilot now sloping steeply away to give an even better field of view, and sections

of the lower wing were cut out to improve downward visibility. The new radiators proved to be useless at cooling the engine so a third design, with radiators mounted on either side of the fuselage, was fitted. Test flights continued throughout July and August with various minor design alterations being made and a report on September 18 praised the new radiators. It also reiterated the praise already given to the Dolphin for its handling and visibility although it added: "Downwards the view is very bad. The gaps in the lower plane are of little value."

DOLPHIN DEVELOPED

Early on in the Dolphin's development it was suggested that in addition to its twin forward-firing Vickers machine guns, the bare rail in front of the pilot's head would be the ideal place to attach a pair of up-angled Lewis guns.

Development work was carried out and the third prototype, when it arrived at Martlesham Heath for testing on October 18, 1917, was fitted with the Lewis guns. The lower wing cut-outs of the second prototype had been deleted from the design and its fin was enlarged. After the first round of tests it suffered engine problems and was grounded.

A fourth prototype was completed and flown to No. 1 Aircraft Depot at St Omer in France on October 29. Here it was concluded that having a pair of Lewis guns on the top wing was unnecessary and instructions were issued to other aircraft depots that production model Dolphins were to be issued with only the right-hand one.

It was decided that 19 Squadron would be the first to receive the Dolphin and the fourth prototype was flown to the unit's base at Bailleul, near Lille, on November 15. A trickle of production model Dolphins followed and the squadron, which had previously flown SPAD VIIs, was fully re-equipped with Dolphins by January 9, 1918, but it was not all plain sailing.

There were problems with the aircraft's 200hp Hispano-Suiza – not least of which was an

A line-up of Dolphins belonging to the Royal Canadian Air Force's 1 Squadron.

alarming propensity for it to suddenly shed its propeller complete with boss and lock nuts while being warmed up at low revs. In addition, combat experience showed that the new position of the radiators on the sides of the aircraft fuselage meant they were being hit by expended bullet cases and links from the Vickers guns.

Wire netting was fitted over the shutter to prevent this from happening before Sopwith redesigned the case chute to stop it entirely. Despite these teething troubles, the pilots of 19 Squadron were generally happy with the Dolphin. One thought persisted in their minds however. Pilot Oliver Stewart wrote: "On getting into the cockpit the writer's first remark was 'This would be an unpleasant machine in which to turn over on the ground'. That remark is recorded because it expressed a thought which passed through the heads of almost all the pilots who flew the machine and led to one or two minor modifications.

"The pilot's head came above the top plane, and he was completely surrounded by longerons, spars, cross-bracing wires and tie-rods, and the feeling of being boxed in with the head exposed in a vulnerable position was experienced at once.

"With the engine in his lap and the petrol tanks in the small of his back, it seemed to the pilot that he had little chance of escaping injury in the event of a bad landing."

The Dolphin's unreliable engine made a forced landing a very real possibility on any given flight and efforts were made to produce a quick release mechanism for the bracing wires at the side of the cockpit. This, it was hoped, would give pilots a better chance of escape in the event of a machine turning over.

It took until May 1918 for the change to be embodied in production machines. Another idea tried was to fit what amounted to a rollover bar – a pair of inverted metal 'V' shapes known as a 'cabane' – to the upper wing. It made little difference. Flight Lieutenant Leslie Hollinghurst wrote: "The introduction of a 'cabane' and a quick release for the centre section wires were concessions

The Achilles heel of the Dolphin was its temperamental Hispano-Suiza engine. Just getting it started could be tricky.

of more moral than practical use.

"Flying Dolphins constantly from November 1917 to March 1919, I saw some 20 or more turned over, but only on one occasion did I see a pilot use the quick release. The great majority of machines when turned over came to rest upside down, with the tail pointing skywards at an angle of about 30°, thus leaving room for the pilot to crawl out."

A second SPAD VII squadron, No. 23, was also re-equipped with Dolphins during the early months of 1918, and a third, No. 79 formed at Beaulieu, Hampshire, moved to France in February 1918. It too began equipping with Dolphins. Finally, 87 Squadron was formed at Hounslow, near London, and was also intended as a Dolphin unit. During the same month, a small number of Dolphins were allocated to Home Defence squadrons, including 141 (Home Defence) Squadron, which had formed at Rochford in Essex on January 1.

The commanding officer of 141 (Home Defence) Squadron, Major Philip Babington, did not get on with the aircraft as a night fighter however. He wrote a report on March 17, 1918, which condemned the Dolphin and afterwards it never saw widespread use in the bomber interception role.

During early to mid-1918 a different means of improving the Dolphin's armament was tried – the upwards firing Lewis guns having largely been removed. Flt Lt Hollinghurst wrote: "For some months pilots either did not

carry the top guns or only carried one for use as a last resource. Eventually, at the suggestion of a flight commander, the Lewis guns were mounted on the bottom main planes just outside the radius of the propeller.

"The Lewis guns were sighted to converge at 100 yards, the Vickers guns at 50 yards. All guns were slightly 'staggered' and a large spread of bullets was thus obtained. All guns were sighted to the Aldis sight and were controlled from the 'joystick'.

"This arrangement of the four guns proved

to be very popular with the pilots. The two Lewis guns, being outside the radius of the propeller, allowed special ammunition to be carried for balloon attack without the risk of late shots and damaged propellers.

"Certain disadvantages are, however, obvious; stoppages could not be remedied and only 97 rounds per gun could be carried, as drums could not be changed in the air, nor could a pilot throw overboard his balloon ammunition if forced to land in enemy territory.

"The position of the guns did not appear to

D3775 was experimentally fitted with its Lewis guns mounted in a fixed forward-firing position on its wings. Having four machine guns all firing directly forwards gave the Dolphin an unprecedented level of firepower.

Dolphins of the RAF's 79 Squadron. Pictured closest to the camera is C8189, one of 200 built by the Darracq Motor Engineering Company.

affect the performance of the machine, nor did the vibration of firing or the extra weight cause any failure of structure. The possibility of sinking guns into the planes and carrying the ammunition between the fabric surfaces on a belt might be considered in the design of future multi-gunned single-seater fighters."

With this ground-breaking development, having two different types of gun mounted on the same machine, all firing forwards, the Dolphin led the world.

THE KAISER'S BATTLE

The Dolphin, designed to dominate the skies in air-to-air combat, had barely arrived in France when it was pressed into service strafing ground targets. On March 21, 1918, the Germans launched Operation Michael – the opening act of the Spring Offensive or Kaiserschlacht 'Kaiser's Battle' against British forces on the Somme front. It was a huge assault preceded by a heavy bombardment of mustard gas, tear gas, chlorine gas and smoke canisters concentrated on the already fog bound British forward trenches. Around 3.5 million shells hit an area 150 miles long during the five hour barrage.

Then 44 divisions, with around 10,000 men per division, advanced through the smoke, gas and fog, some armed with flamethrowers, and overwhelmed British positions all along the line. Falling back ahead of this onslaught, the British Army left men behind manning redoubts and fortresses who were either captured or fought to the last man.

> ## "The high altitude Dolphin was used by necessity to shoot up columns of infantry"

When the morning fog finally cleared, 36 squadrons of RFC aircraft – as many as could be mustered – were scrambled to support the ground forces. Among them were 19, 23 and 79 Squadrons. The high altitude Dolphin with its excellent visibility above and to the rear was used by necessity to shoot up columns of infantry and artillery positions.

The last Dolphin unit, 87 Squadron, was still in Britain when Operation Michael was launched but was soon required to fly to St Omer in France – not to take part in the fighting but simply so its Dolphins could be redistributed to the other three squadrons as sorely needed replacements. The pilots were sent back to Britain and the squadron was forced to re-form when fresh aircraft were available.

As the offensive wore on, there were an increasing number of opportunities for the Dolphin to prove its mettle against enemy aircraft. During Operation Georgette, the follow-on from Operation Michael with the British having managed to establish a new defensive line further to the west, 87 Squadron was sent up to intercept high-altitude German photo reconnaissance aircraft.

The other Dolphin squadrons rapidly began to rack up 'kills' too and the aircraft proved itself time and again to be a highly capable machine when pitted against enemy fighters. By the end of the war, 79 Squadron's Dolphins had accounted for 64 German aeroplanes and eight observation balloons. 87 Squadron had done even better, with a total of 89 kills.

In early 1918, plans were put in place that

Dolphins on the Sopwith production line in 1918. These are part of the huge initial batch of 500. *DH/MG/Brooklands*

A rare photo of an original Dolphin in flight.

could have seen the Dolphin significantly updated. A single example of the type was fitted with a 300hp Hispano-Suiza 8Fb engine – becoming a Dolphin II. Harry Hawker test flew it in France but another pilot crashed it on April 18 so a second Dolphin II, D3615, was created. British trials found it could do an impressive 140mph at 10,000ft and could fly up to 24,600ft.

The RAF was unimpressed by the Dolphin II. The United States Air Service, however, was far keener and ordered 2194 of them, to be built by the Société Anonyme de Constructions Aéronautiques of Paris. It is unknown how many were ultimately built but probably very few since the Armistice then came into force and the order was cancelled before any could be delivered.

Another development, the Dolphin III, was created by simply de-gearing the Dolphin I's 200hp Hispano-Suiza engine to improve its reliability. These machines were being introduced to fly alongside unconverted Dolphins when the war ended.

In 1919, Nos. 19, 23, 79 and 87 Squadrons were all disbanded and their Dolphins were scrapped or put into storage. A total of 1559 had been built – 300 by Darracq, 216 by Hooper and the rest by Sopwith itself. On October 31, 1918, the RAF had 1055 Dolphins

This Sopwith Dolphin replica, based at Old Rhinebeck Aerodrome in New York and pictured here during the 1980s, demonstrates the position of the pilot during flight – high up within the wing and with an excellent field of vision. *The PIPE*

in its possession but 652 were already in storage.

Over a year after the war, on January 8, 1920, the British government gave 10 Dolphins to Poland. They were transferred to Warsaw in May and had been allocated to the 19th Fighter Squadron by early August where they were used in the ground attack role against Russian forces during the Russo-Polish War. By the end of the month, only one of them was still airworthy. Five surviving Dolphins were scrapped in Warsaw in mid-1921.

The Dolphin was officially declared obsolete by the RAF on September 1, 1921. ∎

THE SOPWITH DOLPHIN ACES

Twenty-seven pilots managed to become aces flying the Sopwith Dolphin. The top scorer was an American – Francis Warrington 'Razors' Gillet from Baltimore, Maryland.

Before the United States' entry into the war in 1917, Gillet had graduated from the University of Virginia and joined the United States Air Service. He was too young to be commissioned but managed to get discharged on July 25, 1917, so he could go to Canada and join the Royal Flying Corps.

Having completed his training in England and received his Royal Aero Club Aviator's Certificate, he joined 79 Squadron in France on March 29, 1918. It took him some time to get his tally started however, and his first victory came over four months later on August 3 when he shot down a balloon – one of the most difficult 'kills' to make owing to the formidable defences usually erected around observation balloons.

Two more kills followed that month, both of enemy aeroplanes, and by the end of the war Gillet had shot down 20 German aircraft while flying a Sopwith Dolphin. He survived the war and went on to pursue diverse business interests including liquor distribution, real estate and race horse training.

Another pilot from 79 Squadron was the second highest scoring Dolphin ace – New Zealander Ronald Burns Bannerman. He received his aero certificate while piloting a Curtiss flying boat at the New Zealand Flying School. He joined the Royal Flying Corps on March 29 – the same day Gillet was joining 79 Squadron – and was posted to Gillet's unit during the summer. He had shot down 17 enemy aircraft by the end of the war – his first kill being made a day after Gillet's on August 4.

In third place behind these two was Arthur Whitehair 'Wiggy' Vigers of 87 Squadron. Born in Isleworth, Middlesex, in 1890, Vigers was older than the other two and had originally served as an infantryman with the Royal Engineers, Territorial Force, before being seconded to the RFC.

He originally flew with 15 Squadron as an observer on B.E.2cs before being posted to 87 Squadron. He destroyed 14 aircraft while flying Dolphins and after the war he was briefly a tobacco farmer in Rhodesia before travelling to Australia and becoming a pilot for Qantas in 1924. He later served with the Royal Australia Air Force.

Another 79 Squadron machine, C3901 was from the initial Sopwith production batch.

Chapter 14

ACES HIGH

The most successful Sopwith fighter pilots

A pilot who shot down five or more enemy aeroplanes or balloons became an 'ace'. During the course of the Great War nearly 350 men earned that distinction while flying Sopwith machines – 260 of them in Camels.

Raymond Collishaw was the highest scoring Sopwith Triplane ace of the war, as well as being the overall most successful pilot of Sopwith fighters. He is pictured here in a Camel of 203 Squadron at Izel-lès-Hameau, France, on July 12, 1918.

Major Roderick Stanley Dallas shot down 15 enemy aircraft in a Sopwith Triplane before he was shot down and killed.

The most successful Sopwith Camel pilot was Canadian Donald MacLaren. His total of 54 victories was achieved in a matter of months.

The most successful Sopwith pilot of the Great War was Lieutenant Colonel Raymond Collishaw. He was the sixth most prolific ace of the war, of any nation, and every one of his 60 victories was achieved while flying one of the company's designs.

His first two German machines were sent down while he was flying a 1½ Strutter in 1916. He then downed two more while flying a Pup before beginning an unprecedented spree flying the Triplane and then the Camel.

Collishaw was a natural leader and fought with great skill, but also incredible luck. He was shot down several times, but always survived unscathed. On one occasion, his controls were shattered by enemy bullets and he was forced to sit helplessly while his aeroplane glided down and crashed. On another, he accidentally landed at a German base in heavy fog.

When he saw black crosses painted on stationary machines and then Germans running over to arrest him, he throttled up his machine and took off again.

Immediately after the war, he commanded a squadron sent to help the White Russian forces fight the Bolsheviks – a battle that turned into a rout. Nevertheless, Collishaw still managed to shoot down an enemy machine and destroyed a gunboat by dropping a bomb on it from his Camel.

During the Second World War, he commanded 204 Group in North Africa, fighting Italian forces. He was forced to retire from the RAF in 1943 and died in Vancouver

in 1976, aged 82.

Another Canadian, Major Donald Roderick MacLaren was not far behind Collishaw with 54 kills, but all of his were made using the Camel. While Collishaw's victories began in 1916, MacLaren did not even arrive in France until November 23, 1917, where he joined 46 Squadron.

He did not fight an enemy machine until February 1918, and his first confirmed victory was not until March 6. All of his kills were made during 218 days between then and October 9 – nearly one every four days. The reason his incredible run of victories came to an end was a broken leg sustained during a wrestling match with another pilot from his squadron. He was never injured in combat.

When the war was over, he returned to Canada and formed his own airline, Pacific Airways, which was later acquired by another company and, through a series of further acquisitions and amalgamations, eventually ended up as part of Air Canada. MacLaren died on July 4, 1989, aged 96.

Third highest scorer overall was a third Canadian, William George Barker, whose final fight is detailed in chapter 17. Barker was a farm boy who could ride a horse and already knew how to shoot accurately before he joined the RFC on the Western Front in 1916 as an observer.

He claimed two enemy machines shot down with his observer's gun, though neither was confirmed, and was awarded the Military Cross for spotting a formation of German infantry preparing to launch a counterattack on the British at Beaumont-Hamel on

November 15 and enabling it to be broken up with an artillery attack.

Barker trained as a pilot in January 1917 and joined 15 Squadron, where he claimed another kill which was also disallowed. In August he suffered a head wound from anti-aircraft fire and spent time in England as a flying instructor – still without a single confirmed victory to his name.

He requested to be returned to frontline service and was posted to 28 Squadron, in command of C Flight. The unit moved to France in October and Barker shot down an Albatros D.V on his first patrol, though he did not claim it. His first claimed and recognised kill was on October 20 – an Albatros D.III. Six days later he shot down a pair of Albatros D.Vs.

On November 7, 28 Squadron was posted to the Italian front and it was here that Barker's career as a deadly fighter pilot moved up into high gear. His tally rose steadily, month after month, always flying the same Sopwith Camel – B6313. By March 18, 1918, he had downed 20 enemy machines. In April he joined 66 Squadron and his tally reached 30 on May 24. It was 40 by July 18. His 46th and final kill with B6313 was on September 18. This made B6313 the most successful single aircraft in the history of the RAF right up to the present day.

Barker's total rose to 50 with the battle, which saw him win one of only two Victoria Crosses given to Sopwith pilots during the war on October 27 (see chapter 17).

After the war, Barker formed a business with fellow Canadian ace Billy Bishop – Bishop-Barker Aeroplanes – which lasted three years before he rejoined the Canadian Air Force in 1922. He became its acting director in 1924 and was instrumental in the introduction of parachutes.

After leaving the RCAF, and struggling with pain from his war wounds and alcoholism, he became the president and general manager of Fairchild Aircraft in Montreal – a subsidiary of the American Fairchild corporation. He died aged 35 in 1930 when the Fairchild KR-

An ace with both Pups and Camels, Flight Commander Joseph Stewart Temple Fall is pictured with the Pup of his fellow ace Major Lloyd Samuel Breadner.

21 trainer he was demonstrating for the RCAF crashed. His funeral was the largest in Toronto state history.

One of the most famous Camel aces, though not one of the highest scoring, was Lt Alan Jerrard. Born in Lewisham, south-east London, but educated at Sutton Coldfield, near Birmingham, where his father was a headteacher, Jerrard went to Birmingham University in 1915, but then volunteered to join the Army. He then applied for a transfer to the RFC, graduating as a pilot on June 14, 1917.

Having joined 19 Squadron on July 24, on his second patrol Jerrard lost contact with his formation in heavy fog, raked a column of German infantry with machine gun fire and ended up crashing his SPAD S.7 into a railway embankment from which he had to be dug out by nearby infantry. His nose and jaw were broken in several places.

After surgical attention and a spell back in England, Jerrard returned to the front line with 66 Squadron in Italy on February 22, 1918. A string of victories followed, with Jerrard shooting down an Aviatik D.I, an observation balloon, two more D.Is and an Albatros fighter by March 21.

On March 29, Jerrard stayed up late in the squadron mess and slept in on March 30. When he was called up to fly a patrol he put his overalls over his pyjamas and trudged out to his Sopwith Camel, B5648. At 11.35am, Jerrard and his two comrades, Captain Peter Carpenter and Lt H R Eycott-Martin, spotted

Although he started out on the Western Front, it was fighting on the Italian Front against the Austro-Hungarians that saw William 'Billy' Barker flourish as a deadly ace. He is pictured with his Camel, B6313, the most successful aircraft in the history of the RAF. A tiny demon figure, Barker's mascot can be seen perched above his Vickers guns.

four Albatros fighters escorting a two-seater and attacked.

What happened next depends on whose report you believe. Carpenter and Eycott-Martin reported seeing Jerrard shoot down an Albatros D.III before attacking other machines, shooting up an enemy aerodrome, strafing enemy machines attempting to take off, and then taking on six enemy fighters single-handed before shooting one of them down.

Jerrard then apparently shot down another D.III, though seemed to have been wounded. He was by now being followed by 10 D.IIIs. Jerrard turned and attacked them repeatedly before crashing four miles west of Mansue aerodrome.

On the basis of this report, Jerrard was recommended for the VC and was awarded it on May 1, 1918.

The Austro-Hungarians, who captured Jerrard after he survived his crash unscathed, interrogated him and his own account of the day's combat read: "On March 30, I was flying in formation with two other Camel fighters near the front when we met an Austrian fighter squadron near Mansue. I attacked an Albatros D fighter successfully, then having lost height during the dogfight, my engine started to misfire and run rough. I was pursued by other Austrian fighters and eventually shot down."

The Austro-Hungarian account was closer to Jerrard's than that of Carpenter and Eycott-Martin. He was shot down by the leader of the Albatros flight, Fiala von Fernbrugg, who landed close by and rushed to the crash site to capture Jerrard. Jerrard's Camel was found to have 163 bullet holes in it, including 27 in the fuel tank – which probably saved Jerrard's life since all his fuel had drained away before he crashed.

Finding Jerrard was only wearing his pyjamas under his overalls, the Austrians dropped a note behind Allied lines asking that suitable clothes be air-dropped for him. When 66 Squadron received this, it had two bundles dropped for Jerrard, including his uniform, belt, shoes, socks and cigarettes.

Having seen out the war as a PoW, Jerrard was repatriated and received his VC at Buckingham Palace on April 5, 1919. He remained in the RAF for another 14 years before retiring. He died on May 14, 1968. ■

Alan Jerrard, accompanied by his mother, walks to Buckingham Palace to receive his Victoria Cross.

A stunned and defeated Lt Alan Jerrard photographed close to the wreck of his Sopwith Camel on March 30, 1918. He was later awarded the Victoria Cross – the only Camel ace to receive one.

Sopwith aces of the Great War

Every Camel ace to score 15 victories or more is listed here, along with every Snipe, Dolphin, Triplane, Pup and 1½ Strutter ace. There are not believed to have been aces on any other Sopwith type.

Number of victories	Name and rank	Squadron(s)	Born	Died
Snipe aces (3)				
7 (of 26)	Capt Elwyn Roy King	4 AFC	13.5.94, Bathurst, New South Wales, Australia	28.11.41, Point Cook, Victoria, Australia
6 (of 12)	Capt Thomas Charles Richmond Baker	4 AFC	2.5.97, Smithfield, New South Wales, Australia	Shot down, 4.11.18, near Buissenal
5 (of 7)	Lt Arthur John Palliser	4 AFC	2.3.90, Launceston, Tasmania	Shot down, 5.11.18, Ath, Belgium
Dolphin aces (27)				
20	Capt Francis Warrington Gillet	79	29.11.95, Baltimore, Maryland, USA	21.12.69, Baltimore
17	Capt Ronald Burns Bannerman	79	21.9.90, Invercargill, Southland, New Zealand	2.8.78, Gore, Southland, New Zealand
14	Capt Arthur Whitehair Vigers	15, 87	20.1.90, Isleworth, Middlesex	September 1968, Bunbury, Western Australia
13 (of 28)	Maj Albert Desbrisay Carter		2.6.92, Point de Bute, New Brunswick, Canada	Crashed flight testing a Fokker D.VII, 22.5.19, Shoreham, Sussex
13 (of 23)	Capt Alexander Augustus Norman Dudley Pentland	16, 19, 29, 87	5.8.94, Maitland, New South Wales, Australia	1983, New South Wales, Australia
12	Capt Frederic Ives Lord	79	18.4.97, Manitowoc, Wisconsin, USA	21.7.67, Apple Valley California, USA
12	Capt James William Pearson	23	2.4.95, Bridgeport, Connecticut, USA	26.1.93, Montclair, New Jersey, USA
11	Capt Leslie Norman Hollinghurst	87	2.1.95, Muswell Hill, London	8.6.71, Putney, London
11	Capt Herbert Joseph Larkin	5, 65, 87	8.10.94, Brisbane, Queensland, Australia	10.6.72, St Martins, Channel Islands
10 (of 19)	Capt Arthur Bradfield Fairclough	19, 23	25.7.96, Toronto, Canada	9.12.68
10	Capt Cecil Vernon Gardner	19	14.9.89, Broughton, Oxfordshire	Shot down, 30.9.18, France, died from wounds three days later
9	Capt Roger Amedee Del'Haye	13, 19	9.1.89, Châlons-sur-Marne, France	18.11.44, Montreal, Canada
9	Capt James Donald Innes Hardman	19	21.12.99, Oldham Lancashire	2.3.82
8	Capt Henry Arthur Richard Biziou	42, 87	18.9.96, Unknown	His S.E.5a collided with an Avro 504K, 14.7.19, Farnborough
8 (of 22)	Capt John Leacroft	14, 19	4.11.88, Derby, Derbyshire	26.8.71, Bexhill, Sussex
7	Lt Lewis Hector Ray	19	11.2.88, Montreal, Canada	Unknown
7	Lt Harold Albert White	23	14.2.96, Stogumber, Somerset	December 1970, Aylmer, Ontario, Canada
6 (of 8)	Capt John Dartnell De Pencier	12, 19	12.11.98, Toronto, Canada	Mid-air collision, 17.5.20, Cologne, Germany
6 (of 7)	Lt Norman William Hustings	19	9.6.98, Liverpool	Car crash, 13.4.23, near Thornwood, Essex
5	Lt John Arthur Aldridge	19	9.2.99, Newington, London	November 1988, Hampshire
5	Lt Arthur Winston Blake	19	Unknown	Flying accident, 14.2.23, Dealesville, South Africa
5	Lt Harry Neville Compton	23	9.4.99, Winnipeg, Canada	1951, Toronto, Canada
5	Maj Charles John Wharton Darwin	27, 87	12.12.94, Durham	26.12.41, London
5	Lt Ross Morrison Macdonald	15, 87	3.1.95, Winnipeg, Canada	29.8.60, Winnipeg
5	Capt John Harry McNeaney	79	30.5.97, Jarvis, Ontario	Spanish flu, 1.3.19, England
5	Lt Edgar Taylor	79	9.1.97, Rhode Island, USA	Hit by ground fire while attacking balloon, 24.8.18, France
5	Lt Charles Edward Worthington	87	20.2.97, Leicester	1970, Leicestershire
Camel aces (44 listed out of 260)				
54	Maj Donald Roderick MacLaren	46	28.5.93, Ottawa, Canada	4.7.89, Burnaby, British Columbia, Canada
46 (of 50)	Maj William George Barker	4, 9, 15, 28, 66, 139, 201	3.11.94, Dauphin, Manitoba, Canada	Crash, 12.3.30, Rockcliffe Aerodrome, near Ottawa, Canada
39	Capt William Lancelot Jordan	8N, 201	3.12.96, Georgetown, South Africa	Car crash, 1931, northern England
36 (of 39)	Maj John Ingles Gilmour	27, 28, 65	28.6.96, Helensburgh, Dunbartonshire, Scotland	24.2.28, London
33	Capt Frank Granger Quigley	70	10.7.94, Toronto, Canada	Spanish flu, 20.10.18, Liverpool
30 (of 35)	Capt Henry Winslow Woollett	24, 43	5.8.95, Southwold, Suffolk	31.10.69
29	Capt Arthur Henry Cobby	4 AFC, 71	26.8.94, Prahran, Victoria, Australia	11.11.55
28 (of 36)	Flt Cmdr Joseph Stewart Temple Fall (see also Pup aces)	3N, 9N	17.11.95, Hillbank, British Columbia, Canada	1.12.88, Duncan, British Columbia
27	Lt Clifford Mackay McEwen	28	2.7.97, Griswold Manitoba, Canada	6.8.67, Toronto, Canada
26 (of 33)	Capt Samuel Marcus Kinkead	1N, 47, 201	25.2.97, Johannesburg, South Africa	Crashed during world speed record attempt 12.3.28, Calshot
26 (of 29)	Capt Leonard Henry Rochford	3N, 203	10.11.96, Enfield, Middlesex	17.12.86
24	Capt Peter Carpenter	45, 66	6.12.91, Cardiff	21.3.71, Golders Green, Middlesex
23 (of 60)	Lt Col Raymond Collishaw (see also Triplane aces)	10N, 13N, 47, 203	22.11.93, Nanaimo, British Columbia, Canada	28.9.76, West Vancouver, Canada
23	Capt Harold Alfred Whistler	3, 80	30.12.96, Theddlethorpe, Lincolnshire	Aircraft disappeared, 1.3.40, Gulf of Oman
22	Capt Joseph Leonard Maries White	65	6.1.97, Halifax, Nova Scotia, Canada	Crashed, 24.2.25, Camp Borden, Ontario, Canada
21	Capt Charles Robert Reeves Hickey	4N, 204	10.9.97	Mid-air collision with another Camel, 3.10.18
21	Capt Edgar James Kingston McCloughry	4 AFC, 23	10.9.96, Adelaide, South Australia	15.11.72
20 (of 21)	Capt George Edwin Thomson	46	19.9.87, Rangoon, Burma	Aircraft burst into flames on take-off, crashed, 23.5.18, Oxford
20 (of 27)	Capt Arthur Treloar Whealy (see also Pup aces)	3N, 9N, 203	2.11.95, Toronto, Canada	23.12.45, Ste Marguerite, Quebec, Canada
19	Capt Cedric Ernest Howell	45	17.6.96, Adelaide, South Australia	Crashed into the sea on Hounslow-Australia flight, 10.12.19
19 (of 22)	Capt Cecil Frederick King	43	19.2.99, Sevenoaks, Kent	Mid-air collision, 24.1.19, Sedgeford, Norfolk
19 (of 26)	Capt Elwyn Roy King (see also Snipe aces)	4 AFC	13.5.94, Bathurst, New South Wales, Australia	28.11.41, Point Cook, Victoria, Australia
19 (of 47)	Capt Robert Alexander Little (see also Triplane aces)	3N, 8N, 203	19.7.95, Hawthorn, Victoria, Australia	Shot down by Gotha bomber at night, 27.5.18, France
18 (of 23)	Capt Matthew Brown Frew (see also 1½ Strutter aces)	45	7.4.95, Glasgow, Scotland	28.5.74, Pretoria, South Africa
18	Capt George Chisholm MacKay	13N, 213	17.5.98, Sunderland, Ontario, Canada	4.9.73, Mimico, Ontario
18	Capt Maurice Ashdown Newnham	4, 65	31.8.97, Kensington, London	October 1974, Hampshire
18	Capt John Todd	70	12.1.99, Falkirk, Scotland	1980, Saint Cyrus, Scotland
18	Capt John Lightfoot Trollope	43, 70	30.5.97, Wallington, Surrey	21.10.58, Hove, Sussex
17 (of 20)	Capt Douglas John Bell	3, 27, 78	16.9.93, South Africa	Shot down, 27.5.18, near Thiepval, France
17	Lt Edward Grahame Johnstone	8N, 12N, 208	6.5.99, Tooting, London	Unknown
17 (of 25)	Capt Stanley Wallace Rosevear (see also Triplane aces)	1N, 201	9.3.96, Walkerton, Ontario, Canada	Crashed, 25.4.18, near Arras, France
17	Capt Edwin Swale	10N, 210	28.6.99, Chesterfield, Derbyshire	19.7.78, Chesterfield
16	Capt Owen Morgan Baldwin	73	21.2.93, Twyford, Berkshire	12.1.42, Berkshire
16 (of 17)	Capt Stearne Tighe Edwards	2N, 6N, 9N, 11N, 209	13.2.93, Canada	Seriously injured in crash and died 10 days later, 22.11.18
16	Capt Oliver William Redgate	9N, 209	23.11.99, Nottingham	1929, Nottinghamshire
15 (of 25)	Maj Robert John Orton Compston (see also Triplane aces)	8N, 40	9.1.98, Farnham, Hampshire	28.1.62

Number of victories	Name and rank	Squadron(s)	Born	Died
15	Capt Lawrence Percival Coombes	10N, 12N, 204, 210	9.4.99, Madras, India	2.6.88, Melbourne, Australia
15 (of 16)	Capt Robert Mordaunt Foster	54, 209	3.9.98, Richmond, Surrey	23.10.73, Glemham, Suffolk
15	Capt George Brian Gates	1N, 201	21.7.99	Unknown
15	Lt Harry King Goode	66	22.10.92, Handsworth, Staffordshire	Flying accident, 21.8.42, Northern Ireland
15	Capt John Edmund Greene	13N, 213	2.7.94, Winnipeg, Canada	Shot down, 14.10.18, Belgium
15	Capt Edwin Tufnell Hayne	3N, 203	28.5.95, South Africa	Crashed flying Bristol Fighter, 28.4.19, UK
15	Capt Frank Harold Hobson	70	8.10.94, West Bridgford, Nottinghamshire	1919, Nottinghamshire
15 (of 17)	Capt John William Pinder	9N, 13N, 45, 213	14.2.98, Deal, Kent	Drowned in accident, 16.8.20, Icara, Brazil

Triplane aces (23)

Number of victories	Name and rank	Squadron(s)	Born	Died
34 (of 60)	Lt Col Raymond Collishaw (see also Camel aces)	10N, 13N, 47, 203	22.11.93, Nanaimo, British Columbia, Canada	28.9.76, West Vancouver, Canada
24 (of 47)	Capt Robert Alexander Little (see also Camel aces)	3N, 8N, 203	19.7.95, Hawthorn, Victoria, Australia	Shot down by Gotha at night, 27.5.18
21 (of 29)	Maj Charles Dawson Booker	1N, 8N, 201	21.4.97, Wilmington, Kent	Shot down 13.8.18, Rosières, France
19	Flt Sub-Lt Ellis Vair Reid	10N	31.10.89, Belleville, Ontario, Canada	MIA, later reported killed 28.7.17, France
17 (of 21)	Flt Lt Richard Pearman Minifie	1N	2.2.98, Melbourne, Australia	31.3.69, Melbourne
15 (of 32)	Maj Roderic Stanley Dallas	1N, 40	30.7.91, Mount Stanley, Queensland, Australia	Shot down, 1.6.18, near Liévin, France
10 (of 22)	Capt William Melville Alexander	10N, 210	8.11.97, Toronto, Canada	4.10.88
9 (of 25)	Maj Robert John Orton Compston (see also Camel aces)	8N, 40	9.1.98, Farnham, Hampshire	28.1.62
8 (of 10)	Maj Thomas Francis Netterville Gerrard	1N, 208, 209, 256	13.8.97, Kuala Kubu, Selangor, Malaya	14.7.23
8 (of 25)	Capt Stanley Wallace Rosevear (see also Camel aces)	1N, 201	9.3.96, Walkerton, Canada	Crashed 25.04.18, near Arras, France
8 (of 12)	Capt Reginald Rhys Soar	8N	24.8.93, Castleford, Yorkshire	1971, Wales
7	Flt Lt John Albert Page	3N, 10N	11.7.93, Brockville, Ontario, Canada	Shot down 22.7.17, Becelaere, Belgium
7 (of 8)	Flt Cmdr John Edward Sharman	10N	11.9.92, Oak Lake, Manitoba, Canada	Shot down in N6307 'Black Death' 22.7.17
7 (of 8)	Capt George Goodman Simpson	8N, 9N, 1W	14.9.96, St Kilda, Victoria, Australia	April 1990, Horsham, Surrey
6	Flt Sub-Lt Thomas Grey Culling	1N	31.5.96, Dunedin, Otago, New Zealand	Shot down 8.6.17, Warneton, France
6	Flt Cmdr Cyril Askew Eyre	1N	25.4.96, Codnor, Derbyshire	Shot down 7.7.17
6	Capt Forster Herbert Martin Maynard	1N	1.5.93, Waiuku, Auckland, New Zealand	26.1.76
6	Flt Lt Gerald Ewart Nash	10N	12.5.96, Saltfleet, Ontario, Canada	10.4.76, Welland, Ontario, Canada
6 (of 9)	Lt Anthony George Allen Spence	1N, 201	27.5.97, Toronto, Canada	Unknown
5	Maj Anthony Rex Arnold	8N, 79	26.8.96, Tattenhall, Cheshire	25.5.54, Mozambique
5 (of 8)	Flt Lt Desmond Fitzgerald Fitzgibbon	10N	1.11.90, Hooton, Cheshire	Unknown
5 (of 15)	Capt Harold Thomas Mellings	10N, 210	5.8.99, Bromfield, Shropshire	Shot down, 22.7.18, Ostend, Belgium
5 (of 9)	Capt Herbert Victor Rowley	1N, 201	24.10.97, Audley, Staffordshire	9.4.66

Pup aces (28)

Number of victories	Name and rank	Squadron(s)	Born	Died
11 (of 12)	Capt Maurice Douglas Guest Scott	18, 46, 54, 91	13.11.95, Exeter, Devon	Crashed, 17.3.18, Shoreham
10	Flt Sub-Lt John Joseph Malone	3N	21.12.93, Inglewood, Ontario, Canada	Shot down 30.4.17, France
9	Flt Cmdr Francis Dominic Casey	3N	3.8.90, Clonmel, Tipperary, Ireland	Crashed during test flight, 11.8.17
9	Capt Harold Spencer Kerby	3N, 9N, Walmer HD	14.5.93, Hamilton, Ontario, Canada	8.6.63, London
8 (of 36)	Flt Cmdr Joseph Stewart Temple Fall (see also Camel aces)	3N, 9N	17.11.95, Hillbank, British Columbia, Canada	1.12.88, Duncan, British Columbia
8	Flt Sub-Lt Langley Frank Willard Smith	4N	15.8.97, Philipsburg, Quebec, Canada	Camel lost wing during combat 12.6.17
7	Maj Lloyd Samuel Breadner	3N, 204	14.7.94, Carleton, Ontario, Canada	14.3.52, Boston, Mass, USA
7 (of 8)	Capt Clive Alexander Brewster-Joske	1, 46	October 1896, Fiji	1947
7	Capt Reginald Morse Charley	54	3.8.92, Blakeney, Gloucestershire	1986, Yorkshire
6 (of 10)	Maj Stanley James Goble	5N, 8N, 205	21.8.91, Victoria, Australia	24.7.48, Melbourne, Australia
6	Capt Frank Neville Hudson	15, 54	4.11.97, Beckenham, Kent	Unknown
6 (of 9)	Flt Lt Edmund Pierce	3N, 203	22.10.96, York	April 1985, York
6 (of 7)	Capt Oliver Manners Sutton	21, 54	12.3.96, Westbourne, Sussex	Aeroplane accident, 16.8.21, Suffolk
5 (of 12)	Capt John Oliver Andrews	5, 24, 66, 209	20.7.96, Waterloo, Lancashire	29.5.89, Berkshire
5 (of 13)	Flt Cmdr Frederick Carr Armstrong	3N	13.6.95, Toronto, Canada	Shot down in flames, 25.3.18, France
5 (of 17)	Maj Alfred Williams Carter	3N, 10N, 210	29.4.94, Fish Creek, Alberta, Canada	17.12.86, Vancouver, Canada
5 (of 11)	Flt Cmdr Arnold Jacques Chadwick	4N	23.8.93, Toronto, Canada	Downed 28.7.17, nr Dunkirk after ditching
5 (of 15)	Capt James Alpheus Glen	3N, 10N, 203	23.6.90, Manitoba, Canada	7.3.62, Eton
5	Flt Lt Edward Rochfort Grange	8N, 208	11.1.92, Lansing, Michigan, USA	13.7.88, Toronto, Canada
5	Capt George Hyde	54	1893, Yorkshire	Unknown
5 (of 7)	Capt Arthur Stanley Gould Lee	46	31.8.94, Boston, Lincolnshire	21.5.75, London
5 (of 7)	Capt Stuart Harvey Pratt	46	June 1893, Streatham, Surrey	Lost foot and eye in crash d. date unknown
5	Lt Walbanke Ashby Pritt	44, 66	31.10.97, Leamington Spa, Warwickshire	Car crash, 27.1.28, Bagby, Yorkshire
5	Maj Oliver Stewart	22, 54	26.11.96, London	1976
5 (of 6)	Maj William Victor Strugnell	1, 54	23.7.92, Southampton	Unknown
5	Capt Patrick Gordon Taylor	66	21.10.96, Mosman, New South Wales, Australia	15.12.66, Honolulu, Hawaii
5	Flt Cmdr Herbert Gardner Travers	3N, 211	1.4.91, Kensington, London	16.4.58
5 (of 27)	Capt Arthur Treloar Whealy (see also Camel aces)	3N, 9N, 203	2.11.95, Toronto, Canada	23.12.45, Ste Marguerite, Quebec, Canada

1½ Strutter aces (7)

Number of victories	Name and rank	Squadron(s)	Born	Died
13	Capt Geoffrey Hornblower Cock	45	7.1.96, Shrewsbury, Shropshire	16.2.80, Belford, Northumberland
6 (of 18)	Capt James Dacres Belgrave	45, 60, 61	27.9.96, Kensington, London	Shot down, 13.6.18, east of Albert, France
6 (of 11)	Lt Thomas Montagu Harries	24, 45	16.10.88, Menstrie, Scotland	Unknown
5	Lt George Walker Blaiklock	45	7.12.91, Montreal, Canada	July 1977
5 (of 23)	Capt Matthew Brown Frew (see also Camel aces)	45	7.4.95, Glasgow, Scotland	28.5.74, Pretoria, South Africa
5	Lt John Thompson Murison	45	16.2.89, Islington, London	March 1936
5	2nd Lt John Arthur Vessey	45	1894, Owmby, Lincolnshire	Collision with another 1½ Strutter, 12.6.17

Chapter 15

TRENCH FIGHTERS
Sopwith TF.1 Camel and TF.2 Salamander

Throughout the summer of 1917 and on into the Battle of Cambrai in November and December, the Sopwith Pups and Camels of the Royal Flying Corps had been used to strafe German positions on the ground – resulting in horrendous pilot casualties. Something had to be done to protect the most vulnerable part of these aircraft and Sopwith's design team took up the challenge.

The Battle of Cambrai was another of the Great War's many bloody failures. It was a British offensive against a heavily defended section of the German front line and like several of 1917's major operations it had involved a combined force of infantry, tanks and aeroplanes.

Royal Flying Corps squadrons had been charged with attacking and disrupting German forces on the ground and they had done good work. However, every day the low-flying aircraft were put into action they lost a third of their number to infantry firing from below.

Whole squadrons of experienced pilots flying the latest machines were being completely wiped out every few days and it didn't take a genius to realise that the addition of a few carefully placed armour plates might save many lives that would otherwise be needlessly lost.

The other problem that afflicted low-flying aeroplanes was obstacles and terrain features. Strafing a trench, for example, with forward firing guns mounted directly in front of the pilot meant the aircraft had to be pointed right at the ground. Accuracy was at its greatest at close range and many pilots waited until the last possible second before pulling out of a dive – only to crash into the remains of a tree or wall of a ruined building.

It was therefore considered that machine guns could be fitted to a fighter which pointed at the ground during level flight, enabling the pilot to strafe without having to dive directly on to the target.

Sopwith began work simultaneously on a pair of designs that could improve pilot safety during these most hazardous of missions – a modified version of the already successful Camel and a modified version of its as-yet untried successor, the Snipe.

The TF.1 'Trench Fighter 1' Camel prototype was based on a standard 110hp Le Rhone engined production model built by Boulton & Paul, B9278, though in reality it may have worked up from a hodgepodge of spares including the tail section of another Camel built by Clayton & Shuttleworth.

Both of B9278's forward firing Vickers guns were removed and replaced with a single Lewis gun mounted on the top wing and two more mounted either side of the pilot's seat on the cockpit floor – their barrels protruding at a 45° angle from the bottom of the aircraft.

These downwards and forward firing Lewis guns were fixed in position and had no sights of any kind, which meant they had to be fired blind. A large section of armour plate was fitted along the bottom of the fuselage which covered the whole cockpit and the fuel tank behind the pilot's wicker seat.

The Sopwith Salamander was designed to fly low over the front lines, strafing enemy positions. As a result it was camouflaged to make it more difficult to spot from above and the pilot sat in a bulletproof metal box.
DH/MG/Brooklands

The original 'trench fighter' concept called for a Sopwith Camel to be fitted with a pair of downwards pointing Lewis guns. The underside of the aircraft would have been protected by a hefty sheet of armour plating but the idea was not adopted.

B9278 fully modified by late February 1918 and was flown to France for field testing. Meanwhile, another Camel, B6218, though having no armour and never being formally designated a TF.1, had been used as a guinea pig to test a set of periscope style arrangement of mirrors intended to give the pilot of a 'Trench Fighter' some idea of what he was shooting at. This too was sent to France.

The TF.1 was largely overtaken by time and by the parallel development of the TF.2. Tests in France revealed that the two downward firing Lewis guns covered less of an area than guns being fired forwards and were considerably less accurate too.

In addition, time had passed and the Camel itself was beginning to approach obsolescence as a front line fighter. It was therefore left to the Snipe offshoot to continue as the Sopwith 'Trench Fighter'.

A Salamander fitted with a Bentley engine.

RISE OF THE SALAMANDER

Sopwith had put its proposal for the ground attack version of the Snipe into official hands on February 1, 1918, even before the TF.1 was complete. This was updated on February 11 when the company gave revised details of the armour it intended to install on the aircraft – an 8mm thick plate at the front, an 11mm thick plate across the bottom, 6mm on the sides and a double wall behind the pilot of 4mm and 2.6mm thicknesses.

All of this armour combined weighed a hefty 605lb – the equivalent of carrying four additional average sized men in the aeroplane's fuselage. As with the TF.1 also being worked on, it was envisioned that the TF.2 Snipe would have a pair of downwards firing Lewis guns with five 97-round drums of ammunition each. It would also have a single forwards firing Vickers with 300 rounds.

Unlike the TF.1, six prototypes were ordered for the TF.2 on March 20, 1918. By now the report from France was in on the TF.1's downwards firing Lewis guns and all six were ordered to have a pair of fixed forwards firing Vickers guns instead, with 1000 rounds between them.

The name Salamander was approved for the TF.2 on April 9, 1918, and the first prototype, E5429, made its first flight on April 27. It looked very much like a Snipe – though the two types were already diverging from their common ancestry – for example on April 23, it was decided that the Salamander's Vickers guns should be staggered to allow more room for their oversized ammunition boxes.

It was overoptimistically reported on April 24 that all future Salamanders would now be able to carry 1850 rounds of ammunition. They would also, as of May 8, be able to carry a rack of four 20lb bombs – though Sopwith had some difficulty in finding a way for the release mechanism's control cables to pass through the pilot's armour plating and into the cockpit.

The RAF was less than enthusiastic about the Salamander at this stage, feeling that Sopwith had gone overboard and provided too much protection for its pilots. Controller of Aircraft Production Brigadier General Robert Brooke-Popham wrote on April 19: "This machine has about 500lb of armour but will probably be unsuitable owing to its poor view and the fact that it will not be very handy. I pointed out that all we had ever asked for was a lightly armoured single-seater machine and a heavily-armoured two-seater machine, and that the TF.2 did not fulfil either of these two requirements. With regard to the distribution of the armour on the Camels, I pointed out that it had been agreed that up to 100lb of armour was permissible, and it was obvious that complete protection could not be afforded but that as much protection as possible should be afforded to a) pilot b) carburettors c) magnetos. Petrol tanks should be protected by being covered with rubber i.e. self-sealing tanks."

The first prototype E5429 was flown to France for testing on May 9 and arrived with 3 Squadron on May 17.

It then went to 65 Squadron on May 19 but was damaged beyond economic repair when it crashed while its pilot was trying to avoid a vehicle crossing the aerodrome to reach the scene of another crash.

The 65 Squadron report on the Salamander stated: "The machine gets up a tremendous speed with the nose slightly down, and for this reason I do not think that it will ever be well suited for trench strafing owing to the fact that it will be impossible to dive anything approaching vertically as the speed obtained would be too great."

The Air Ministry ignored this report and ordered 500 Salamanders at the end of May. While the first Salamander prototype had been fitted with 'soft' steel armour plates, those of all subsequent aircraft had 'hardened' plates made by four firms – William Beardmore & Co of Glasgow, Thomas Firth & Sons and Sir Robert Hadfield & Co of Sheffield, and Vickers.

It proved very difficult to obtain steel plates that were of sufficient quality for use in an aircraft however. The hardening process tended to distort them, making them awkward if not impossible to fit.

Sopwith itself complained that an engine back plate supplied by Firths would not fit because it was too deformed. Firths said it simply couldn't rectify this problem and knew of no viable solution to it. Worse, it seemed that apparently straight plates could still spontaneously distort even after the aircraft had been completed.

After the war, on January 6, 1919, it transpired that one aircraft, F6599, had shifted badly out of its proper internal alignment for no obvious reason.

It was flown in this distorted state by Captain Copeland to determine just how much of a problem this distortion might pose to an aircraft in service. He reported on June 17, 1919: "Taking off it was very difficult to get the tail up.

"When I did the machine went up and almost stalled and I had to push the stick half forward and throttle the engine back a little.

"I climbed to about 1500ft without turning, I then turned. The machine is flying right wing low. I tried the machine with varying throttles taking my hand off the joystick to see what would happen.

"She went up every time and stalled. I tried it with the engine off. It did the same thing. I then landed and taxiing up I had to put on full left rudder and hard right aileron to make her go straight. This, though, may have been due to the length of the grass on the aerodrome, which is very long and almost dangerous.

"The throttle controls were very loose and vibrated closed as soon as they were left alone. The machine is not safe to fly as it is."

JUST A LITTLE TOO LATE

Three months after the original Salamander prototype was wrecked in France, another example was tested at Brooklands. It was naturally found to be heavy on the controls but still capable of being looped and turned without too much trouble. With the engine on full revs it was deemed "easily manageable" when flying close to the ground, though visibility was poor.

Tests had shown that its metal plates, except those on the sides, would deflect a German armour piercing bullet fired directly at them from 150ft away. The weaker plates on the sides would stop a bullet at anything over a 15° angle.

Its Vickers guns had 750 rounds each and it could carry the same bomb load as a Camel – four 20 pounders or a single 112lb bomb. The pilot testing the Salamander concluded: "Practically the only way in which the machine

An external view of the Camel TF.1, B9278, showing the barrels of its two Lewis guns pointing towards the ground.

could be brought down would be by explosive bullets in a main spar – two flying wires shot away – or a direct hit from anti-aircraft."

Many still believed at this stage that the Salamander was simply an armoured Snipe but the truth was that the two types now had few parts in common. The only interchangeable parts were apparently the tail skid and rudder. The primary reason for this difference was the need to give the Salamander strengthened parts that could take the strain of its enormous weight.

This was underlined when a mistake on the production line led to Snipe centre sections being used instead of Salamander ones. At a glance, they no doubt looked the same but there was a big difference in strength.

On December 28, the Technical Department wrote to the RAF to say: "I am directed to

inform you that it has been ascertained that all Salamanders hitherto delivered by Messrs Sopwith have been provided, by an error on the part of the firm, with Snipe centre sections, which reduce the factor of safety to 3.1 in the case of the front spar and 2.8 in the case of the rear spar, instead of the required factors of 7 and 5 respectively.

"As the machine is clearly dangerously weak, it will be necessary to withdraw machines at once from service, and to have instructions issued that they are not to be flown until rectified. I have to request you for immediate information as to whether this rectification can be made by units, or whether the machines will have to be returned for this purpose to depots or to the makers.

"In the latter case, it may be possible to arrange for correct centre sections to be

A side view of the camouflaged Sopwith Salamander without any identifying markings.

The third Salamander prototype, E5431.

The hefty armoured shell within the Salamander's fuselage offered the pilot and fuel tank relatively good protection but in practice made the aircraft extremely unwieldy. *DH/MG/Brooklands*

supplied for this purpose by the makers."

The war was over before the Salamander saw service but it was still in production by 1919 and squadrons had begun re-equipping with it. Sopwith built at least 337 Salamanders, the Air Navigation Company built at least 100, the Glendower Aircraft Company built 50 and at least 10 were made by Palladium Autocars. A total of 1400 Salamanders had been on order at the time of the Armistice.

The first Salamander unit was to have been 157 Squadron but despite receiving 24 Salamanders by October 31, the war was over before it could be transferred over to France and it was disbanded. Another squadron, No.

96, was also allocated a number of Salamanders but it is doubtful whether it ever received them.

In 1919, the Salamanders already produced were retained by the RAF rather than being scrapped and a small number were used for testing camouflage schemes designed to make them less easily seen from above while flying at low altitude. A couple of examples were still flying at the Royal Aircraft Establishment for this purpose at the beginning of 1920 and the type was listed alongside the Snipe, Cuckoo and Ship's Camel as being in service with the RAF in February, 1922.

A single Salamander, F6533, went to the US for testing that year and it survived until 1926. ∎

EXPERIMENTS IN CAMOUFLAGE

The losses of Cambrai in 1917 didn't just teach the British about the need for armour when flying low over the enemy – they highlighted the need for protection from enemies flying above too.

British fighters tasked with daytime missions had, up to that point, generally been painted in mixtures of iron oxide and lampblack which resulted in a sort of drab brown colour. This was used for doping (painting) specifications PC10 and PC12. Also used were battleship grey and clear varnish.

After Cambrai, the Central Flying School's Experimental Flying Section at Orford Ness on the Suffolk coast was set the task of devising a doping scheme that would break up a trench fighter's outline and make it harder to see.

The Salamander was naturally an ideal guinea pig for this work and J5913, built by the Glendower Aircraft Company, was the subject of several test schemes. Patches of brown and green were painted on the upper wing and fuselage with black lines to separate them. The circular markings on the upper wing were made darker than usual and the white ring normally applied around the outside was painted in grey-green instead.

There were no markings on the fuselage or stripes on the tail and the lower wings were painted an earthy brown. The grey-green colour was also applied to the fuselage sides. On the aircraft's underside, the cockades were made larger to prevent British troops on the ground opening fire on the trench fighter by mistake.

While it was too late in the war for these schemes to be applied to aircraft already fighting at the front, notes were taken and when Britain's fighters were camouflaged in 1938 ahead of the Second World War, similar schemes were applied.

Chapter 16

TORPEDO BOMBER
Sopwith T.1 Cuckoo

After the colossal naval duel that was the Battle of Jutland, the German fleet retreated to port for repairs. It was battered but unbeaten and continued to pose a serious threat to Allied shipping. The Admiralty approached Sopwith to see whether air power could help finish the job.

The first torpedo bomber built by Sopwith, 1914's Type C, was underpowered and unsuitable for its intended role. Its successor, the Type 860, was equally unsuccessful and the Admiralty latched on to its competitor, the Short Type 184, for quantity production instead. But even this ended up being far more use as a spotter than a torpedo launcher.

Aviation pioneer Commodore Murray Sueter, who was the Navy's most prominent supporter of torpedo-launching aircraft as a concept, was hopeful however that a successful example would eventually be developed.

When another opportunity to commission a dedicated carrier-based torpedo bomber presented itself, he jumped at the chance.

Technology had moved on by 1916 and in the wake of the Battle of Jutland, a climactic showdown between the best battleships, cruisers and destroyers of Britain and Germany, Sueter felt that the time had come to give the concept another try.

The German High Seas Fleet was licking its fairly extensive wounds in the docks at Wilhelmshaven; and if a sizeable force of torpedo-equipped aircraft could be assembled, it could be flown from aircraft carriers to catch the enemy vessels off guard and unable to escape.

Sueter sent Tommy Sopwith a letter which read: "Will you please go into the question, with as little delay as possible, regarding a torpedo carrying aeroplane with four hours'

fuel and pilot (1) to carry 1 x 1000lb locomotive torpedo, (2) to carry 2 x 1000lb locomotive torpedoes. Torpedo aeroplane will probably be discharged by catapult, giving machine an acceleration of 90ft/sec in 60ft. Details of Short 225 seaplane attached."

The 'Short 225' was actually the Short Type 184 but was frequently 'nicknamed' 225 due to the power output of its engine. Ironically, a single Type 184, No. 8359, had been flown during the Battle of Jutland where its pilot and observer, Flight Lieutenant Frederick 'Rutland of Jutland' Rutland and Assistant Paymaster G S Trewin respectively, won plaudits for spotting four German cruisers and reporting back – rather than firing a torpedo at them.

Sopwith gave the single torpedo carrier project the designation T.1 and the twin torpedo type was the T.2, but this was quickly dropped as impractical. The T.1 was designed by Herbert Smith and was worked on in conjunction with the B.1 bomber project (outlined in Chapter 18). A necessarily large prototype, N74, was built with separated front wheels for ease of attaching and dropping the torpedo.

Fitted with a 200hp Hispano-Suiza engine, N74 was ready for testing by June 6, 1917. Trials were carried out at the Isle of Grain on the northern coast of Kent throughout July and the Admiralty was so impressed it placed an order for 100 T.1s – the attack force required to scupper the German fleet.

Since the Sopwith factories were already operating at maximum capacity building fighters, the work was subcontracted to Pegler & Co of Doncaster and the Govan-based Fairfield Shipbuilding & Engineering Co. Neither had any experience of building aircraft and struggled to find any staff who had – which posed something of a problem when attempting to fulfil a major order for advanced torpedo bombers.

While these two tried to get themselves

A Sopwith T.1 launches its torpedo. The original reason for building the T.1 was to attack the German High Seas Fleet while it was in port for repairs after the Battle of Jutland.

In profile, the T.1 was a handsome machine with clean lines that belied its sheer size.

A key feature of the T.1 Cuckoo was its folding wings, enabling it to be stored on an aircraft carrier, even if it couldn't be landed back on one after take-off. *DH/MG/Brooklands*

Launching a torpedo at low altitude could be extremely hazardous for the pilot of a T.1 Cuckoo. There was a danger that the subsequent splash could swamp the whole machine. *DH/MG/Brooklands*

geared up for production, a third contractor was brought in, Blackburn, which already had a wealth of experience, having built 186 Sopwith Baby seaplanes. It swiftly retooled in readiness for building T.1s based on Sopwith design drawings.

Blackburn was also entrusted with developing the torpedo dropping and aiming gear with the aid of Navy torpedo specialists.

"The huge T.1 could even be looped when it wasn't carrying a torpedo"

At the same time, plans were being laid to prepare the carriers *HMS Argus*, *HMS Furious* and *HMS Campania*, and the converted cruisers *HMS Courageous* and *HMS Glorious*, to carry the T.1 force to its target.

Testing continued using the N74 machine in January of 1918 and since the required version of the Hispano-Suiza engine would not be available, another powerplant was picked – the 200hp Sunbeam Arab.

Within a month, N74 had had one of these fitted but this made it nose heavy so alterations to the tail were needed. Next, tests were carried out to see just how easily a T.1 could take off from the deck of an aircraft carrier. For this purpose a section of airfield was marked out to the right size and shape with straight lines running across it to clearly indicate distance.

In order to simulate the weight of a torpedo, use of a real one being deemed too risky, a wooden box full of lead shot was slung beneath the aircraft. On the second day of these tests, while it was being flown 1000ft

above the airfield, N74's propeller shaft sheared off and the huge two-bladed propeller made of solid wood span away, slicing through part of the port wing and damaging the engine's radiator as it went.

The pilot was able to glide the machine down but this was not the end of the T.1's teething troubles. When the first production aircraft N6950 was delivered, it was found that part of its undercarriage had fractured on landing along with the tail skid and rudder post – and it hadn't even been carrying the weight of a torpedo.

It was back to the drawing board for the T.1 and construction blueprints already completed and sent out to Pegler, Fairfield and Blackburn had to be withdrawn. The tail required a major redesign but the clock was ticking so it was decided that the first 10 aircraft, which were already in production at the various manufacturing facilities, would be completed to the original design and modified later.

In readiness for delivery of the first production batch, the RNAS formed the Torpedo Development Squadron at Gosport in Hampshire. This was to have six T.1s and four Airco DH.4 bombers and would work out how best to successfully launch a 1000lb 18in Mk.IX torpedo from the air without putting the crew of the aircraft at risk. Pilot training also took place over the Firth of Forth in Scotland from the aerodrome at East Fortune in East Lothian.

Those who flew the early T.1s reported that they tended to pull to the right so Sopwith altered the design again to incorporate a larger rudder and a slightly offset fin. While it was possible to launch a torpedo from a T.1, it was soon determined that this couldn't be done below 50ft. If it was, the splash made by the weapon came up over the aircraft – potentially swamping it.

In addition, although it could certainly be launched from an aircraft carrier, it was impossible to land on one. The T.1 had to be flown off the deck close to its target and once its mission had been completed it had to make its way to a friendly airfield as quickly as possible before its fuel – enough for four hours in the air – ran out.

It was highly manoeuvrable though and could even be looped when it wasn't carrying a torpedo. Unfortunately, it also presented a large target and was unarmed except for its anti-shipping payload. Nevertheless, pilots apparently liked it because of its sturdy

construction and the fact that it was capable of a relatively safe landing in the ocean if necessary.

While the technology and techniques for using air-launched torpedoes were being developed, time ran out for Commodore Sueter's planned attack on the German fleet. The war moved on.

T.1s of 185 Squadron were embarked on *HMS Argus* in November 1918 but hostilities came to an end before they could take part in any combat operations. Orders had been placed for 350 T.1s by this point but those that had yet to be built were immediately cancelled.

The type remained in service however and was given the name Cuckoo after the war. Its Sunbeam Arab engine suffered from an unpleasant level of vibration and a relatively small number of the 233 T.1s produced were retrofitted with 200hp V8 Wolseley Vipers instead, becoming Cuckoo IIs in the process.

They also had flotation bags installed in their fuselages to prevent them from sinking when ditched, larger rudders, extra-large tailskids and a modified exhaust system that vented hot engine gases to the torpedo to prevent its mechanisms from freezing up.

By 1922 there were still 24 T.1 Cuckoo IIs in squadron use by Britain's armed forces, another six being used for training and a further 15 being kept in store. The last British unit to fly the Cuckoo, 210 Squadron, was disbanded at Gosport on April 1, 1923.

The Imperial Japanese Navy was presented with six Cuckoo IIs in 1921 by the British Air Mission and two years later it was operating the Mitsubishi B1M torpedo bomber. This aircraft designed by Herbert Smith, who went to work for Mitsubishi after Sopwith was dissolved in 1920, bore a remarkable resemblance to the Cuckoo. ∎

A head-on view of the T.1 with its wings folded back for storage. The type's independent front landing gear is shown clearly. *DH/MG/Brooklands*

Chapter 17

Next GENERATION

Sopwith 7F.1 Snipe

The ultimate wartime Sopwith fighter was the Snipe. Unlike the oddball Dolphin it took the familiar shape of the Camel and expanded upon it. The result was a heavy and powerful, though less manoeuvrable, machine. It served only briefly on the front line but soon found itself in some tricky situations as the postwar mainstay of the RAF.

Intended as a direct successor to the incredibly successful Sopwith Camel, the Snipe featured a similarly squat fuselage but lacked its predecessor's manoeuvrability. *Paul Le Roy*

Not long after work had begun on the Sopwith Dolphin as the direct successor to the Camel, the Air Board issued a new fighter specification to Britain's aircraft manufacturers.

It wanted a machine that had one seat and a tractor engine, two fixed synchronised machine guns firing through the propeller with 750 rounds of ammunition between them, and the option of a third with 250 rounds that could fire upwards.

It also had to have an Aldis optical sight, oxygen equipment, an armoured shield to protect the pilot's back, a top speed of no less than 135mph and the ability to climb from 10,000ft to 20,000ft in 10 minutes or less.

The specification was issued in April 1917

Sopwith Snipe replica produced by film director Peter Jackson's company The Vintage Aviator flying in New Zealand. *Paul Le Roy*

Sopwith Snipe prototype B9966 had a number of features that would become standard on the production version, such as a larger rudder, bigger fuel and oil tanks, a new fuel system and an adjustable tailplane.

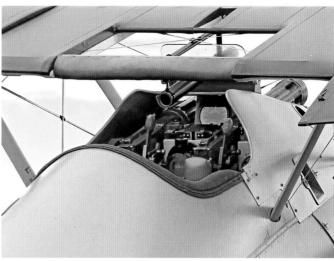

The cockpit of a Sopwith Snipe was snug, like those of its predecessors, but refinements like the small windscreen, through which the Aldis gun sight projected, the upper wing cut-out for improved visibility and easy access to the guns for clearing jams made pilots' lives easier. *Paul Le Roy*

and by August 14, Sopwith's Herbert Smith had drawn up plans for a new fighter he called the Snipe. It was very similar to the Camel, with engine options that could hardly have hit the Air Board's ambitious targets – the 150hp Bentley BR1, a 150hp Gnome, a 130hp Clerget or a 110hp Le Rhone. Still, work on the Snipe progressed.

A month later Tommy Sopwith himself had decided that the Snipe should have the BR1 engine and on October 19, the War Office ordered six Snipe prototypes. These were to be fitted with the powerful new 230hp Bentley BR2 engine.

The first of these had been completed by November 1 and underwent a series of test flights at Brooklands before crashing on November 19. After repairs it went to Martlesham for official tests but crashed again on December 23. This prototype, serial B9965, initially bore a strong resemblance to the Camel but when it reappeared on January 25, 1918, it was substantially different with longer wings and a host of other more minor revisions.

The Snipe was approaching its final form; a compact, almost stubby, fuselage with long wings and a very tall undercarriage.

By now the Air Board had issued a new requirement – now it wanted a machine with the same guns but 1200 rounds rather than 750, enough oxygen for two and a half hours, a carrier for five 25lb Cooper bombs, a fuel load of 40 gallons and provision for

While it was designed primarily as a fighter, the Snipe could also carry a rack of underslung 25lb Cooper bombs. *Paul Le Roy*

the pilot to wear an electrically heated suit.

This time it was a straight competition between four BR2-powered machines. Sopwith entered its Snipe, Austin its AFT3 Osprey triplane, Boulton & Paul the oddly named Bobolink and British Nieuport the BN1 – which had been designed by the man behind the successful SE5, Henry Folland.

After tests had been carried out, the Snipe was found to fall far short of requirements. In a report on February 22, 1918, examiner Wing Commander Alec Ogilvie found it was too slow, carried too little ammo – just 900 – and regarding its flying qualities he wrote: "As the machine was tested its flying qualities were bad, there being a strong

Sopwith Snipe E8015 'E' was flown by E Mulcair of A Flight, 43 Squadron, between October and November 1918. He scored two victories with it.

A contemporary view of one of the Snipe prototypes undergoing testing in March 1918. It took months to prepare the Snipe for front line duty, by which time the war was almost over.

This machine, E6615, flew with the RAF's 23 Squadron.

tendency to get the nose down on turns. The rigging is being altered with a view to getting over this trouble."

He recommended that the Snipe should have its wings moved back and an adjustable tailplane added; its wheel track needed widening too and both fuel tank and magazines needed to be bigger. A decision on the competition winner was put off until March 15 but a further undated report stated that in terms of production and maintenance ease, the Nieuport and Austin machines were the best.

"This great roaring engine had taken possession of the situation"

The Nieuport machine, however, used an unusual wing structure which raised some concerns and then the only prototype was destroyed by fire on March 10.

Ultimately, the Sopwith machine came out on top after it was witnessed in action by then Chief of Air Staff Major General Hugh Trenchard and Brigadier Robert Brooke-Popham. B9965 was taken to France on March 18 for field testing by pilots from 43 Squadron and contracts for 1700 Snipes were drawn up two days later.

While contractors for the Snipe were being organised, work on B9965 continued and it was given a new engine cowling in May 1918. The next prototype in the series, B9966, was fitted with an adjustable tailplane, bigger fuel and oil tanks and a new fuel system. A larger rudder was fitted too.

The first production models were rolling off Sopwith's production line by mid-August, albeit without the modifications

A costumed re-enactor with the RAF Museum's replica or 'composite' Snipe, E6655. *RAF Museum*

that had been made to B9966 which were later made standard.

Unsurprisingly, 43 Squadron was the first to operate the Snipe. It could put 14 of them in the air by September 24, 1918, and by the end of October there were 97 Snipes in France. The Armistice put an end to the Snipe's career on the Western Front before, with one notable exception (see 'Barker's battle'), it had really begun.

Work had begun on a naval version of the aeroplane and E8068 had had a hydrovane – a sort of narrow sideways-on water ski – fitted ahead of its jettisonable wheels to enable it to ditch in the sea more safely. This project was abandoned when hostilities ended, along with plans to introduce the Snipe as a Home Defence fighter. It had been due to enter service in that capacity in January 1919.

A derivative of the Snipe that did see service with the RAF was the Mk.1a long distance Snipe. This was intended to escort and protect bombers on missions deep inside German held territory, although that requirement had already evaporated by the time it entered service. It had an enlarged fuel tank behind and beneath the pilot's seat that was capable of carrying 50 gallons compared to the standard Snipe's 32. The wings were slightly swept back to readjust the centre of gravity and areas of the fuselage were strengthened.

The first Mk.1a was Snipe E8089, which had these modifications plus the tail unit of a Sopwith Dolphin – a feature that was not carried forward for the production Mk.Ia. The Mk.1a machines that were produced in quantity suffered badly from the extra weight, despite the measures taken to mitigate its effects, and pilots were warned against 'stunting' them.

Around 40 two-seater trainer versions of the Snipe were also built and every squadron operating the fighter after the war had at least one. The trainers were still being used by flying training schools as late as 1928, two years after the fighter itself had been retired from squadron service.

The other two main sub-types of the Snipe, the Salamander and the Dragon, are dealt with in chapters 15 and 18 respectively.

SOLDIERING ON AFTER THE WAR

When the war ended, numerous contracts for Snipe production were cancelled almost immediately. Even so, a total of 1550 were built and it was used to equip 22 squadrons. From November 1918 to September 1919, Snipe units were posted in Germany as part of the army of occupation.

In addition, surplus Snipes were given away to Britain's Allies. India received 40 of them even though there were no plans for an Indian Air Force and they rotted away in storage for several years before being scrapped.

The postwar Royal Canadian Air Force got just two – E8102 and E8213 – and one was given to the Americans, E7649. New Zealand preferred not to take them at all.

For the RAF, however, the Snipe became a way of life for a generation of young pilots. Training typically took place in a sedate and old fashioned Avro 504K before the cadet was moved into the powerful Snipe. One pilot described his experiences in forthright terms: "After completing the necessary hours of solo on 504Ks, the day came when one was introduced to the dual control Sopwith Snipe.

"Two cockpits in so short a fuselage? Impossible! But in this stubby machine the impossible was achieved. Following the usual pre-flight palaver, instructor and pupil, the latter in the forward cockpit, harnessed themselves in.

"The change from the 504K's safety belt to a Sutton Harness presaged new possibilities but hardly prepared the novice for what was to come. The exaggerated nose-up position of the Snipe at rest, due to the very short fuselage and high undercarriage, infused a sense of urgency and power – and this even before the engine was started. Taxiing out for take-off was a jerky ride, every irregularity of the ground

The Snipe was designed to make full use of the Bentley BR2 rotary engine. *Paul Le Roy*

being transmitted through the tail-skid to the cockpits in the short fuselage. Instructions were given that on take-off full rudder should be applied before opening up the engine, to be followed by rudder in the opposite direction as the tail lifted into flying position.

"This was to correct the combined effect of deflection of the fin and rudder by the slipstream and the terrific gyroscopic

moment impacted by the great mass of the rotating BR2.

"Also the stick had to be pushed right forward to quickly lift the tail into flying position and then eased back.

"The wheels unstuck after a brief run and as airspeed was built up, assisted by the guiding hand of the instructor on the stick, the aircraft was put into, what seemed at the time, very nearly a vertical climb."

Sopwith Snipe E8213 was presented to Canada by the city of Leicester on January 21, 1919. It was taken on strength by the fledgling RCAF on August 5, 1919. It was entered into a Toronto-New York air race by an 'H S Quigley' but crashed on August 25 while being tested in Toronto ahead of the race.

He said this experience was both disturbing and disorientating to a pilot more used to the leisurely pace of the Avro 504K.

"After being alarmed at losing sight of the horizon, confidence was restored on finding it somewhere near the leading edge of the lower main plane. This great, roaring engine had taken possession of the situation and was, in a few brief seconds, completely revising the pilot's opinion of flying. Although some hours were flown in single-seat Snipes, that first dramatic rocketing into the blue is a lasting memory which recalls the amazing and famous climbing quality of the Snipe as no other thing ever did.

"In most manoeuvres, the gyroscopic effect of the large rotary engine could always be felt; in fact, it was so immense that at the top of a loop it was necessary to apply full rudder to prevent the aircraft turning on its back. All controls were very sensitive, the aircraft giving immediate response to any movement of the control column and rubber-bar, a feature which made the Snipe highly suitable for aerobatics.

"It was, due to its sensitive qualities, not an easy aircraft to fly. The low inherent stability in the air and the narrow wheel base and short fuselage in landing and taxiing called for unrelaxed attention on the part of the pilot."

During the 1920s, the Snipe saw action both in Ireland and Iraq. The former saw Snipes being used during the Irish War of Independence to seek out and attack IRA militiamen trying to ambush British Army units. On one occasion in 1921: "A patrol of this type of aeroplane recently located in Ireland an ambush, and the result was disastrous for the ambushers, five of whom were killed by our airmen."

The situation in Iraq also required the RAF's Snipes. The country had become a League of Nations mandate under British control on November 11, 1920, and the following year the British asked Faisal bin Hussein bin Ali al-Hashimi to become king

as Faisal I. He agreed. This move had been fostered as a way of preventing insurrection but in that it was a failure.

Kurdish leader Sheikh Mahmud Barzanji had initially been appointed by the British

as governor of the area north of Baghdad but he resented the British for promises he believed had been made to the Kurdish people during the Great War and then broken. By early 1923, he was holding officials hostage and beginning a series of insurrections against British rule.

"They forced the tribesmen to retreat by repeatedly strafing their ranks"

A cavalry regiment unit was sent to put down the Kurds but its commanders had failed to appreciate the scale of the Kurdish movement and it was soon surrounded by a huge host of armed tribesmen. The situation looked desperate for the British until a flight of Sopwith Snipes from 1 Squadron, based at Hinaidi, arrived overhead. They dived on the tribesmen and forced them to retreat by

As the mainstay of the postwar RAF, the Snipe ended up being fielded all over the world. This flight of 1 Squadron Snipes is pictured over Baghdad, Iraq, in early 1923.

Snipe E6939 was stationed in Baghdad, Iraq, with 1 Squadron at Hinaidi in the 1920s.

repeatedly strafing their ranks with machine gun fire. Thereafter, the Snipes flew patrols overhead to provide the cavalry column with continuous aerial support.

Despite the aircraft's widespread military use, there were still too many Snipes for the British military's purposes and the RAF began to dispose of them as early as 1920. The Aircraft Disposal Company began offering complete examples for sale to other countries with a price tag of £700. The book price of the BR2 engine alone was £880.

There were no takers. Eventually, in May 1922, Brazil bought a dozen which were duly delivered and put to work by the Brazilian navy.

It used 10 of them to equip its Flotilha de Caca at Rio de Janeiro. Six of these were still flying by January 1929.

In the RAF, the Snipe had already been replaced by the Gloster Grebe – another Folland design – in 1926.

The Snipe had been the RAF's last serving Sopwith machine. ∎

Another 1 Squadron Snipe stationed in Hinaidi. Snipes were used to strafe Kurdish tridesmen during an insurrection.

BARKER'S BATTLE

The most famous aerial battle involving the Snipe took place on October 27, 1918, and involved the highest scoring Sopwith Camel ace of the war – Major William 'Billy' Barker.

Barker, a Canadian, had been an observer and a pilot since 1916 before being posted to Italy in 1917 where he racked up 46 victories before returning to England in October 1918. He had been given a training position and was returned to the Western Front for a 'refresher course' in air combat tactics – something he was unlikely to have required.

It was a thinly veiled excuse to have one last scrap in France before he was effectively forced to retire from the front line for good. He was temporarily attached to 201 Squadron based at Beugnatre, near Bapaume on the Somme Front, which operated the new Snipe, but bad weather kept him grounded for most of his stay.

His last flight was supposed to be back to the air supply depot at St Omer away to the north-west but he was determined to add another kill to his score. He headed directly east for about 40 miles until he crossed the front line – which had just been pushed five miles further east by the Battle of Selle River. He spotted a two-seater Rumpler C reconnaissance machine flying over Mormal Woods near Le Quesnoy at 8.25am. It was the classic 'lure' and Barker fell for it.

He swooped down and shot it out of the sky but failed to notice a flight of Fokker D.VIIs that had been shadowing it. One of these then fired into his machine, seriously wounding him. What happened next is hotly contested but Barker was awarded the Victoria Cross for his actions and his VC citation reads: "He was wounded in the right thigh, but managed, despite this, to shoot down the enemy aeroplane in flames. He then found himself in the middle of a large formation of Fokkers, which attacked him from all directions and he was again severely wounded in the left thigh, but succeeded in driving down two of the enemy in a spin.

"He lost consciousness after this and his machine fell out of control. On recovery he found himself being again attacked heavily by a large formation. Singling out one machine, he deliberately charged and drove it down in flames.

"During this fight his left elbow was shattered and he again fainted, and on regaining consciousness he found himself still being attacked; but, notwithstanding that he was now severely wounded in both legs and his left arm shattered, he dived on the nearest machine and shot it down in flames.

"Being greatly exhausted, he dived out of the fight to regain our lines but was met by another formation which attacked and endeavoured to cut him off; but after a hard fight he succeeded in breaking up this formation and reached our lines where he crashed on landing.

"This combat, in which Major Barker destroyed four enemy machines (three of them in flames), brought his total successes up to 50 enemy machines destroyed, and is a notable example of the exceptional bravery and disregard of danger which this very gallant officer has always displayed throughout his distinguished career."

Barker crashed near a British kite balloon winch crew who were able to bring him the medical aid that undoubtedly saved his life. Even so, he was unconscious for 10 days afterwards. Few credible eyewitnesses came forward and since the combat began at 12,000ft – the point at which Barker suffered his first critical and debilitating wound – even those directly below would have struggled to see what exactly was going on.

Precisely how many Fokkers Barker engaged varies from newspaper reports of 60 to a more credible 15 down to just a handful. He never spoke about the battle publicly – in fact it may be that the only person who heard the full tale was his superior officer who then wrote his combat report for him.

All he would say was: "I was severely wounded and shot down."

Chapter 18

THE ZOO
Sopwith experimental types

A huge number of prototype and experimental aircraft were produced during the Sopwith Aviation Company's eight years of manufacturing. This proliferation of types most of them named after animals, led some to refer to the 'Sopwith zoo'. The machines detailed here are those not featured elsewhere in this publication and they are presented in chronological order.

Hispano Triplane

The Sopwith works was a hive of activity towards the end of 1915 as both the 1½ Strutter and Pup were taking shape. While the experimental fitting of a Pup fuselage with three sets of narrow wings resulted in the production model Clerget-engined Triplane, the 1½ Strutter fuselage also got the triplane treatment, this time with a Hispano-Suiza engine.

Delays in the production of its engine hampered the Hispano Triplane, although the two examples built, N509 and N510, still flew in 1916 before the Pup-derived Triplane had entered serial production. N509 had a 150hp direct drive engine and N510's was a 200hp geared type.

The Hispano Triplane's cockpit was positioned back behind the wings but behind a much longer engine this resulted in poor forward visibility. During trials at Eastchurch in December 1916, N510's tailplane broke off in mid-air, destroying the machine; and during testing of 509 shortly afterwards, tail vibration was noted. The second machine was also written off at Manston on October 29, 1917.

It seems likely that the Hispano Triplane, particularly when fitted with the 200hp engine, would have been able to carry substantially more weight than its diminutive cousin, the Triplane, but even so it was only ever tested with a single synchronised Vickers gun.

L.R.T.Tr

One of the most unlikely looking fighters ever built, the Sopwith L.R.T.Tr triplane, was designed for long range reconnaissance missions. Fitted to its top wing was a streamlined nacelle for a gunner – one of three crew members – and it had four wheels rather than the more usual two.

The additional wheels at the front were intended to prevent the aircraft from nosing over with particularly dire consequences for the unfortunate gunner. Even though the aircraft usually sat on all four wheels, it also had a tail skid and skids towards the ends of the lower wings on either side too.

The top gunner, exposed though he was in his pod, would have had an unparalleled field of fire and although existing photographs never show the L.R.T.Tr fitted with a gun mounting, it seems likely that rather than a Vickers or Lewis, the pod would have been fitted with a large Davis-type recoilless gun which fired 2lb balls of lead suitable for punching through the skin of Zeppelins.

A second gunner with a Lewis gun would have sat directly behind the pilot for more conventional air-to-air defence. The L.R.T.Tr's engine was the first Rolls-Royce to be fitted into any Sopwith machine – the 250hp Rolls-Royce Mk.I.

Only a single example was made, and its development soon stalled and was never resumed after it suffered structural damage during its first landing.

Bee

The smallest manned aeroplane built by Sopwith, the Bee was constructed using largely Pup components but with a very short wingspan of just 16ft 3in compared to the Pup's 26ft 6in. It took over from the SL.T.B.P. as Harry Hawker's 'runabout' but was in reality a development and research machine.

Built in 1917, it was fitted with a then-outdated and underpowered 50hp Gnome engine and had a large cutout in the top wing for the pilot's head. The latter was of most interest to Sopwith's designers since there were concerns that removing such a large area of wing would result in a loss of lift. Rather than ailerons, a relatively new technology in 1917, the Bee had 'old-fashioned' wing warping instead.

It has been suggested that the Bee's short wingspan, under-powered but cheap and readily available engine and unsophisticated control mechanism might have been the result of involvement in the programme intended to produce an unmanned flying bomb.

All three features would have been seen in such a weapon to keep costs down in an essentially expendable single-shot device. Indeed, the type's name, Sopwith Bee, might have been a rather unsophisticated but effective camouflage for Sopwith 'B.' or Sopwith Bomb. Certainly, conventional Sopwith bombers were given the 'B.' initial in their type name.

Another suggestion links 'Bee' with the aircraft's powerplant, or rather its intended powerplant.

The final refinement of the flying bomb programme, the Sparrow, was fitted with the 45hp ABC Gnat engine and ABC also produced the 60hp Gadfly and 170hp Wasp, not to mention the notorious 320hp Dragonfly. It is possible that the Bee was intended for another ABC development that never saw the light of day.

B.1/B.2

A parallel development to the T.1 Cuckoo, the B.1 was a bomber, as the single letter in its name suggests. Powered by a 200hp Hispano-Suiza, it was a large single seater which could carry up to 560lb of bombs in a compartment directly behind the pilot.

Structurally, it was very similar to the T.1 except for its landing gear, which was the conventional axle type, and its cockpit/bomb compartment section.

Test flights of the first B.1 began in early April 1917 and it proved to be such a promising design that both the British and French governments showed an interest. Field testing began at Dunkirk in May and pilots found it tiring to fly, although they rated its performance as "very good".

Minor modifications made to the second example, B1496, including external elevator cables, were deemed sufficient for it to be given the type number B.2.

The B.1/B.2's bomb bay was accessed via an external panel on the fuselage and its load typically comprised nine British 50lb bombs, loaded nose up. Alternatively, French 50kg 'Gros-Andreau' anilite bombs, as detailed in chapter 5, could be carried.

After testing at Dunkirk, the first B.1 was sent to Port Victoria in Kent where it was modified to incorporate folding wings, a wireless set, hydrovane landing gear and a second cockpit behind the pilot. Given the number N50, this was the first of a new type, the P.V. Grain Griffin. It was found that numerous alterations were still necessary and when a production run of seven Griffins was eventually arranged, the resulting aircraft deviated quite substantially from the original B.1, although the familial resemblance was still evident.

3.F2 Hippo

A two-seat fighter, the Hippo was intended as a replacement for the hundreds of Sopwith 1½ Strutters entering French service in early 1917. Its most striking feature was a strong backwards stagger to its wings – with the upper wing being set much further back than the lower. It was set so far back, in fact, that the pilot's head was actually in front of it.

The rear gunner, equipped with a Lewis gun, sat almost within the wing thanks to a large wing cutout to improve his field of vision. The pilot had a pair of fixed forward firing synchronised Vickers machine guns.

Wings aside, the Hippo was a parallel development to the more conventional 2FR.2 Bulldog.

Sopwith's Hippo design drawings were completed on April 30, 1917, and the first example, fitted with a 200hp Clerget 11Eb engine, was sent to France for testing in September. A new set of wings was fitted in December and further trials commenced in January 1918 at Martlesham Heath. The prototype Hippo by this time carried the number X11. It is believed that the Hippo as first tested may have carried the number X10.

The report from Martlesham Heath stated: "The machine is very slow and heavy on lateral control, also the pilot and passenger are too far apart for easy communication, these points being disadvantages to a fighting machine."

Official interest in the Hippo waned in February 1918, although Sopwith continued to develop it. Another example, or possibly the same one but heavily modified, was flying in June 1918 under the number X18.

2FR.2 Bulldog

A two-seat reconnaissance fighter, hence the 'R' in its name, the Bulldog had a Dolphin-like position for the pilot – with his head within and slightly above the top wing. As with the Hippo, the rear gunner sat behind the upper wing.

The original Bulldog design specified not only a camera but also a wireless set. Its wings were to be slightly longer than those of the Hippo – 40ft 3in compared to 38ft 9in – which would have improved its performance at the higher altitudes required for photo recce missions. Weight was reduced by giving the pilot one Vickers gun rather than two.

In its first built form however, the Bulldog had only a stubby 26ft 6in wingspan and twin Vickers guns instead of just the one. Like the Hippo, it was powered by a 200hp Clerget 11Eb – they were the only two Sopwith designs to use it. The rear gunner got a pair of Lewises, one at either end of the cockpit rather than side by side.

The first example was designed between August and September 1917 and testing began in November, new longer wings being fitted on November 13. Now the prototype became number X3. A second Bulldog, X4, was fitted with an ABC Dragonfly engine in June 1918, by which time the Bulldog was no longer considered a viable prospect for full scale production. X4 was still flying at Farnborough as an experimental machine as late as March 1919.

2B.2 Rhino

The Rhino was a relatively small two-seat triplane bomber powered by a tall and very narrow 230hp Beardmore-Halford-Pullinger (BHP) engine. Its load of four x 112lb, nine x 50lb or 20 x 20lb bombs was located below the pilot in the very deep fuselage and could be winched into position all in one go in a cellular bomb 'crate'.

The first Rhino, numbered X7, was tested at Brooklands in October 1917 before undergoing official trials at Martlesham Heath in January 1918. A second Rhino, X8, followed on February 1918. X7 had a synchronised Vickers gun mounted immediately ahead of the pilot, with its fairing providing him with some protection. On X8, the gun was further away from the pilot, allowing the fitment of a full windscreen.

Unfortunately the aircraft's wing configuration made it very difficult for the crew to accurately aim their payload. In addition, its performance in the air was unimpressive and the type got no further than more tests at Martlesham in February and March 1918.

AT and Sparrow

Controlling vehicles using a wireless signal was a concept that had fascinated inventors for some years before the Great War. Radio-controlled boats and airships had been developed but no one had been able to overcome the problem, for military purposes, of a hostile operator jamming the signal, or even hijacking it and the remotely controlled vehicle itself into the bargain.

When war broke out, leading the field of wireless control in Britain was Professor Archibald Low. The RFC tasked him with developing a pilot-less aircraft – a guided flying bomb. It would have to be small, simple and cheap. The programme was codenamed 'AT' for 'Aerial Target', the idea being to convince the Germans that this weapon was actually merely a training vehicle.

Low started out in a garage in Chiswick but then moved to Brooklands where he had ready access to aeroplanes. Before long, it was discovered that a 50hp Gnome rotary generated too much interference. The radio control gear worked fine – but only when the engine was switched off.

Sopwith began to develop its own 'AT' shortly thereafter, in parallel with a number of other companies, and ABC Motors developed a small throwaway engine to power it. This 35hp horizontally opposed twin-cylinder powerplant was designed to run for just two hours but that, it was deemed, would be sufficient for the AT to take off and be flown directly into a Zeppelin.

The Sopwith AT, top right, had a 14ft wingspan and the radio control box was positioned in a glass topped 2ft 3in by 9in wooden box on rubber supports in the tail, well away from the engine. Contacts made in the control box caused, via mechanical relays, the control surfaces to move. The rest of the fuselage was filled with fuel tanks, batteries and the explosives. The aerials were wound round the rear of the fuselage and the outboard sections of the upper wings. The AT was damaged while it was being assembled at Feltham and never flown. Its successor, bottom right, was the Sopwith Sparrow – apparently a development of the same SLTBP design that resulted in the Pup. It had a 25ft wingspan, the 35hp ABC engine, and wing-warping for control. Like the AT, the Sparrow never went into production and such was the secrecy involved in the project little is known about its later development.

8F.1 Snail

The Snail was a single-seat fighter that was smaller than either the Pup or the Camel. It was designed around a new type of engine – the 170hp seven-cylinder radial ABC Wasp – and the two prototype examples built differed quite significantly from one another.

The first order for four Snails was made by the Government on October 31, 1917, but less than a month later, on November 23, this was expanded to six but with the additional two having a monocoque fuselage made of plywood. In a monocoque structure, most or all of the load is taken by the shell-like outer skin, hence the name 'Snail', which came also to apply to the conventionally structured 8F.1.

The first conventional

fuselage Snail, C4284, below right, and the first monocoque one, C4288, below left, were built at the same time. The top wing of C4284 was positioned further back than the lower one, a stagger of 5in, while the top wing of C4288 was staggered forwards of the lower one by 22in. In C4288 there were internal differences too, with the pilot sitting further back.

This meant that the upper wing, which on C4284 had a large centre section cut-out similar to that seen on the Dolphin, only had a cut-out at its trailing edge on C4288. Both had the horizontal tail surfaces of a Snipe.

While C4288 appears never to have had any weapons fitted, C4284 had a pair of Vickers guns positioned one either side of the pilot with only the muzzle ends poking out from the almost conical nose fairing.

The ABC Wasp engine suffered delays and C4284's example was not delivered until March 18, 1918. C4288 was finished by April 27, 1918, but work on the other prototypes was halted before they were complete. Tests revealed the Snail's handling to be poor at low speeds, though the type was fast and climbed well – when its engine worked.

Buffalo

Like the Sopwith Salamander, the Buffalo was heavily armoured, but unlike the Salamander, which was a single seat 'trench fighter', the Buffalo had two seats and was designed for 'contact patrols' rather than strafing German positions.

'Contact patrols' were extremely hazardous missions where a two-man crew had to fly at low level to visually assess concentrations of enemy troops, defensive positions and weaponry. With this in mind, the Buffalo gave its crew a good field of view both above and below. The pilot sat within a rectangular upper wing cut-out right behind the engine up front, while the observer/gunner sat close behind him.

The engine was a powerful 230hp Bentley BR2 and the fuselage was narrow to present a smaller target for enemies firing from the ground. The pilot had a fixed forward-firing

Vickers gun and the observer got a Lewis gun. Top speed was 110mph and service ceiling was 9000ft.

A pair of prototype Buffalos, H5892 and H5893, were ordered on September 6, 1918, the first of which was already nearly finished. H5892 first flew at Brooklands on September 18 and it was flown to France for testing on October 20. Changes were

suggested but it is likely that the war ended before they could be implemented.

The second Buffalo had an extended conical engine fairing, extra armour for the rear cockpit, cut-outs in the lower wing for improved downwards visibility and an altered tail rudder shape. There was a strong interest in the Buffalo but when the war ended so did its chances of entering production.

Scooter and Swallow

The Scooter was completed as a 'runabout' for Harry Hawker in July 1918. It had the fuselage of a standard 130hp Clerget-powered Sopwith Camel but with an entirely new swept back monoplane wing mounted on top of it very close to the fuselage. As with every aeroplane regarded as a 'mere runabout' for Hawker to ferry himself about in however, the Scooter was a template or testbed for something else – the Swallow.

The Swallow, which at first glance looked almost identical to the Scooter, was intended as a naval fighter. It was deemed that its

parasol style monoplane wing would improve its potential for landing on the decks of aircraft carriers – a practice that few had previously dared to undertake.

It differed from the Scooter in having larger, longer, stiffer wings set slightly higher above the fuselage. A pair of synchronised Vickers guns was fitted in front of the pilot though they were more widely spaced than those of the Camel and lacked any sort of faired-over 'hump'.

Where the Scooter had a Clerget engine, the Swallow had a 110hp Le Rhône, but in any

case it was too late. The first tests did not take place until May 1919 after delays caused by fuel-system problems.

Hawker actually bought the Scooter from the remains of the Sopwith company in April 1921. It had been given the civilian registration G-EACZ. After Hawker's death just three months later, it was placed into storage before being overhauled by a 'C Clayton' of Hendon and given a new certificate dated August 1, 1925. A year later it was sold to Dudley Watt who flew it for a couple of months before it was sold for scrap.

Dragon

Six prototype Snipes were ordered, as detailed in chapter 17, and the last of them, B9967, was fitted with the promising new ABC Dragonfly engine. This 'Dragonfly Snipe' was ready to go in April 1918 and was sent to Farnborough for tests on May 11, 1918. It remained thereafter as a flying testbed for the engine – which was already beginning to display certain teething troubles.

Another converted Snipe, E7990, is regarded as the first true Sopwith Dragon since it can be seen in photographs that the company painted the name 'Dragon' on the side of its fuselage and it had a lengthened rear fuselage that characterised the full production model. In spite of the problems associated with the engine, and in the hope that these could swiftly be overcome, a production contract for 30 Dragons was given to Sopwith in June 1918.

The production version of the Dragon had most of the later upgrades made to the Snipe. It had a pair of Vickers guns tightly wedged in behind the large engine and a 1.8in Aldis gun sight. While the Dragon was listed as a standard RAF type in 1921, it never equipped a squadron and was 'withdrawn' in 1923.

Snark

Another triplane design, this time with a monocoque fuselage, the Snark was also another machine cursed by the installation of an ABC Dragonfly engine. It was built as a single-seat high-altitude fighter and its armament was twin Vickers guns built into the sides of the fuselage behind the powerplant, plus four Lewis guns – two mounted in each lower wing. This made it the most heavily armed fighter to be designed during the Great War.

A trio of Snarks was ordered in April 1918, F4068, F4069 and F4070, and work on the first example had been completed by October but it lacked a serviceable engine. One was finally delivered in December but it wasn't fitted until April 1919. This engine proved to be useless so a second was fitted in July and trials at Brooklands did not take place until September 1919.

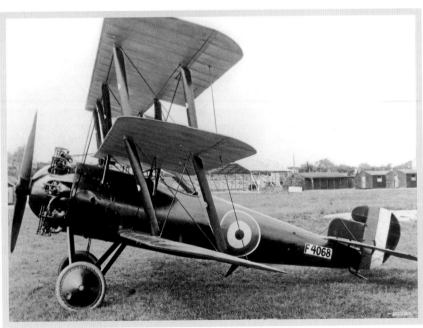

By then, both of the other Snarks had also been completed. F4068 was delivered to Martlesham Heath for testing on November 12 – a year after the war ended – but had to be sent back to Sopwith for yet another new engine. Tests resumed in March 1920. There are few records of F4069's fate but F4070 finally flew in 1921 with a very large spinner mounted on its nose.

When F4068 was fitted with its final engine, a Dragonfly 1A, it became a Snark Mk.II. None of the three Snarks survived very long since their monocoque fuselages deteriorated rapidly and all had been scrapped by 1922.

Snapper

The final Sopwith single-seat fighter built was a straightforward biplane that was a near contemporary of the Snark. Another high-altitude fighter, the Snapper, had a conventionally constructed fuselage but it also had a Dragonfly engine. Its weaponry was a pair of fixed forward-firing Vickers guns set ahead of the pilot.

Three Snappers were ordered in early 1918, F7031, F7032 and F7033, but F7031 was not completed and ready to fly until April 1919. Tests were carried out at Martlesham Heath in September 1919. All three completed Snappers were at the Royal Aircraft Establishment at Farnborough in June 1920, since the RAF was keenly interested in the type, but ultimately it lost out to the Nieuport Nighthawk, which was faster and could fly higher.

F7032 and F7033 were used for static load testing with sand – presumably until they broke. The eventual fate of F7031 is unknown but it was presumably scrapped.

Cobham

The last military aircraft ever produced by the Sopwith Aviation Company was not a fighter – it was a twin-engined three-seat triplane bomber. Furthermore, rather than being given an animal name, it was instead called the Cobham – after the town in Surrey.

The ABC Dragonfly was the intended powerplant for the Cobham, which was designed in the early summer of 1918 as a short to medium range bomber. It was proposed that it would be able to carry a payload of up to 750lb.

A mock-up of the aeroplane was built in August and three Cobhams were ordered – H671, H672 and H673. The troubles of the Dragonfly engine resulted in the first Cobham, H671, being fitted with high compression 290hp Siddeley Pumas instead. It was thereafter referred to as the Cobham Mk.II, while the second Cobham, H672, which eventually received Dragonfly 1As, was the Mk.I.

H671 first flew in mid-1919 but its undercarriage was damaged during tests and it was sent to Brooklands for repairs in November. H672 first flew in January 1920 before being sent to Martlesham in February. It was sent to Farnborough for disposal in June.

The third Cobham, H673, was completed with Dragonfly 1As and joined H672 at Martlesham in February before being sent back to Sopwith for modifications or repairs in May. It too was sent to Farnborough in June and both Dragonfly Cobhams had been scrapped by the time H671 finally arrived at Farnborough on November 29, 1920. It flew there on January 27, 1921, before it too was scrapped. ∎

Chapter 19

SOPWITH around the world

Aircraft in service with foreign nations

Sopwith machines flew all over the world with pilots of numerous nationalities at the controls. Among the largest foreign users were France, with its 4500 licence-built 1½ Strutters; the US, which acquired large stocks of Strutters and Camels from the French and British respectively; and Russia, which churned out hundreds of unlicensed Strutter copies.

Afghanistan
A single Sopwith 1½ Strutter, albeit a copy of the design manufactured in Russia by Dux of Moscow, was transported to Afghanistan in September 1921 in a caravan that included three elephants. A few more Russian-built Strutters were sent in 1925.

Argentina
Two 1½ Strutters entered the civilian register in Argentina in 1928 as R-105, later LV-BAA, and R-106, later LV-CAA. One of these still exists (see chapter 21).

Australia
One Blackburn-built Sopwith Baby was used by the Royal Australian Navy, N1014. It was delivered in April 1917 and operated for just three months from the cruiser *HMAS Brisbane*. The navy also operated a pair of Pups – one each aboard *HMAS Sydney* and *HMAS Australia*.

In 1914, an Australian Flying Corps had been established in parallel to the Royal Flying Corps. It was operating four squadrons by 1918 – two of them fighter units. A single Sopwith 1½ Strutter was used for training by 2 Squadron and more by 4 Squadron, which was equipped with the Camel as its front line fighter. The AFC's 6 (Training) Squadron used 1½ Strutters in England.

The Camels of 4 Squadron were replaced with Snipes in September 1918. After the war, the Royal Australian Air Force chose to operate S.E.5s rather than Snipes, but did request Sopwith Pups for use as advanced trainers.

In June 1920, Pup C523 was displayed at the Melbourne Exhibition Air Show and in 1921, 11 Pups (C521-C528, C530-C532) were handed over to No. 1 Flying Training School in Australia as intermediate fighter trainers. Another Pup, C476, entered the civilian register as G-AUCK and was still flying as VH-UCK in 1944.

Captured from the forces of White Russian General Anton Denikin, this Camel was pressed into service by the Red Army with a star on its tail and an unusual batwing design on its fuselage.

Belgium
At least 38 1½ Strutters were used by the Belgian Air Force. Eight were delivered from the RNAS in March 1917 – N5235-N5242 – and other examples or at least components are believed to have been delivered from the RFC. The Belgians renumbered the RNAS examples S1-S8 and used them for reconnaissance with the 6 Squadron based at Houtem. A few weeks later Belgium received 30 French-built 1½ Strutters and allocated them to 2, 3 and 4 Squadrons. They were replaced by SPAD XIs before the end of the war.

In mid-1917, six Pups were delivered to Belgium and it allocated them to 3 Squadron to escort Farman observation aircraft. They were withdrawn when around 50 Camels were acquired and took up the same duties.

Brazil
Three 1½ Strutters were used by the Brazilian Air Force for liaison duties and in May 1922 Brazil bought 12 Snipes through the Curtiss Aeroplane Export Co of New York for $6500 (£1600) each. These probably originated with the Aircraft Disposal Company (ADC) and went to the Brazilian Navy. Ten of them were based in Rio de Janeiro, but they suffered a series of accidents due in part to the poor quality of the airfield, but also to a lack of spares. Just six remained by January 1929.

The ADC, led by Frederick Handley Page, bought up the entire stock of the Aircraft Disposals Board on March 15, 1920 – 10,000 aircraft including Sopwith Pups, Camels, Dolphins and Snipes, as well as Avro 504Ks, Bristol Fighters, DH.6s, DH.9s, DH.9As, DH.10s, S.E.5s and many more, plus 35,000 engines and 500-1000 tons of ball bearings, 350,000 sparking plugs, 100,000 magnetos and huge quantities of nuts and bolts! The company paid £1million for stock which, on paper, was worth £5.7m.

The firms that had made the aeroplanes in the first place received nothing from their subsequent sale – at knock down prices and in competition with their own new designs – since they were government property.

Canada

An independent Canadian Air Force was formed before the end of the war and its first squadron, 1 Squadron, was equipped with Sopwith Dolphins. Another Sopwith machine was already serving with Canadian forces however – Canada had acquired a single Camel, B3772, from the US for its Canadian School of Aerial Fighting on October 2, 1918.

The fledgling Canadian Air Force was disbanded following the Armistice and reformed as the Royal Canadian Air Force. It took into service at least five Dolphins and a pair of Snipes – E8102 and E8213. The former was Canadian ace William Barker's machine, and was dismantled soon after its arrival in Canada. Another Snipe, E7649, was acquired from the US in 1921, but crashed on October 22, 1923.

Another seven Camels, 2F.1s including N7367, were also picked up from the US and one of them survived until mid-1928.

Chile

Before the war, Chile had placed orders with British companies for warships, which were then never delivered due to the conflict. In 1919, Britain offered 50 aircraft by way of compensation. Included in the number were 11 seaplanes – two of them Sopwith Babies. One of these, with the Chilean serial N2103, made the first flight of a Chilean naval aircraft on July 3, 1919, in the bay of Talcahuano in the hands of English instructor Victor Huston.

Estonia

The Estonians flew a single ex-Soviet 1½ Strutter and after the war were sent a 2F.1 Ship's Camel, N6616, formerly of *HMS Vindictive*. It was delivered to Björkö, Estonia, on July 20, 1919, with an RAF pilot to fly it – Captain Claude Emery. It was flown against Bolshevik forces until the following year.

Numerous Sopwith 1½ Strutters served with the Red Army's air forces. This one was named 'Red Victor' and the slogan on the side reads 'red eagles of all countries – fly together'.

A Sopwith 1½ Strutter in Belgian service as S08. This ex-RNAS Mann, Egerton & Co built machine (N5236) has had a hard life – its fin is from an ex-RFC Ruston, Proctor & Co machine (A8166) and its rudder is from something else entirely! *Daniel Brackx*

France

Seven French firms licence-built an estimated 4500 Sopwith 1½ Strutters, which were used to equip 72 squadrons either wholly or in part. The French Navy operated 33 Sopwith Babies from 1916-1919, but wanted to create its own fighter squadron at Saint-Pol-sur-Mer, near Dunkirk. It was unable to get the aircraft it needed from the French Air Force so it placed an order for 10 Triplanes directly with the Sopwith company. These machines were not given British serial numbers, and their Clerget 130hp engines and Vickers machine guns were supplied by the French Navy.

The first delivery was made on December 11, 1916. The 10 machines were given temporary serial numbers for transit – F.1-F.10 – which they kept, but were supplemented by squadron letters and numbers.

F.1 SP.9, F.2 SP.12 and F.4 SP.4 were the first aircraft delivered, then F.5 SP.11 arrived on December 30, 1916. F.3 SP.10 on January 15, 1917, F.7 SP.13 on January 29, F.9 SP.14 on February 2, F.6 SP.15 on February 14, and both F.8 SP.17 and F.10 SP.16 on March 1.

In mid-1917, five extra Triplanes were supplied by the RNAS, which did have British serials – B5384-B5388. They became F.11-F.15. There was an F.16 too, though its background is uncertain.

Eight of the 16 were destroyed in accidents, and F.15 was shot down by German fighters on September 3, 1917. The remaining seven machines were transferred to the RNAS in October and November. F.5 was given the serial N541, F.9 became N542 and F.10 was N543. Another survivor became N524. N5384, N5387 and N5388 reverted to their original serials.

After the war, the civilian register was flooded with ex-French military 1½ Strutters. There were still 55 in civilian hands by 1922.

Georgia

Having been part of the Russian Empire since 1801, Georgia declared independence in the middle of the Russian Civil War on May 26, 1918. At least one Sopwith Camel was flown by the Democratic Republic of Georgia's air force. It is likely to have been one of several sent over by Britain, since Georgia was nominally under British protection from 1918 to 1920.

Germany

After Greece, Germany was Sopwith's second overseas customer, having ordered a Bat Boat Type 2 in November 1913. Delivered in spring 1914, the aircraft was given serial No. 44 in the German Naval Air Arm and was used as a trainer at Kiel-Holtenau. Once the war had begun, German forces occasionally captured a Sopwith machine intact or with only light damage and pressed it into service. These included at least one example each of a Sopwith Schneider, 1½ Strutter (serial A1914), Pup (N6161), Triplane (N5429) and Camel. The latter was flown by German pilot Otto Kissenberth, who used it to shoot down a British S.E.5a on May 16, 1918.

Greece

Sopwith's first foreign customer, Greece ordered three SPGn Pusher Seaplanes, which were delivered, then a further six, one of which was built as a Type 880 tractor seaplane. These were all pressed into service by the British when the war began. The three Pushers were delivered and flown from the Eleusis Air Station in Greece. The Greeks were also given a Sopwith Bat Boat Type 2.

From 1918/19 the Hellenic Navy operated 19 Babies and six 1½ Strutters, which it used during the Asia Minor Campaign against Turkey. Two Pups, N6470 and N6471, were given to Greece in 1917.

A handful of Camels served with the Greek Z Squadron against the German-backed Turks in early 1918. Z was then split into four – H1 based at Thassos, H2 at Mudros, H3 at Stavroupolis and H4 at Mytilene. H2 was equipped with Camels and continued to use them until 1923.

India

When the war was over, the British government offered 100 aircraft each to its dominions to form the basis for an independent air force. For its Imperial Gift, India chose 40 Sopwith Snipes and 60 Airco DH.9s, but there were never any plans for an Indian air force at this stage so the Snipes were put into storage at Karachi, where they rotted away.

Italy

Two Sopwith Babies, 8214 and 8215, were sent to the Italian government for evaluation in April 1916, and were tested at the Venice naval air station in October. A generally favourable report convinced the Italians to fund licensed production of the type, but the government's favoured contractor, Società Italiana Transaerea, was unable to take up the work and another firm, Ansaldo, agreed to do it instead. It signed a contract to build 100 Babies under licence on January 26, 1917, and was supposed to supply the government with 35 machines in July 1917 and 45 in August.

At the end of the year, Ansaldo had built 150 aeroplanes, but only four were Babies – the rest were the firm's own SVA type. The government wrote to ask where its Babies were and Ansaldo complained about a lack of raw materials. Eventually, by September 30, 1918, all the Babies, plus 14 sets of spares, had been delivered, the completed machines having the serials 5005-5104.

They were powered by 120hp Le Rhone 9J rotaries in completely circular cowlings, and during the latter part of their career, some Ansaldo Babies had six large vents cut in the mid-lower portion for additional cooling. The Babies served as trainers from December 1917 until 1923, by which time all had been wrecked or scrapped. The remains of 8214 and 8215 were returned to Britain.

The Italian government paid Sopwith £4477/2/9d in royalties in September 1920 and the remaining £7022/16/3d owed was written off as a bad debt.

Japan

A single Sopwith Baby, 8201, was sent to Japan for evaluation in 1916 at the request of the Imperial Japanese Naval Air Service. The Imperial Japanese Army Air Service received at least 15 1½ Strutters from Britain, but also bought 'a large number' from France.

In 1919, Japan received 49 Pups with the serials C-481-499, C503-C509, C-533-C535, C537-C538, C1496, D4144-D4152, D4155-D4156, D4160, D4163, D4165 and D4168-D4169.

The Baby was known as So-Shiki Model 1, the Strutter as Model 2 and the Pup as Model 3. 'So' is the Japanese character for the beginning of the name 'Sopwith' and 'Shiki' means 'type'.

Six Viper-powered Sopwith Cuckoos were also sent to Japan, in 1921, and served as trainers for torpedo-carrying operations. In addition, at least seven Japanese 1½ Strutters ended up on the civilian register.

Latvia

The Soviet Latvian Air Force operated seven ex-Russian 1½ Strutters from 1918/19. Following its breakaway from the USSR in 1918, the Republic of Latvia was given seven 2F.1 Ship's Camels in January and March 1920. One of these, N8137, suffered engine failure and was destroyed in the resulting crash on May 2. The remaining six Camels survived until 1927.

Lithuania

During a battle with the Bolsheviks on February 5, 1919, the Lithuanians captured a single 1½ Strutter. This became Lithuania's first fighter aircraft. It was first flown on August 3, 1921, and crashed on September 21, 1928, after its engine caught fire.

Mexico

The Arma de Aviación Militar operated one 1½ Strutter, serial 1-S-68, from around 1920 to 1924.

Netherlands

While maintaining a strict neutrality during the war, the Netherlands attempted to buy new aircraft from both the Allies and the Germans, but was not successful since both sides wanted every airworthy machine for themselves. Therefore, the Dutch waited for machines to land on their territory and then impounded them before pressing them into their own service.

The first such 'catch' was an RNAS Sopwith Baby, 8149, which became stranded off the Dutch coast on April 27, 1916. In service with the Dutch navy, it was given the serial T-1 and was operated until 1919.

Two 1½ Strutters, 9396 and 9420, followed on August 25, 1916, and September 17, respectively. These got the serials LA-33 and LA-38 (later S-24). Next, the Dutch netted an RFC Pup, A6164, on March 1, 1917. This became LA-41, later S-212. Then came a trio of 1½ Strutters – 9376 on April 22, N5154 on May 12 and French-made No. 115 on July 17. These became LA-42/S-412, LA-34/S-413 and LA-45/S-701.

The Dutch nearly got a Camel on September 28, 1918, the RAF's C1542, but it was destroyed on landing. Finally, they scooped a working Camel on October 7, 1918 – C1537, which became S-226.

The pilots were imprisoned, but were allowed back to Britain on parole. In the end, the Dutch even paid the British government £1700 each for the 1½ Strutters, which was a great deal considering they had only cost £1750 each brand new.

Norway

The Royal Norwegian Navy Air Service bought 10 Sopwith Babies in 1917 – the first four arriving that year and the remaining six following in 1918. They were given even numbered serials from F.100 to F.118 and whenever one of them crashed and was written off, the Norwegians simply built an unlicensed copy to replace it. F.104 and F.114 each got replaced twice, while F.108, F.110, F.116 and F.118 were each replaced once.

In winter, the Norwegians found that the Babies' floats made good skis, although one was tested with proper skis in February 1921. Another was tested with wheels in March 1922. Arctic explorer Roald Amundsen used the second Norwegian-built version of F.104 – a two seater – during an unsuccessful flight from Alaska in the US to the Norwegian archipelago of Svalbard in 1923.

Two Norwegian Babies, Sopwith-built originals F.100 and F.102, accompanied Amundsen's attempt to rescue the crew of the airship *Italia* in 1928 – during which he disappeared in a Latham 47 flying boat, never to be seen again.

Five Babies, F.100, F.102, F.106, the second F.116 and the second F.118 survived until February 2, 1932, when they were scrapped.

Poland

Poland operated three 1½ Strutters, captured from the Soviets in 1919/20, and five or six Camels were given to Poland in 1919. At least one of these was still in service by 1922. The British government decided on

German forces made use of several Sopwith machines during the war. This Triplane is most likely N5429. It was captured virtually intact on September 13, 1917, south of Wervicq, France, after being driven down by Kurt Wüsthoff of Jasta 4. It was his 15th victory of an eventual 27. The pilot was Flight Sub-Lieutenant John R Wilford of 1 (Naval) Squadron.

The Norwegians loved their small fleet of 10 Sopwith Babies – so much so that whenever one crashed they simply built a new one to replace it and gave it the same serial. There were two F.108s – the Sopwith original and its Norwegian clone. This may well be the latter.

January 8, 1920, to send Poland 10 Dolphins to help it fight Bolshevik forces.

Six were packed onto *SS Neptun* – F7128, J153, J162, J169, J178 and J181 – and set off on April 1. The other four, E4815, F7120, J139 and J151, set sail aboard the *SS Warszawa* on April 21. The first six arrived at Lwów on May 19, before being transferred to Warsaw. They had all been assembled by July and given Polish numbers 21.01 to 21.10.

The Dolphins were used on a series of ground attack missions throughout August, and by the end of the month only 21.04 was still airworthy. In October, 21.04, 21.09 and 21.10, the latter two presumably repaired, were operated by the 18th Squadron and by March 1921 only one was still serviceable.

The following month, five Dolphins were brought together and enough parts were recovered to make 21.08 airworthy again, but it never flew. A few months later all remaining Polish Dolphins had been scrapped.

Romania

The Royal Romanian Air Force was supplied with 20 1½ Strutters by Britain during the war.

Russia/Soviet Union

A small number of Sopwith Tabloid copies were built in Russia in 1915 as the Lebed VII, but by far the most common Sopwith, in both Imperial and Soviet Russia, was the 1½ Strutter. The precise number of ex-RFC/RNAS 1½ Strutters supplied to pre-revolution Imperial Russia is unknown, but it was at least 190, possibly 204. An unknown number of unlicensed copies were also built under the Soviet regime by Dux of Moscow and V A Lebedev of Novaya Derevnya, St Petersburg.

It is known that the latter received an initial order for 50 1½ Strutters followed later by another order for 140. A last batch of 22 was built in the Soviet National Aircraft Factory in 1922. Soviet 1½ Strutters had a modified undercarriage of Russian design. A lack of engines resulted in some Soviet-built Strutters being scrapped before they could enter service.

The Red Air Fleet of Workers and Farmers took over at least 34 British-built Strutters in 1917, and some 130 examples were still in use in 1920, the number dropping to 82 the following year. Ten survived until 1929. British-built 1½ Strutters also served with White Russian forces.

At least one Pup, N6204, was given to Imperial Russia in 1917 and used by Soviet forces, specifically the 14th Reconnaissance Air Detachment of the Soviet 10th Army in 1919. A single Triplane, N5486, was sent to Imperial Russia on May 4, 1917, and was fitted with skis on its arrival.

At least seven Sopwith Camels served with White Russian forces against the Bolsheviks in 1918/19 and at least one was captured and served with the Soviet forces.

A single Snipe was also captured by the

The Chilean navy operated a trio of Sopwith Babies, including this one which was given the serial N-2103.

Bolsheviks – E6351. Nicknamed 'Nelly', it was flown by Soviet pilot Grigoriy Sapozhnikov until it crashed on September 8, 1922.

Sweden

Just a single 1½ Strutter flew in Sweden – one that had been bought from Switzerland (see below).

Switzerland

A pair of 1½ Strutters entered the civilian register in Switzerland. CH-53 was registered on April 9, 1921, but struck off on October 9, 1923. CH-67 was registered on December 5, 1923, but its registration was cancelled in December 1926 as it was sold to Sweden.

Ukraine

A single 1½ Strutter was acquired from Russia in 1918 and the 1st Zaporski (Ukrainian) Squadron received two Polish Dolphins, 21.01 and 21.03, and took them to fight the Bolsheviks on October 24, 1920. When the Ukrainians were forced to retreat the Dolphins were handed back to the Poles.

USA

The US acquired 130 French-built SOP 1B2 two-seat bombers and 384 SOP 1A2 observation machines in February 1918 – a total of 514 1½ Strutter types. The latter equipped the 90th and 99th Aero Squadrons in June of that year. The 88th Aero Squadron received 18 1½ Strutters in July as an interim type. The bombers were declared obsolete before entering service.

The US also received 325 British Camels during the war, of which 143 were used by the 17th and 148th Aero Squadrons attached to the RAF in July 1918. The 185th Aero Squadron began using the Camel as a night fighter on October 18 and a third day fighter unit, the 138th Aero Squadron, started using Camels just as the war came to an end in November.

Most of the 143 Camels ended up wrecked. The remaining 182 were used by the US Army and Navy after the war.

The US Navy's first Sopwiths were a Schneider, which originally had the RNAS serial 3765 and a Baby that had been 8209. Both had been transferred from the RNAS to the Canadian navy, which then passed

Latvia's Camels sported swastikas – a symbol known to the Latvians, long before the Nazis got hold of it, as either ugunskrusts 'the fire cross', when used counter-clockwise, or pērkonkrusts 'the thunder cross' when used clockwise.

them on to the US. The Americans gave them the serials A394 and A407, respectively. Two more Babies became A869 and A872. The American government placed orders for 2194 Sopwith Dolphin IIs – the type fitted with the 300hp Hispano-Suiza engine – in July 1918. These were to be built in France by Société Anonyme de Constructions Aéronautiques (SACA) and the company soon received a batch of five British-built Dolphins to re-engine for the Americans. None of the 2194 were built, but SACA did manage to re-engine the British Dolphins, which had been part of a batch of eight allocated to the US – E4662, E4663, E4645-E4650. The five were shipped out on January 1, 1919, but none were used in active service. Only one Dolphin received a US Army number, 94071. A single Salamander was tested in the US.

The US Navy also operated Pups A5655 and A5656 (US serials). From the US Army it received F.1 Camels A5658 (formerly RAF serial C8228), A5659, A5729 and A5730; Ship's Strutters A5660, A5749 and A5750; and 15 1½ Strutters, A5734-A5748. Of these, A5658 was flown from the turret of the battleship *USS Texas* on March 9, 1919.

A5734 crashed on takeoff from the USS Arizona, killing a man on deck, and A5738 force landed with engine trouble on April 6, 1920, and was wrecked while being hoisted aboard *USS Sandpiper*. A5739 was written off after being damaged while being hoisted onto the *USS Oklahoma* at Guantanamo on March 12, 1920, and A5740 was wrecked aboard the *USS Pennsylvania* on January 29, 1920.

A small number of Camels entered civilian use in the US, including British Caudron-built N6254 – an American civil registration rather than a military serial (see chapter 21). ∎

Dozens of French 1½ Strutters were sold to civilian operators after the war. This one was flew from Aérodrome du Bourget, near Paris, 'pour tourisme' as the original caption said.

Chapter 20

AFTER THE WAR
Final designs, dissolution and Hawker

The British government was taken by surprise when Germany's forces collapsed and the war ended. Sopwith and its contractors had been building Snipes, Salamanders, Dragons and Cuckoos when suddenly nearly every order was cancelled. There were no more fighters or bombers needed – so what now for Sopwith?

A series of large-scale Allied assaults begun in August 1918 finally drove the Germans back beyond the Hindenburg Line – a well defended fallback position constructed during 1916-1917.

The Allies believed that the Germans would continue to resist and began preparations for a final push in 1919. The Germans, however, had reached the end of their rope. They were short on food and equipment, winter was approaching and morale was at rock bottom. So they called for an armistice and were forced to accept unconditional surrender.

The knock-on effect of this abrupt end to hostilities was dramatic for the Sopwith Aviation Company and the many companies building its machines under licence. The Government cancelled almost all the orders it had placed for military aeroplanes, many in mid-flow. While work on some Snipes and Salamanders continued, many of these now had only to be delivered as kits of parts rather than completed aircraft.

Overall, Sopwith designs had accounted for 25% of all British aircraft built during the war and 60% of all single-seat fighters.

Now Sopwith's only customer and the source of its revenue had gone. Yet it was operating a large factory in Canbury Park Road, Kingston-upon-Thames, and leasing the vast National Aircraft Factory No. 2 near Ham Common on the road between Kingston and Richmond. It had also retained its original former roller skating rink facility and its sheds at Brooklands for a grand total of some 14 acres of factory space.

Before the Armistice, the company had more than 3500 workers – 1000 of them women – but with the war over many simply left, including most of the women. The remainder were retained as new peacetime opportunities were explored.

Even before 1918 had ended, Sopwith had secured the rights to manufacture ABC motorcycles under licence – a new venture. ABC Motors and Sopwith had previously been closely associated, despite ABC's chief engineer

Granville Bradshaw's Dragonfly engine having caused Sopwith numerous problems.

There was a substantial amount of retooling required to switch to motorcycle production but once it was under way the newly renamed Sopwith Aviation & Engineering Company produced some 2200 ABC 398cc motorcycles. A London office was established at 67 South Molton Street to provide a city address and showroom, and production also switched to saucepans, car bodies, furniture and even toys.

The aviation side of the business was not forgotten, however. During late 1918, Thomas Sopwith turned his attention to a challenge with a cash prize that had lain unclaimed throughout the war years – £10,000 offered by the Daily Mail for the first nonstop transatlantic flight.

The rules stated that the flight had to be between any point in Great Britain and any point in Canada, Newfoundland (it only became part of Canada in 1949) or the US, it had to be direct and it had to be accomplished within 72 hours.

The Sopwith Rainbow racer accelerates on take-off. It had an ABC Dragonfly engine, although it may also have been fitted with the similar looking Cosmos Jupiter at some stage.
DH/MG/Brooklands

Shortly after the end of the war, the Daily Mail attempted to revive interest in its transatlantic challenge. The Atlantic was Sopwith's ill-fated contender for the prize. Note the propeller protruding from the side of the fuselage to generate electricity for the aeroplane's wireless set. *DH/MG/Brooklands*

> *The King asked his son: "What are you doing flying with this man?" The Prince replied: "Well you know father, he is a very gallant man and you gave him the VC so I supposed it was all right." The King banned him from ever flying again.*

With huge design and manufacturing facilities now at his disposal, a very different scenario from his prewar days of competition flying, Sopwith was able to have a suitable machine built and be ready to fly by February 1919. It was a large machine, similar in size to the Sopwith Cuckoo, and had a very deep fuselage containing the enormous fuel tanks necessary for the trip.

There was room for two crewmen and it was powered by a 375hp Rolls-Royce Eagle VIII engine, which was chosen for its reliability. The undercarriage was designed to be jettisoned once the machine was airborne to reduce drag and there was a wireless set with a wind-powered generator on board for emergencies. Another safety feature was the decking over the rear fuselage which, when removed, doubled up as a lifeboat.

Hawker volunteered to be the pilot and his navigator was Lieutenant Commander Kenneth Mackenzie-Grieve. It was decided that they would fly from Newfoundland to Britain.

After news of the Sopwith attempt was publicised, the Newfoundland Post Office sent the company a letter enquiring about the possibility of carrying some letters on the flight. The company wrote back accepting the proposal on condition that up to 110 letters could be carried rather than the originally proposed 10.

Carrying 95 letters, the Sopwith aeroplane, dubbed the 'Atlantic', set off on May 18 at 6.45pm from Mount Pearl flying field, St John's, Newfoundland. It was the first ever attempt at an airborne transatlantic crossing.

The weather was unexpectedly foggy but the aircraft performed well and Hawker and Mackenzie-Grieve were soon cruising at 100mph at 10,000ft, having jettisoned the undercarriage as they passed the Newfoundland coastline. The Rolls-Royce was thumping along but it gradually became

apparent to Hawker that the machine's cooling system was not working very well.

The problem got worse and Hawker decided he had no option but to ditch, having first flown on as long as possible in the hope of sighting a ship. The Danish steamer *SS Mary* was spotted on the following morning, May 19, and Hawker put the Atlantic down into the water safely. Unfortunately, the *SS Mary* had no salvage gear so even though Hawker and Mackenzie-Grieve were rescued after just half an hour, the Atlantic had to be left where it was.

The *SS Mary* had no radio either, so the Atlantic's crew were feared dead by those awaiting them in Britain. The King even sent Hawker's wife a telegram offering his condolences. On May 23, the *SS Lake Charlottesville* saw the wreck of the Sopwith Atlantic and salvaged it.

The Royal Navy received a telegram from Lieutenant Commander A C Wilvers of the *SS Lake Charlottesville* which read: "Near the top of the plane was lashed a brown postage bag which was marked 'Newfoundland GPO'. It contained mail mostly addressed to prominent British peers, the royal family and one addressed to His Majesty the King. The mail was very soaked and otherwise damaged."

The *SS Mary* arrived at the Hebrides on May 25 and the authorities were notified that Hawker and Mackenzie-Grieve were safe. The *SS Lake Charlottesville* arrived at Falmouth on May 28 and the wrecked Atlantic was handed over to customs and excise officials. The mail entered the British postal system on May 30. Daily Mail owner Lord Northcliffe gave Hawker £5000 as a consolation prize and the King gave both him and his companion the Air Force Cross.

The wreck of the sole Sopwith Atlantic was later displayed on the roof of Selfridges department store in London.

MAKING CIVILIAN AEROPLANES

While it was built as a competition machine, the Sopwith Atlantic was also considered to be a prototype for a future commercial transport that the company would build if there proved to be sufficient demand.

At the same time, two other civilian types were being designed and constructed. The first was the Dove. This was referred to as a 'sporting two-seater' and was aimed both at wealthy gentlemen who fancied a runabout and flying schools.

The Dove was very similar to, but not the same as, the Pup. The obvious difference was the second seat, with the pilot sitting at the front, but the wingspan was also shorter by 1ft 8½in, the wings were swept back and the machine was heavier at 1065lb empty, compared to the Pup's 787lb. The fin, rudder and tailplane were also a different shape to those of the Pup. Both, however, had an 80hp Le Rhone engine.

Work on the prototype Dove was completed by early May 1919 and with Harry Hawker away in Newfoundland, an alternative test pilot was needed. Major William George Barker, still with his arm in a sling from his Victoria Cross-winning battle in a Snipe the previous October (see chapter 17), was available and as a passenger he brought along the Prince of Wales, later Edward VIII.

Barker and Wales had previously become acquainted when the prince visited 139 Squadron on the Italian front on April 16, 1918. Barker had, without King George V's knowledge or consent, taken the Prince up for a spin in a two-seater. Now, on May 10, 1919, he repeated the feat, still without the King's knowledge, in the Dove. Photographs from the day show Thomas Sopwith himself nervously watching the two men climb into their seats. The Dove, however, performed faultlessly.

Bowler-hatted Thomas Sopwith looks on nervously as the Prince of Wales, centre, and Major William Barker prepare to take flight in the prototype Sopwith Dove. Barker's left arm is still in a plaster cast from an epic aerial battle fought the previous year. This stunt would earn the Prince a 10 year flying ban.

WHERE DID ALL THE DOVES GO?

Just 10 Sopwith Doves were built. Here's what became of each one as far as is known:

K-122 / G-EACM / G-CAAY

The prototype Dove had the fin and rudder of a Sopwith Camel. It was the machine flown by Major Barker with the Prince of Wales as a passenger; and Barker took it to Canada in May 1920 when he formed Bishop-Barker Aeroplanes Ltd with fellow Canadian ace and VC holder Billy Bishop. It was reported in the Quebec Telegraph on Friday, September 16, 1921, that G-CAAY had crashed: "Aviator Albert Highstone, while piloting a Sopwith Dove plane, crashed 1200ft in a trial flight, but escaped with minor injuries. The machine was to have been an attraction at the fair here and was being placed in readiness for a series of flights. It landed in a tree near the wireless station and will be almost a total loss."

K-133 / G-EACU / S-AFAA

Sold to Major Olaf Enderlein of the Swedish Air Force in January 1923.

K-148 / G-EAFI / S-AYAA

Sold to a customer in Norway during 1921, resold to Oscar Bladh in Sweden in August 1924.

K-157 / G-EAGA

Sold in Australia in September 1919. Photographed at Warrnambool, Victoria, on January 20, 1920, and later at Glenhuntly, Victoria.

K-168 / G-EAHP

Operated in Australia in September 1919 by the Larkin-Sopwith Aviation Company.

The most numerous of Sopwith's postwar aeroplanes was the Gnu. The prototype pictured here had an open cockpit for the pilot at the front and a fully enclosed cabin with side-by-side seating for two passengers to the rear. Most of the production machines dispensed with the glazed cabin roof. *DH/MG/Brooklands*

G-EAJI / G-AUDN / VH-UDN

Operated in Australia by the Larkin-Sopwith Aviation Company as G-EAJI, then the Aviation Service Company, then by E O Cudmore from 1921-22 as G-AUDN. Changed to VH-UDN on March 28, 1929, then owned by T J E Stratton of Sydney and others up to March 16, 1934, when it was scrapped after a forced landing on February 22 of the same year.

G-EAJJ / G-AUJJ

Operated in Australia by the Larkin-Sopwith Aviation Company. Scrapped June 27, 1925.

G-EAKH / G-AUKH

Operated in Australia by the Larkin-Sopwith Aviation Company. Scrapped June 19, 1928.

G-EAKT / G-AUDP

Operated in Australia by the Larkin-Sopwith Aviation Company, then by A L Long of Hobart, Tasmania. It was destroyed in a crash before he could officially register it.

G-EBKY

Owned by D L Hollis Williams up to 1930, then sold to British Aircraft Company founder Charles Herbert Lowe-Wylde of West Malling, England, who used it for towing gliders; then bought by Richard Ormonde Shuttleworth of Old Warden in July 1937 and converted into a Sopwith Pup.

The following day, after photographs of the occasion appeared in the national press, the Prince was summoned for an interview with his father, who asked him: "What are you doing flying with this man?" The Prince reportedly replied: "Well you know father, he is a very gallant man and you gave him the Victoria Cross, so I supposed it was all right for me to fly with him." The King responded by forbidding his son to ever fly again – a ban that was only lifted 10 years later.

Despite all the publicity, there were no orders for the Dove from British customers. At least 10 were built, including or possibly in addition to one single-seat example.

The third civilian type being worked on by the Sopwith Aviation & Engineering Company in early 1919 was the Gnu – a three-seater passenger aeroplane powered, initially, by a Bentley BR.2. The two passengers sat side by side in a fully enclosed cabin with large windows to the rear while the pilot had an open cockpit at the front.

While the Dove was for training or personal touring and stunting, and the Atlantic was a pure transport, the Gnu was a sightseeing or short distance passenger aircraft.

The first example was completed and ready to fly at Brooklands on March 31, 1919. Harry Hawker, having returned from his disastrous transatlantic crossing attempt, flew it from Brooklands to Hendon on May 29 accompanied by a second Gnu – this being fitted with a far weedier 110hp Le Rhone engine.

It was the latter engine that was fitted to a Gnu sold to Australian dried fruit entrepreneur Jack De Garis in 1920 for £1800. This machine was being piloted by RFC veteran F S Briggs during a takeoff from a small clearing near the River Murray in South Australia on one occasion when one cylinder of the Le Rhone cut out.

The Gnu stalled and as Briggs put his hand over the side to switch off the engine his hand got caught and his finger broken by the side of the fuselage. The machine fell 60ft into a gum tree and Briggs was drenched in 18 gallons of fuel which, though it failed to ignite, badly stung his skin.

Gnus produced after the prototype, including Briggs' machine, dispensed with the enclosed cabin and had an open passenger compartment instead. A total of 13 were built. Notable examples include G-EAGP, used by Flight Lieutenant Walter Hunt Longton to win the first race for the Grosvenor Cup Challenge in 1923 (the rules only admitting British machines with engines under 150hp), and G-EAIL, which survived in Essendon, Victoria, Australia, until it was damaged beyond repair during a wind storm on April 19, 1946.

THE AUSTRALIAN CHALLENGE

The Sopwith Aviation & Engineering Company placed a strong emphasis on trying to win sales in Australia almost from the outset of civilian production so when the Australian government announced a £10,000 prize for the first Australian to fly a British or Commonwealth-made machine from Britain to his native land before the end of the year and within 30 days, Sopwith jumped at the chance.

Another competition machine was built that was similar in many respects to the Atlantic. It was powered by the same Rolls-Royce Eagle VIII engine and was known as the Wallaby. It had only half the fuel capacity of its forebear however, since the trip would be made in a series of legs rather than all in one go.

The cockpit arrangement also differed – there was no partition between the two crew members and each had a seat mounted on a vertical frame, enabling them to be independently raised or lowered and then locked in position. There was also a sliding roof panel over the cockpit, so that the pilot/navigator in the front seat could raise himself up to look out over the engine or lower his seat and slide the hatch towards himself and over his head to create a completely enclosed cabin.

The pilot's controls were also duplicated to the rear – the crewman not flying the machine able to detach his control column and fasten it onto the side of the cockpit. Beneath his instruments, the pilot got a locker holding two plywood trays onto which maps could be pinned. The trays also had parallel rulers, dividers and other instruments clipped to them so that the pilot could also perform his navigation duties. The second crew's designated role was 'mechanic'.

Triplex windows were fitted into the Wallaby's sides and there was another small window in the floor beneath the pilot's feet. A novel instrument featured for the first time was a turn indicator. An azimuth mirror was included for navigation along with three compasses. Smoke bombs were fitted on racks along the sides of the fuselage – the idea being that when they were dropped the drift of the smoke would help with orientation.

A high proportion of Sopwith's postwar output ended up in Australia. G-EAJI is seen here as operated by the Aviation Service Company.

The crew were Australians Captain George Campbell Matthews and Sergeant Thomas D Kay. They took off from Hounslow Heath Aerodrome in the Wallaby, G-EAKS, at 11.44am on October 21, 1919. Bad weather causing significant delays at Cologne and Vienna and then disaster struck when the pair were arrested and imprisoned as suspected Bolsheviks in Yugoslavia.

Once that mess had been sorted out, there were further delays at Belgrade caused by snow, at Constantinople due to a cracked engine cylinder and Aleppo due to yet more bad weather. The Wallaby was wrecked on landing at Grokgak on Bali on April 17, 1920, and Matthews was injured.

The challenge was over but G-EAKS was shipped to Australia and rebuilt as an eight-seater, gaining the new serial G-AUDU. It was operated by Australian Aerial Services carrying mail and eventually written off after a forced landing at Bowning, New South Wales, on October 13, 1928.

Similar to the Sopwith Atlantic, the Sopwith Wallaby was built to fly to Australia in 30 days. The flight was dogged by bad weather and almost came to a sticky end when the Wallaby's crew, Australians Captain George Campbell Matthews and Sergeant Thomas D Kay, were arrested as suspected Bolsheviks in Yugoslavia. *DH/MG/Brooklands*

CIVILIAN SOPWITHS IN BRITAIN

Upwards of 18,000 Sopwith machines were manufactured altogether but only 46 entered the civil register in Britain after the war:

Type	Number	Serials
1½ Strutter	1	G-EAVB
Antelope	1	G-EASS
Camel F.1	2	G-EAWN (ex-H2700), G-EBER (ex-F6302)
Dolphin 5F.1	1	G-EATC (ex-D5369)
Dove	10	(detailed in separate panel)
Gnu	13	G-EAAH, G-EADB, G-EAEP, G-EAFR, G-EAGP, G-EAGQ, G-EAHQ, G-EAIL, G-EAIM, G-EAME, G-EAMF, G-EAMG and G-EAMH
Grasshopper	1	G-EAIN
Pup	8	G-EAVF (ex-3210), G-EAVV (ex-C440), G-EAVW (ex-C312), G-EAVX (ex-B1807), G-EAVY (ex-C438), G-EAVZ (ex-C540), G-EBAZ (ex-C1524), G-EBFJ (ex-C242)
Rainbow/1919 Schneider	1	G-EAKI
Scooter	1	G-EACZ
Snapper	1	G-EAFJ
Snipe 7F.1	5	G-EATF (ex-J365), G-EAUU (ex-J459), G-EAUV (ex-J453), G-EAUW (ex-J455), G-EBBE (ex-J461)
Wallaby	1	G-EAKS

The elegant Sopwith Grasshopper was similar in size and shape to the 1½ Strutter but competition from hundreds of cheap war surplus Avro 504Ks took away any hope of it attracting sales. Nevertheless, its owners enjoyed flying it and its striking green paintwork was a common sight at Brooklands for years. *DH/MG/Brooklands*

Having built the Atlantic and the Wallaby, Sopwith decided to go ahead and build another machine based on the same basic template for the civilian market – the Antelope. Only a single prototype was made and like the Gnu it had a pilot up front and two passengers in a cabin behind.

The engine, however, was a war surplus water-cooled 200hp inline Wolseley Viper which offered improved fuel consumption and lower maintenance costs. The undercarriage was initially a traditional V-type but this was swapped for a four wheeled structure to "protect the propeller and prevent the machine from nosing over on landing", according to the Sopwith literature.

There was a door in the side of the fuselage so passengers did not have to climb up on to the fuselage to take their seats, the side windows provided a good view and one of the two passenger seats could even be raised up so that the occupant could put their head through a sliding roof hatch above and experience the thrills of open cockpit flying.

To modern eyes it appears ungainly and perhaps too similar in function to the Gnu but at the time the Antelope was highly regarded – winning second prize in the Air Ministry Small Commercial Aeroplane Competition of 1920 at Martlesham Heath, which was a not inconsiderable £3000.

It was also flown to victory by Freddie Raynham in the Surrey Open Handicap Race in June 1922. Temporarily re-engined with a Siddeley Puma and given a new registration, G-AUSS, it was transferred to the Larkin-Sopwith Aviation Company in Australia in April 1923. It then flew mail runs alongside the Sopwith Wallaby. It was withdrawn from use on February 27, 1935, and presumably scrapped.

THE END AND THE BEGINNING

Sopwith's final attempt at a commercial machine was a two-seat tourer with simple classic good looks known as the Grasshopper. Its tail was similar to that of the Camel and it was powered by a 10-cylinder 100hp Anzani radial engine. Larger than the Dove but smaller than the Gnu, of all Sopwith's machines it was closest in size and shape to the 1½ Strutter.

The sole Grasshopper, G-EAIN, was completed by July 31, 1919, but did not receive its Certificate of Airworthiness until March 22, 1920, possibly due to problems with its engine. Sopwith made little effort to promote the Grasshopper, probably because it was in direct competition with the Avro 504K two-seater of which dozens of cheap war surplus examples were flooding on to the market.

In fact, a total of 304 Avro 504Ks entered the civil register – effectively burying any hopes that the Grasshopper might win sales orders. G-EAIN was finally sold in December 1922 to London sports car enthusiast Loftus Claude Gerald Moller Le Champion, then to Earnest Arthur Douglas Eldridge in May 1923, who wanted it to replace his Sopwith Gnu, G-EADB. Next it was sold to John Cobb in February 1925 and then Dudley 'Dangerous Dan' Watt six months later, who rebuilt it.

In 1926, J King flew Dangerous Dan's machine around the Brooklands circuit at extremely low level, passing beneath the Byfleet bridge. G-EAIN was sold for the last time to female pilot Constance Leathart in February 1928. It was based at Cramlington but after its last Certificate of Airworthiness expired in May 1929 it was not renewed.

The last Sopwith machine of all was one of its most remarkable. With the end of the war, the Schneider Cup competition was revived – the trophy still being in Britain's possession following Howard Pixton's victory in the Sopwith Schneider in 1914. The race date was set for September 10, 1919, at Bournemouth and Sopwith was honour-bound to compete.

Though not the prettiest of aeroplanes to modern eyes, the Sopwith Antelope nevertheless embodied a number of important features – it had an inline engine for better fuel economy, a side door for passengers and safety measures such as loops at its wingtips to stop them hitting the ground and four wheels to prevent a noseover. *DH/MG/Brooklands*

A rear view of the 1919 Sopwith Schneider seaplane. Its floats, similar to those of the wartime Sopwith Baby, were its weak point.

The sleek Sopwith Schneider was built for the 1919 race. The last time the event had been held, in 1914, a Sopwith machine won it. The new Schneider seaplane is seen here being prepared for a test flight. The man pictured second from right may be Harry Hawker.

Once again, the company's designers got to work and produced a sleek seaplane that undoubtedly looked the part. Power was to be provided by a new radial engine – the huge 450hp Cosmos Jupiter. The forward fuselage was covered in aluminium panels with each of the Jupiter's cylinder heads protruding from its forward fairing. The wings were relatively short in span and the seaplane's floats were similar to those seen on the Baby.

Like its predecessor it was named the Schneider and given the civil registration G-EAKI. The first flight was on August 29 at Hythe with Harry Hawker at the controls. Unfortunately, the positioning of the floats was incorrect and the machine nosed over in the water, causing damage that took two days to repair.

When the competition date rolled around, the Sopwith Schneider lined up against machines from new challengers Fairey and Supermarine, each powered by a 450hp Napier Lion and the Italian Savoia S.13bis. Entries from Nieuport, SPAD and Avro failed to start. During an elimination round, the Sopwith machine reached 180mph but its floats were damaged on landing.

Hawker had the floats removed and put them into his motorboat to take them back to Southampton, where he was staying, for repair. The boat was built for only two people but Hawker crammed in his wife, her sister and two mechanics as well. It capsized and all five were dumped into the water, along with the floats.

The race itself was a fiasco due to poor weather. Heavy fog off the sea obscured the turning points and Hawker, having damaged the Schneider's floats again on landing at Bournemouth, retired. The Italian entry was the only one to complete the course but was disqualified for missing markers. Eventually however, its pilot Guido Janello was declared the winner.

Afterwards, the Schneider was re-engined and reconfigured as a landplane. It got a new name too – the Rainbow. The engine was none other than the notorious ABC Dragonfly. Hawker flew the Rainbow at the 1920 Aerial Derby on July 24, for which G-EAKI was given the race

number 13. A report of the race in *Flight* magazine stated: "Another machine approached the aerodrome, and we recognised Hawker's Sopwith.

"To everyone's surprise, instead of making the required half-circuit of the aerodrome, Hawker flew straight in to the aerodrome past No. 1 pylon, but not across the line. It was obvious by his time of arrival that he would have found a place in the handicap, so there was much disappointment at his not finishing correctly.

"On landing he said he thought the finish was the same as last year's, hence the mistake. Well, Hawker, do not have No. 13 next time!"

The Rainbow's failure was not just unlucky however, it heralded the end for the Sopwith Aviation & Engineering Company. Its civilian machines had failed to sell, its diversified business was not enough and to cap it all the Government threatened the company with a potential demand for Excess Profits Duty. Employees were told that the factories would close for two weeks starting on September 3, 1920, then on the 10th they were informed that the business was being wound up.

After entering voluntary liquidation, the Sopwith Aviation & Engineering Company paid its creditors 20 shillings in the pound – in other words they got everything they were owed. A year earlier the company had had reserves of £900,000 and even now the receiver's statement showed assets to the value of £862,630 with liabilities of just £583,510.

Less than two months later, on November 15, 1920, a new company was brought into being: the H G Hawker Engineering Company. Among its first directors were T O M Sopwith, engineer, H G Hawker, aeroplane pilot and F Sigrist, engineer. Even though the personnel remained the same, it was felt that a different name on the letterheads would serve to distance the new organisation from any potential demands on Sopwith.

The first thing that the H G Hawker Engineering Company did though was to acquire all the rights to Sopwith company products and the remaining assets of that company – including mountains of spare parts for in-service aeroplanes such as the Snipe.

The following year, on July 12, Harry Hawker was practising for the 1921 Aerial Derby, due to be held at Hendon four days later. He was flying a one-off racer – the Nieuport Goshawk – which was powered by an ABC Dragonfly. It is believed that the illness that had plagued him during his early flying career – diagnosed during a post-mortem examination as spinal tuberculosis – finally caught up with him. A large abscess had burst causing paralysis of Hawker's legs and severe pain. He lost control of the machine at 2500ft and it veered to the left before crashing to the ground and catching fire. Having suffered severe burns and fractures, Hawker died 10 minutes later.

Following his death, the company that bore his name carried on with Thomas Sopwith at the helm. A new aircraft, the Hawker Woodcock, went into serial production in 1923 and designs such as the Hart and Fury followed. The firm's name was changed to Hawker Aircraft in 1933 and two years later the Hawker Hurricane took its first flight. ∎

The Sopwith Dove was based on the Pup but had two seats and gently swept wings. Just 10 were made. *DH/MG/Brooklands*

Chapter 21

Survivors and replicas
Sopwith aircraft today

A century is a long time for aeroplanes designed to last only a few years. There are perhaps 20 surviving Sopwith machines, but some have been assembled from the components of two or more incomplete examples. An ever-growing legion of replicas demonstrates the marque's enduring appeal.

TABLOID
No surviving original example.
Replicas:
· Replica floatplane version at Brooklands Museum, near Weybridge, Surrey. www.brooklandsmuseum.com
· G-BFDE, built 1977, RAF Museum, Hendon. www.rafmuseum.org.uk
· Replica kit available from Airdrome Aeroplanes of Holden, Missouri, for $14,995. At least one built. www.airdromeaeroplanes.com

BABY
There are no complete surviving machines, but nominally original Sopwith Baby N2078 is a composite of parts from two machines – 8214 and 8215.

Both sets of parts apparently survived because they were sent to the Italian government as pattern aircraft in July 1916. They enabled Genoa-based engineering firm Ansaldo to produce the 100 Babies it made the following year.

Prior to that, 8214 and 8215 had been delivered to the Central Supply Depot at White City in April 1916. The parts were noted as being part of the Nash Collection at London Airport in 1961. They were moved to Upavon in 1963 and arrived at RNAY Fleetlands to be rebuilt in 1966 as N2078.

Today, N2078 is at the Royal Navy Fleet Air Arm Museum at Yeovilton in Somerset. www.fleetairarm.com
Replicas:
· BAPC-137, formerly at Thorpe Park, Surrey, sold 1987, current whereabouts unknown.
· Replica kit available from Airdrome Aeroplanes of Holden, Missouri, for $14,995. At least one built, but with wheels rather than floats.

1½ STRUTTER
Four original Sopwith 1½ Strutters are known to exist. S85 is on display at the Koninklijk Legermuseum/Musée Royal de l'Armée in Brussels. It was a two-seater, modified to accept either a third crew member or heavy photographic equipment.

French-made No. 556 Sop 1A2 is suspended from the ceiling of a hall at Musée de l'Air et de l'Espace at Paris Le Bourget airport and a second French machine, No. 2897 Sop 1B2, has been restored to flying

condition at the Association Memorial Flight at La Ferté-Alais near Paris. http://memorial.flight.free.fr/indexuk.html

Finally, a 1½ Strutter operated by Argentina until 1928 is currently undergoing restoration work at film director Peter Jackson's The Vintage Aviator Limited in New Zealand, having previously been owned by Kermit Weeks' Fantasy of Flight Museum at Polk City, Florida.
Replicas include:
· G-BIDW 'A8226', built 1980, RAF Museum, Hendon.
· 'B619', built 2005, RAF Manston History Museum, Kent. www.rafmanston.co.uk
· C-FSOP '9739', The Great War Flying Museum/Ontario Aviation Historical Society, Canada. http://greatwarflyingmuseum.com
· OK-NUP-01, 85% scale replica, privately owned, Czech Republic.
· N4088H, Military Aviation Museum, Virginia Beach, Virginia, US.
· No serial (still under construction April 2014), National Museum of Flight, East Fortune, Scotland.

PUP/DOVE
There are three surviving original Pups and one Sopwith Dove that was converted to Pup configuration. N5182 was built by Sopwith in 1916 and flown in Belgium and Northern France by several RNAS squadrons. It was kept in store by the French Air Force until 1959 when it was acquired by Desmond St Cyrien and restored to airworthy condition, registered as G-APUP. It first flew in restoration in Surrey on August 11, 1973. It was acquired by the RAF Museum in 1982 and is now on display at Hendon.

St Cyrien also found and restored a second Pup, N5195, which was registered as G-ABOX and flew during the 1990s. It is now on display at the Museum of Army Flying in Middle Wallop, Hampshire. www.armyflying.com

The third Pup, B1807, was built by the Standard Motor Co in 1917 and served with a Home Defence squadron. It was originally fitted with a 100hp Gnome Monosoupape engine, but refitted with an 80hp Le Rhone the following year. It was sold at Croydon in 1920 and entered the civil register as G-EAVX in the middle of an alphabetical sequence of five civilianised Pups, running from G-EAVV

Brooklands Museum's Camel replica, registered as G-BFCZ and displayed as B7270, has an original 130hp Clerget engine. *Alexander Power*

to G-EAVZ. It was ground-looped at the 1921 Aerial Derby at Hendon, its wings were removed and its fuselage was stored in a barn in Dorset. Rediscovered in 1973, the fuselage went to the Royal Navy Fleet Air Arm Museum at Yeovilton and is being restored.

For about 50 years – from the 1930s to the 1970s – it was believed that no original Pup had survived. The closest thing to a real Pup was Sopwith Dove G-EBKY, bought in 1936 by Richard Shuttleworth and converted into a Pup. Today it still flies as part of the Shuttleworth Collection, based at Old Warden, Bedfordshire. www.shuttleworth.org
Replicas include:
· G-AWYY 'N6401', built 1969, Fleet Air Arm Museum, RNAS Yeovilton, Somerset. www.fleetairarm.com
· G-BIAU 'N6452', built 1983, Fleet Air Arm Museum.
· G-BZND 'N5199', built 2006, privately owned, Oakley, Wiltshire.
· G-BIAT 'N6460', built 1986, Air Force Museum, New Zealand. www.airforcemuseum.co.nz
· 'A653', privately owned, Kent.
· G-EAGA (Dove replica), privately owned, Essex.

- CF-RFC, B2127/L, Canadian Warplane Heritage Museum, Ontario, Canada. www.warplane.com
- PH-SOP 'N1915K', Early Birds Foundation, Lelystad, the Netherlands. www.vroegevogels.org/en
- VH-NHD 'B1727', privately owned, Serpentine airfield, Western Australia.
- VH-PSP 'D4170', RAAF Museum, Point Cook, Australia. www.airforce.gov.au/raafmuseum
- VH-SOR, Fleet Air Arm Museum, Australia. www.navy.gov.au/history/museums/fleet-air-arm-museum
- ZK-SPH 'A6192', Chariots of Fire Fighter Collection, Blenheim, New Zealand.
- ZK-PPY 'N6205', The Vintage Aviator, Masterton, New Zealand.
- NX6018 'B1843', Museum of Flight, Seattle, US. www.museumofflight.org
- 'N6183 Mildred H', Golden Age Air Museum, Pennsylvania, US. www.goldenageair.org
- 'N6184 Judy L', privately owned, Oshkosh, Wisconsin, US.
- N914W, Frontiers of Flight Museum, Dallas, Texas, US. www.flightmuseum.com
- N1612U, built 1965, privately owned, Florida, US.
- 'B1795', Planes of Fame Museum, Chino, California, US. http://planesoffame.org
- 'N6465', Combat Air Museum, Topeka, Kansas, USA. www.combatairmuseum.org
- 'N5139', Owls Head Transportation Museum, Rockland, Maine, US. http://owlshead.org
- Replica kit available from Airdrome Aeroplanes of Holden, Missouri, for $12,495. At least one built.

TRIPLANE

Two original Triplanes survive. N5912 was one of the three built by Oakley in 1917. It served with No. 2 School of Aerial Fighting in North Yorkshire and after the war went on display at the Imperial War Museum in London until 1924. It was acquired by the RAF in 1936 and restored. It is currently on show at the RAF Museum, Hendon.

The Russian government received the other survivor, N5486, as an evaluation machine in May 1917. It was fitted with skis and later served in the Red Air Force. It is now on show, painted in horrendous blue, at the Central Air Force Museum, Monino, Russia. www.monino.ru

Replicas include:
- G-BOCK 'N6290', Shuttleworth Collection, Old Warden, Bedfordshire.
- G-PENY/G-BWRA 'N500', built 1988, part of Great War Display Team, UK.
- BAPC-111 'N5459', Fleet Air Arm Museum, RNAS Yeovilton, Somerset.
- ZK-SOP '533' The Vintage Aviator, Masterton, New Zealand.
- 'N6302/N5487' Calgary Aerospace Museum, Ottawa, Ontario, Canada.
- CF-CBM 'N5492', Canada Aviation and Space Museum, Canada.

- 'N6291' MAPS Air Museum, North Canton, Ohio, US.
- G-BHEW, built 1979, privately owned, Paso Robles, California.
- N38057, Museum of Flight, Seattle, US.
- Replica kits were offered by American firm St Croix Aircraft in the late 1990s for $26,000 apiece.

CAMEL

Seven original Sopwith Camels, two of them naval configuration 2F.1s, survive today. Beardmore-built 2F.1 N6812, which was used to shoot down Zeppelin LZ100 on August 11, 1918, is on display at the Imperial War Museum in London and Boulton & Paul-built F6314 is on display at the RAF Museum, Hendon.

The other 2F.1, N8156, was built by Hooper & Co and is at the Canada Aviation and Space Museum, having been bought by the RCAF in 1924. B7280, the last of a batch of 100 built in Lincoln by Clayton & Shuttleworth has been restored and is on display at the Polish Aviation Museum in Krakow. It served with the RAF, during which time it was used by Flying Officer J H Foreman to shoot down two German machines, and by Flight Lieutenant H A Patey to shoot down nine more. Patey had to make a forced landing behind German lines in B7280 and it was captured by the Germans, later being displayed in Berlin.

A second Clayton & Shuttleworth machine, B5747, is on show at the Koninklijk Legermuseum/Musée Royal de l'Armée in Brussels. An unidentified British Caudron-built Camel that was sold to a buyer in the US in 1920 and given the American civil registration N6254 is now owned privately in New Zealand.

Sopwith Aviation Company-built B6291 was apparently bought by two former RFC officers after the war who planned to use it for 'barnstorming' in the Lincoln area. When the venture failed it ended up in a barn just south of Lincoln until 1963.

It was restored in the UK and spent some time at the Shuttleworth Collection before its owner sold it to a buyer in the US. It is currently owned and flown privately in Paso Robles, California.

Replicas include:
- G-AWYY 'B6401', Fleet Air Arm Museum, RNAS Yeovilton, Somerset.
- G-BFCZ 'B7270', Brooklands Museum, near Weybridge, Surrey.
- G-BPOB 'N8997/B2458', built 1973, privately owned, Marlow, Buckinghamshire.
- BAPC-59 'B5577', Montrose Air Station Heritage Centre, Scotland.
- ZK-JMU 'B3889', The Vintage Aviator, Masterton, New Zealand.
- 'B6289', Canadian Museum of Flight, Langley, British Columbia, Canada.
- N2257J, Stamp and Vertongen Museum, Antwerp, Belgium.
- 'B7220', Luftfahrt Museum, Laartzen, Germany.
- OK-NUL-36 'B7270', Letajici Cirkus, Brno-Turany, Czech Republic.

- N7157Q 'B6299' Old Rhinebeck Aerodrome, New York, US.
- 'F6034', USAF Museum, Wright-Patterson Air Force Base, Ohio, US.
- No serial, Evergreen Aviation Museum, Oregon, US.
- 'N8343', privately owned, Paso Robles, California, US.
- 'N6330', Museum of Flight, Seattle, US.
- 'B7260', Cavanaugh Flight Museum, Dallas, Texas.
- N62103, built 1993, privately owned, Daytona Beach, Florida, US.
- 'A5658', National Naval Aviation Museum, Pensacola, Florida, US.
- No serial (still under construction April 2014), Shuttleworth Collection, Old Warden, Bedfordshire.
- Replica kit available from Airdrome Aeroplanes of Holden, Missouri, for $13,695. At least one built.

DOLPHIN

No complete survivor, but in early 2012 the RAF Museum at Hendon unveiled newly completed composite airframe C3988, based on 6ft of rear fuselage from C3988, plus components from D5329, C4033 and D3725, all of which had been kept in storage.

Replica:
- N47166 Old Rhinebeck Aerodrome, New York, US.

SNIPE

Three Snipes have survived, though one of them, E8102, exists only as a fuselage. It was the machine flown by Major William Barker during his Victoria Cross winning combat on October 27, 1918 (detailed in chapter 17), and having been riddled with bullet holes, was shipped to Canada after the war. It is on display at the Canadian War Museum in Ottawa, Ontario.

The second original Snipe, E8105, is far more complete, and is displayed at the National Air and Space Museum in the US. Built in August 1918, it was exported to the US in the early 1920s and passed through various hands until it ended up at Cole Palen's Old Rhinebeck Aerodrome in New York in 1951. He bequeathed it to the museum on his death in 1993.

The third Snipe, E6938, is also at the Canadian War Museum. Built postwar, it was delivered to the RAF on January 31, 1919. Exported to the US, it appeared in the 1930 Howard Hughes-directed film Hell's Angels. Restored in the early 1960s, it was bought by the museum and moved to Canada in 1964.

Replicas:
- 'E6655', RAF Museum, Hendon.
- VH-SNP 'E8050', privately owned, Victoria, Australia.
- 'E6837', Museum of Flight, Seattle, US.
- ZK-SNI 'F2367', The Vintage Aviator, Masterton, New Zealand.
- 'E8102', Fantasy of Flight Museum, Polk City, Florida, US.
- 'N8263', privately owned, Port Hueneme, California, US. ∎

Chapter 22

Bought, built and flown

Sopwiths given military serials and who made them

When the Great War began and orders for aircraft started flooding in, the Sopwith Aviation Company was forced to bring in an army of subcontractors to keep production lines rolling. Here are all Sopwith-designed machines given British military serial numbers and who built them…

Military serial number(s)	Manufacturer	Type	Number ordered	Number made	Notes
27	Sopwith	Hybrid	1	1	Sold to the Navy
33	Sopwith	D	1	1	Shown at 1913 Olympia show before sale to the Navy
38	Sopwith	Bat Boat I	1	1	Served with Naval Wing
58-60	Sopwith	HT (Hydro Tractor) or Anzani Tractor Seaplane	3	3	Served with Naval Wing
61	Sopwith	S	1	1	Served with Naval Wing
93	Sopwith	GPH pusher seaplane	1	1	Served with Naval Wing
103-104	Sopwith	D	2	2	Served with Naval Wing
118	Sopwith	Bat Boat I	1	1	Shown at 1913 Olympia show before sale to the Navy
123-124	Sopwith	SPGn Pusher Seaplane	2	2	Served with Naval Wing
127	Sopwith	Bat Boat II	1	1	Served with Naval Wing
137-138	Sopwith	137	2	2	Served with Naval Wing
149	Sopwith	Sociable/Churchill	1	1	Served with Naval Wing
151	Sopwith	Tractor Seaplane	1	1	Rebuilt from 1913 Circuit of Britain machine
157-159	Sopwith	FTS.200 / C	3	3	Served with Naval Wing
160	Sopwith	Single Seat Biplane	1	0	Apparently never delivered
167-168	Sopwith	SS	2	2	904 and 905 renumbered
169	Sopwith	St.B	1	1	Prototype of 'Tabloid', ex-RFC 604
170	Sopwith	Special Torpedo Seaplane	1	1	Served with Naval Wing
243	Sopwith	D2	1	1	Served with Military Wing
246-247	Sopwith	D2	2	2	Served with Military Wing
300	Sopwith	D2	1	1	Served with Military Wing
315	Sopwith	D2	1	1	Served with Military Wing
319	Sopwith	D2	1	1	Served with Military Wing
324-325	Sopwith	D2	2	2	Served with Military Wing
326	Sopwith	SS	1	1	Served with Military Wing
333	Sopwith	D2	1	1	Served with Military Wing
362	Sopwith	SS	1	1	Served with Military Wing
378	Sopwith	SS	1	1	Served with Military Wing
381	Sopwith	SS	1	1	Served with Military Wing
386-387	Sopwith	SS	2	2	Served with Military Wing
392	Sopwith	SS	1	1	Served with Military Wing
394-395	Sopwith	SS	2	2	Served with Military Wing
604	Sopwith	St.B	1	1	Prototype of 'Tabloid', sent to RNAS as 169 (see above)
611	Sopwith	SS	1	1	Served with Military Wing
654	Sopwith	SS	1	1	Served with Military Wing
801-806	Sopwith	806 Gunbus	6	6	Built for RNAS
807-810	Sopwith	807	4	4	Built for RNAS
851-860	Sopwith	860	10	10	Built for RNAS
879	Sopwith	Bat Boat II	1	1	Went to RNAS
880	Sopwith	D3 / 880	1	1	Built for 1914 Circuit of Britain race
896	Sopwith	D3 / 880	1	1	Built for Greek government but pressed into RNAS service
897-901	Sopwith	SPGn Pusher Seaplane	5	5	Built for Greek government but pressed into RNAS service
904-905	Sopwith	SS	2	2	Formerly RFC 394 and 395 (see above)
906	Sopwith	D	1	1	Built for RNAS
919-926	Sopwith	807 (Folder Seaplane)	8	8	Built for RNAS
927-938	Sopwith	860	12	6-12	Nos. 927, 932, 934, and 936-938 not delivered, poss not built
1051-1074	Sopwith	D5 / Two-seater Scout (Spinning Jenny)	24	24	Built for RNAS
1201-1212	Sopwith	SS3	12	12	Built for RNAS
1213	Sopwith	SS	1	1	Pressed into RNAS service

Military serial number(s)	Manufacturer	Type	Number ordered	Number made	Notes
A5138-A5237	Wells Aviation Co	9901 (Pup)	100	0	Order cancelled
A5238-A5337	Wells Aviation Co	1½ Strutter	100	100	Built for RFC
A5950-A6149	Morgan & Co	9700 (1½ Strutter)	200	100	Built for RFC, some transferred to RNAS, last 100 cancelled
A6150-A6249	Whitehead Aircraft	9901 (Pup)	100	100	Built for RFC
A6901-A7000	Hooper & Co	9700 (1½ Strutter)	100	100	Built for RFC, some transferred to RNAS
A7301-A7350	Standard Motor Co	9901 (Pup)	50	50	Built for RFC
A8732-A8737	Sopwith	9901 (Pup)	6	0	Serials allocated for intended transfer to RFC
A8141-A8340	Ruston, Proctor & Co	1½ Strutter	200	200	Built for RFC
A8726-A8731	Unknown	1½ Strutter	6	0	Serials allocated for intended transfer to RFC
A8726-A8793	Vickers	1½ Strutter	50	50	Built for RFC
A8970-A8973	Sopwith	Sparrow	4	4	Serials may have been allocated so machines could be struck off
A9000-A9099	Clayton & Shuttleworth	Triplane (Clerget engine)	100	0	RFC order cancelled
A9813-A9918	Clayton & Shuttleworth	Triplane (Clerget engine)	106	0	RFC order cancelled
B331	Sopwith	9901 (Pup)	1	0	Order cancelled
B381	Sopwith	F.1 Camel	1	1	Prototype
B1496	Sopwith	B2	1	1	Built for RFC
B1701-B1850	Standard Motor Co	9901 (Pup)	150	150	Built for RFC
B2151-B2250	Whitehead Aircraft	9901 (Pup)	100	100	Built for RFC, mostly with 100hp Monosoupape engines
B2301-B2550	Ruston, Proctor & Co	F.1 Camel	250	250	Built for RFC, 11 transferred to RNAS
B2551-B2600	Ruston, Proctor & Co	1½ Strutter	50	50	Built for RFC
B3751-B3750	Sopwith	F.1 Camel	200	200	Built for RFC, 104 transferred to RNAS
B3977	Sopwith	F.1 Camel	1	1	Formerly N6338
B4601-B4650	Portholme Aerodrome	F.1 Camel	50	50	Built for RFC
B5151-B5250	Boulton & Paul	F.1 Camel	100	100	Built for RFC
B5251-B5400	Whitehead Aircraft	9901 (Pup)	150	150	Built for RFC
B5401-B5450	Hooper & Co	F.1 Camel	50	50	Built for RFC
B5551-B5650	Ruston, Proctor & Co	F.1 Camel	100	100	Built for RFC, 19 transferred to RNAS
B5651-B5750	Clayton & Shuttleworth	F.1 Camel	100	100	Built for RNAS
B5901-B6150	Standard Motor Co	9901 (Pup)	250	250	Built for RFC training
B6151-B6200	Sopwith	F.1 Camel	50	0	Renumbered as 2F.1s N6600-N6649
B6201-B6450	Sopwith	F.1 Camel	250	250	Built for RFC, 131 transferred to RNAS
B7131-B7180	Portholme Aerodrome	F.1 Camel	50	50	Built for RFC, 21 transferred to RNAS
B7181-B7280	Clayton & Shuttleworth	F.1 Camel	100	100	Built for RNAS, three given to Belgium
1214	Sopwith	Gordon Bennett racer ('Tabloid' derivative)	1	1	Pressed into RNAS service
1215	Sopwith	Gordon Bennett racer (slim fuselage)	1	1	Pressed into RNAS service
1280-1299	Sopwith	860	20	0	Ordered cancelled
1347-1350	Sopwith	860	4	0	Ordered cancelled
1436-1447	Sopwith	Schneider	12	12	Built for RNAS
1556-1579	Sopwith	Schneider	24	24	Built for RNAS
3686	Sopwith	9400 (1½ Strutter)	1	1	Prototype
3691	Sopwith	9901 (Pup)	1	1	Prototype for RNAS
3698-3699	Sopwith	Biplane (150hp)	2	0	Order cancelled
3707-3806	Sopwith	Schneider	100	100	Built for RNAS
3833-3862	Robey & Co	806 Gunbus	30	30	All delivered but at least 13 as spares
5719-5721	Sopwith	1½ Strutter	3	3	Former RNAS machines for RFC
7762-7811	Ruston, Proctor & Co	1½ Strutter	50	50	Built for RFC
7942	Sopwith	1½ Strutter	1	1	Former RNAS machine for RFC
7998-8000	Sopwith	1½ Strutter	3	3	Former RNAS machines for RFC
8118-8217	Sopwith	Baby	100	100	Built for RNAS
9376-9425	Sopwith	9400 (1½ Strutter)	50	50	15 transferred to RFC
9496-9497	Sopwith	9901 (Pup)	2	2	Pre-production machines for RNAS
9651-9750	Sopwith	9400 & 9700 (1½ Strutter)	100	100	49 transferred to RFC
9891	Sopwith	1½ Strutter (trainer version)	1	1	Built for RNAS
9892-9897	Sopwith	1½ Strutter	6	6	One transferred to RFC
9898-9900	Sopwith	9901 (Pup)	3	3	Pre-production machines for RNAS
9901-9950	Wm Beardmore & Co	9901a (Ship's Pup)	50	50	Built for RNAS
A377-A386	Sopwith	1½ Strutter	10	10	Former RNAS machines for RFC
A626-A675	Standard Motor Co	9901 (Pup)	50	50	Built for RFC
A878-A897	Sopwith	1½ Strutter	10	10	Former RNAS machines for RFC
A954-A1053	Fairey Aviation Co	1½ Strutter	100	100	Built for RFC
A1054-A1153	Vickers	1½ Strutter	100	100	Built for RFC
A1902-A1931	Sopwith	1½ Strutter	30	30	Former RNAS machines for RFC
A2381-A2430	Ruston, Proctor & Co	1½ Strutter	50	50	Built for RFC
A2431-A2432	Sopwith	1½ Strutter	2	2	Former RNAS machines for RFC
A2983-A2991	Sopwith	1½ Strutter	9	9	Former RNAS machines for RFC

Military serial number(s)	Manufacturer	Type	Number ordered	Number made	Notes
B7281-B7480	Ruston, Proctor & Co	F.1 Camel	200	200	Built for RFC, six transferred to RNAS
B7481-B7580	Whitehead Aircraft	9901 (Pup)	100	100	Built for RFC training
B9131-B9330	Boulton & Paul	F.1 Camel	200	200	Built for RFC
B9962-B9967	Sopwith	Snipe	6	6	Prototypes
B9990	Sopwith	F.1 Camel	1	1	Formerly N6344
C1-C200	Nieuport & General Aircraft Co	F.1 Camel	200	200	Built for RFC, 81 transferred to RNAS
C201-C550	Standard Motor Co	9901 (Pup)	350	350	Late machines from this batch went directly to storage
C551-C750	British Caudron Co	F.1 Camel	200	0	Order cancelled
C1451-C1550	Whitehead Aircraft	9901 (Pup)	100	100	Some transferred to RNAS
C1551-C1600	Hooper & Co	F.1 Camel	50	50	Built for RFC
C1601-C1700	Boulton & Paul	F.1 Camel	100	100	Built for RFC
C3281-C3380	Boulton & Paul	F.1 Camel	100	100	Built for RFC but delivered to RAF
C3707-C3776	Whitehead Aircraft	9901 (Pup)	70	70	Built for RFC
C3777-C4276	Sopwith	Dolphin	500	500	First order of Dolphins
C4284-C4289	Sopwith	Snail	6	2	Only C4284 and C4288 completed
C6701-C6800	British Caudron Co	F.1 Camel	100	100	Built for RFC
C7901-C8200	Cubitt	Snipe	300	0	Believed to be mistaken allocation of serials
C7901-C8000	Fairfield Engineering	Cuckoo	100	0	Given serials N7000-N7099 instead
C8001-C8200	Darracq Motor Engineering Co	Dolphin	200	200	Built for RFC
C8201-C8300	Ruston, Proctor & Co	F.1 Camel	100	100	Built for RFC
C8301-C8400	March Jones & Cribb	F.1 Camel	100	100	Last three may not have been delivered
D1776-D1975	Ruston, Proctor & Co	F.1 Camel	200	200	Deliveries started to RFC, ended to RAF
D3276-D3325	Pegler	Cuckoo	50	0	Order cancelled
D3326-D3425	Clayton & Shuttleworth	F.1 Camel	100	100	Built for RNAS
D3576-D3775	Sopwith	Dolphin	200	200	Built for RFC
D4011-D4210	Whitehead Aircraft	9901 (Pup)	200	200	Built for RFC training
D4211-D4360	Wm Beardmore & Co	F.1 Camel	150	0	Order cancelled
D5201-D5400	Hooper & Co	Dolphin	200	200	Built for RFC
D6401-D6700	Boulton & Paul	F.1 Camel	300	300	Deliveries started to RFC, ended to RAF
D8101-D8250	Ruston, Proctor & Co	F.1 Camel	150	150	Built for RAF
D9381-D9530	Ruston, Proctor & Co	F.1 Camel	150	150	Built for RAF
D9531-D9580	Portholme Aerodrome	F.1 Camel	50	50	Built for RAF
D9581-D9680	Clayton & Shuttleworth	F.1 Camel	100	100	Built for ex-RNAS units of RAF
E1401-E1600	Ruston, Proctor & Co	F.1 Camel	200	200	Built for RAF
E4374-E4423	Clayton & Shuttleworth	F.1 Camel	50	50	Built for ex-RNAS units of RAF
E4424-E4623	Sopwith	Dolphin	200	200	Built for RAF
E4629-E5128	Sopwith	Dolphin	500	200	Last 300 cancelled
E5129-E5178	Portholme Aerodrome	F.1 Camel	50	50	Built for RAF
E5429-E5434	Sopwith	Salamander	6	6	Prototypes
E6137-E6536	Boulton & Paul	Snipe	400	370	Last 30 believed cancelled
E6537-E6686	Coventry Ordnance Works	Snipe	150	110	Last 40 believed cancelled
E6787-E6936	Napier & Son	Snipe	150	135	Last 15 believed cancelled
E6937-E7036	Nieuport & General Aircraft Co	Snipe	100	100	Built for RAF
E7137-E7336	Ruston, Proctor & Co	F.1 Camel	200	200	Built for RAF
E7337-E7836	Ruston, Proctor & Co	Snipe	500	472	Last 28 cancelled
E7987-E8286	Sopwith	Snipe	300	300	Built for RA
E8307-E8406	Portholme Aerodrome	Snipe	100	100	Built for RAF
E9997	Sopwith	Dolphin	1	1	Possibly a prototype
F1301-F1550	Boulton & Paul	F.1 Camel	250	250	Built for RAF and US Air Service
F1883-F1957	Boulton & Paul	F.1 Camel	75	75	Built for RAF
F1958-F2007	Portholme Aerodrome	F.1 Camel	50	50	Built for RAF
F2008-F2082	Ruston, Proctor & Co	F.1 Camel	75	75	Built for RAF
F2083-F2182	Hooper & Co	F.1 Camel	100	100	Built for RAF
F2210-F2229	Made in France	Ship's 1½ Strutter	20	20	Converted by 2 (Northern) Area Repair Depot at Coal Aston, near Sheffield
F2333-F2532	Sopwith	Snipe	200	200	Built for RAF
F3096-F3145	Clayton & Shuttleworth	F.1 Camel	50	50	Built for ex-RNAS units of RAF
F3196-F3245	Nieuport & General Aircraft Co	F.1 Camel	50	50	Built for ex-RNAS units of RAF
F3918-F3967	Nieuport & General Aircraft Co	F.1 Camel	50	50	Built for ex-RNAS units of RAF
F3968-F4067	Ruston, Proctor & Co	F.1 Camel	100	100	Built for RAF
F4068-F4070	Sopwith	Snark	3	3	Prototypes
F4974-F5073	Clayton & Shuttleworth	F.1 Camel	100	100	Built for ex-RNAS units of RAF
F5174-F5248	March Jones & Cribb	F.1 Camel	75	75	Built for RAF
F6301-F6500	Boulton & Paul	F.1 Camel	200	200	Built for RAF
F6501-F7000	Sopwith	Salamander	500	102	Last 398 cancelled
F7001-F7030	Sopwith	Dragon	30	30	Built for RAF
F7031-F7033	Sopwith	Snapper	3	3	Prototypes

Military serial number(s)	Manufacturer	Type	Number ordered	Number made	Notes
F7034-F7133	Darracq Motor Engineering Co	Dolphin	100	100	Built for RAF
F7144-F7146	Sopwith	F.1 Camel	3	0	Order cancelled
F7547-F7596	Made in France	Ship's 1½ Strutter	50	50	Converted by 2 (Northern) Area Repair Depot at Coal Aston, near Sheffield
F7601-F7750	Wolseley Motors	Salamander	150	0	Order cancelled
F7801-F7950	Air Navigation Company	Salamander	150	0	Order cancelled
F8231-F8280	Blackburn	Cuckoo	50		Given serials N6950-N6999 instead
F8496-F8595	Nieuport & General Aircraft Co	F.1 Camel	100	100	Built for ex-RNAS units of RAF
F8646-F8695	Portholme Aerodrome	F.1 Camel	50	50	Built for RAF
F9446-F9495	British Caudron Co	F.1 Camel	50	0	Order cancelled
F9846-F9995	Coventry Ordnance Works	Snipe	150	0	Order cancelled
H351-H650	Ruston, Proctor & Co	Snipe	300	98	Last 202 cancelled
H671-H673	Sopwith	Cobham	3	3	Prototypes
H734-H833	Hooper & Co	F.1 Camel	100	100	Built for RAF
H2646-H2745	Boulton & Paul	F.1 Camel	100	100	Built for RAF. Later machines went directly to storage
H3996-H4045	British Caudron Co	F.1 Camel	50	46	Last four cancelled
H4865-H5064	Sopwith	Snipe	200	98	Last 102 cancelled
H5892-H5893	Sopwith	Buffalo	2	2	Prototypes
H7343-H7412	Hooper & Co	F.1 Camel	75	75	Built for RAF
H8513-H8662	Nieuport & General Aircraft Co	Snipe	150	0	Order cancelled
H8663-H8762	Portholme Aerodrome	Snipe	100	53	Last 47 cancelled
H9964-H9966	Sopwith	Snipe	3	0	Given serials E8089-E8091 instead
J1-J150	Hooper & Co	Dolphin	150	109	Last 41 cancelled
J151-J250	Darracq Motor Engineering Co	Dolphin	100	65	Last 35 cancelled
J301-J400	March Jones & Cribb	Snipe	100	0	Order cancelled
J451-J550	Boulton & Paul	Snipe	100	25	Last 75 cancelled
J651-J680	British Caudron Co	F.1 Camel	30	0	Order cancelled
J681-J730	March Jones & Cribb	F.1 Camel	50	10	Last 40 cancelled
J2392-J2541	British Caudron Co	Snipe	150	0	Order changed to Nieuport Nighthawks
J2542-J3041	Grahame-White Aviation Co	Dragon	500	0	Order changed to Nieuport Nighthawks
J3042-J3341	Gloucestershire Aircraft	Snipe	300	0	Order cancelled
J3617-J3916	Sopwith	Dragon	300	100	Last 200 cancelled
J3917-J3991	Barclay Curle & Co	Snipe	75	0	Order cancelled
J4092-J4591	National Aircraft Factory No. 3	Snipe	500	0	Order cancelled
J5892-J5991	Glendower Aircraft	Salamander	100	50	Last 50 cancelled
J5992-J6091	Palladium Autocars	Salamander	100	0	Order cancelled
J6092-J6491	National Aircraft Factory No. 1	Salamander	400	0	Order cancelled
J6493-J6522	Kingsbury Aviation	Snipe	30	30	Delivered straight into storage
N4-N5	Sopwith	1½ Strutter	2	0	Order cancelled
N4-N5	Sopwith	FS1	2	2	N5 used as prototype 2F.1 Camel
N50	Sopwith	B1	1	1	Built for French government
N74	Sopwith	Cuckoo	1	1	Prototype
N300	Blackburn	Baby	1	1	Built as replacement for 8201 from initial production batch when it was sent to Japan
N500	Sopwith	Triplane (Clerget)	1	1	Prototype
N503	Sopwith	Pup (110hp Le Rhone)	1	0	Order cancelled
N504	Sopwith	Triplane (Clerget)	1	1	Second prototype
N509-N510	Sopwith	Triplane (Hispano)	2	2	Prototypes
N517-N518	Sopwith	F.1 Camel	2	2	Built as prototypes for Navy
N524	Sopwith	Triplane (Clerget)	1	1	Bought back from French government
N533-N538	Clayton & Shuttleworth	Triplane (Clerget)	6	6	Built for RNAS with twin Vickers guns
N541-N543	Sopwith	Triplane (Clerget)	3	3	Bought back from French government
N1010-N1039	Blackburn	Baby	30	30	Five for French government
N1060-N1069	Blackburn	Baby	10	10	Built with 110hp Clerget engine
N1100-N1129	Blackburn	Baby	30	30	Built with 100hp Clerget engine
N1190-N1219	George Parnall & Co	Hamble Baby	30	30	Built with 130hp Clerget engine
N1320-N1329	Fairey Aviation Co	Hamble Baby	10	10	Built with 110hp Clerget engine
N1330-N1339	Fairey Aviation Co	Hamble Baby	10	10	Built with 130hp Clerget engine
N1340-N1359	Sopwith	Daily Mail	20	0	Order cancelled
N1410-N1449	Blackburn	Baby	40	40	Built with 130hp Clerget engine
N1450-N1479	Fairey Aviation Co	Hamble Baby	30	30	Built with 130hp Clerget engine
N1960-N1985	George Parnall & Co	Hamble Baby	26	26	Built with 130hp Clerget engine
N1986-N2059	George Parnall & Co	Hamble Baby Convert	74	74	At least 53 delivered straight into storage
N2060-N2134	Blackburn	Baby	75	75	Built with 130hp Clerget engine
N5080-N5119	Sopwith	9400S and 9700 (1½ Strutter)	40	40	Built for RNAS
N5120-N5169	Westland Aircraft Works	9700 (1½ Strutter)	50	50	Built for RNAS
N5170-N5179	Sopwith	9400S (1½ Strutter)	10	10	Built for RNAS
N5180-N5199	Sopwith	9901 (Pup)	20	20	Initial production batch

Military serial number(s)	Manufacturer	Type	Number ordered	Number made	Notes
N5200-N5219	Mann, Egerton & Co	9700 (1½ Strutter)	20	20	Built for RNAS
N5220-N5249	Mann, Egerton & Co	9400S (1½ Strutter)	30	30	Built for RNAS
N5350-N5389	Clayton & Shuttleworth	Triplane (Clerget)	40	40	Built for RNAS
N5420-N5494	Sopwith	Triplane (Clerget)	75	75	Built for RNAS
N5500-N5549	Sopwith	9700 (1½ Strutter)	50	38	Built for RNAS, last 12 cancelled
N5550-N5559	Sopwith	1½ Strutter	10	0	Order cancelled
N5550-N5559	Sopwith	Triplane (Clerget)	10	0	Order cancelled
N5600-N5624	Westland Aircraft Works	9400S and 9700 (1½ Strutter)	25	25	First five Type 9700, the rest 9400S
N5630-N5654	Mann, Egerton & Co	9400S and 9700 (1½ Strutter)	25	25	Six Type 9700, the rest 9400S
N5910-N5934	Oakley & Co	1½ Strutter	25	0	Order changed to Sopwith Triplanes
N5910-N5934	Oakley & Co	Triplane (Clerget)	25	3	Last 22 cancelled
N5940-N5954	Sopwith	1½ Strutter	15	0	Order cancelled
N6100-N6129	Wm Beardmore & Co	9901 (Pup)	30	0	Order changed to WB.III
N6160-N6209	Sopwith	9901 (Pup)	50	50	Built for RNAS
N6290-N6309	Sopwith	Triplane (Clerget)	20	20	Built for RNAS
N6330-N6379	Sopwith	F.1 Camel	50	50	Built for RNAS
N6430-N6459	Wm Beardmore & Co	9901a (Ship's Pup)	30	30	Built for RNAS
N6460-N6529	Sopwith	9901 (Pup)	70	20	Last 50 cancelled
N6530-N6579	Sopwith	F.1 Camel	50	0	Order cancelled
N6600-N6649	Sopwith	2F.1 Camel	50	50	Built for RNAS
N6750-N6799	Wm Beardmore & Co	2F.1 Camel	50	50	Deliveries started to RNAS, ended to RAF
N6800-N6849	Wm Beardmore & Co	2F.1 Camel	50	50	Built for RAF
N6900-N6929	Blackburn	Cuckoo	30	30	Originally allocated serials D3276-D3325
N6930-N6949	Pegler	Cuckoo	20	10	Last 10 believed cancelled
N6950-N6999	Blackburn	Cuckoo	50	50	Initial production batch
N7000-N7099	Fairfield Engineering	Cuckoo	100	50	Last 50 cancelled
N7100-N7139	Wm Beardmore & Co	2F.1 Camel	40	40	Built for RAF
N7140-N7149	Arrol Johnston	2F.1 Camel	10	10	Subcontracted from Wm Beardmore
N7150-N7199	Blackburn	Cuckoo	50	50	48 built as Mk.1, two as Mk.2
N7200-N7299	Fairey Aviation Co	2F.1 Camel	100	0	Order cancelled
N7300-N7349	Pegler	2F.1 Camel	50	0	Order cancelled
N7350-N7399	Arrol Johnston	2F.1 Camel	50	25	Last 25 cancelled
N7650-N7679	Wm Beardmore & Co	2F.1 Camel	30	0	Order cancelled
N7850-N7979	Frederick Sage & Co	2F.1 Camel	150	0	Order cancelled
N7980-N8079	Blackburn	Cuckoo	100	32	Last 68 cancelled
N8130-N8179	Hooper & Co	2F.1 Camel	50	35	Last 15 cancelled
N8180-N8229	Clayton & Shuttleworth	2F.1 Camel	50	25	Last 25 cancelled

FRANKENSTEIN'S SOPWITHS

Sometimes aeroplanes were so badly damaged in the field they could not be rebuilt in their original form. When this happened, they were stripped for serviceable components, which were then used to build 'new' machines at repair depots both in England and France. They were then given unique new serials.

These reconstituted aircraft included:
21 Sopwith 1½ Strutters: B711, B714, B715, B729, B744, B745, B762, B816, B827, B862, B4016, B4044, B7914-B7916, B7946, B8911, B8912, B9910, C4300.

34 Sopwith Pups:
B735, B803-B805, B849, B1499, B4082, B4128, B4131, B4136, B7752, B8064, B8784-B8786, B8795, B8801, B8821, B8829, B9440, B9455, B9931, C3500-C3503, C4295, C8653, C8654, C9990, C9991, C9993, E9996, F4220.

577 Sopwith Camels:
B778, B802, B847, B885, B886, B888, B889, B893, B898, B900, B3977, B4122, B7728, B7732, B7733, B7736, B7742-B7746, B7755, B7757, B7760, B7766, B7769, B7772, B7774, B7776, B7777, B7783-B7786, B7789-B7791, B7793, B7797, B7798, B7806-B7808, B7817, B7820-B7822, B7828, B7829, B7834, B7835, B7856, B7859, B7860, B7862-B7864, B7867-B7870, B7873-B7875, B7889, B7895-B7897, B7905-B7907, B7923, B8013, B8025, B8055, B8830, B8920, B8921, B8926, B9990, E9964-E9983, F2189-F2208, F4170, F4175, F4177-F4190, F4193, F4194, F4196, F4197, F4199-F4205, F4207-F4216, F5913-F5960, F5964-F5970, F5981-F5994, F6021-F6039, F6051-F6053, F6055, F6056, F6058, F6061-F6064, F6067-F6069, F6076, F6082-F6084, F6086-F6090, F6100, F6102, F6105-F6107, F6110, F6111, F6115, F6117, F6122, F6123, F6126, F6129, F6132, F6135, F6138, F6140, F6147-F6157, F6175-F6177, F6180, F6182-F6185, F6188-F6194, F6197-F6202, F6210, F6211, F6216, F6219-F6221, F6223-F6228, F6230, F6238, F6240-F6247, F6249-F6253, F6255-F6265, F6267-F6269, F6271, F6272, F6275, F6281, F6282, F6285, F6287, F6290-F6298, F6300-F6349, F6466-F6479, F6489 (the last 64 were later given new serials within the H6843-H7342 block), F9407, F9410, F9411, F9413, F9417, F9548, F9574-F9576, F9579, F9588, F9592, F9608, F9617, F9623, F9624, F9628, F9630-F9632, F9634-9637, F9695, H6844, H6847, H6848, H6850-H6856, H6860-H6864, H6867-H6869, H6871, H6872, H6874-H6878, H6884, H6886, H6889-H6892, H6897-H6899, H6901-H6904, H6993-H7016, H7077-H7117, H7151, H7205, H7207-H7226, H7234-H7241, H7255, H7269-H7290, H8200-H8202, H8253, H8258-H8262, H8264, H8271, H8291-H8294.

24 Sopwith Dolphins:
B7849, B7851, B7855, B7861, B7876, B7877, B7927, B7928, B7937, B7953, B7955, B7978, B8189, F5961, F5962, F6020, F6144-F6146, H6866, H7243-H7246.

10 Sopwith Snipes:
H6846, H6880, H6894, H6895, H7149, H7150, H7152-H7154, H7227.

Chapter 23

The details
Technical specifications of the Sopwith aeroplanes

For a company that only lasted eight years, Sopwith produced a huge variety of different aeroplane types. Some became famous, a few infamous, and some were short-run types that were designed for a particular competition or contract. Presented here are outline technical details of most, where known, and a 'total built' figure based on the information in chapter 22. Costs, where given, exclude weapons and instruments.

Tractor biplane 'The Hybrid' (built 1912)
Function: Two-seat general purpose tractor biplane
Total built: 1 (Sopwith)
Engine: Gnome, 70hp
Armament: None
Weight (lb): 950
Endurance: 3 hours, 30 minutes
Speed at altitude: 55mph
Ceiling: N/A
Notes: First complete Sopwith design. Given Navy serial No. 27 and rebuilt as a Type D in spring 1913

Type D (built 1912-1914)
Function: Two or three seat general purpose tractor biplane
Total built: 12 (Sopwith)
Engine: Gnome, 80hp or Green, 100hp
Armament: None
Weight (empty/loaded in lb): 1060/1810 (Gnome), 1100/1550 (Green)
Endurance: 2 hours, 30 minutes
Speed at altitude: 73.6mph (Gnome), 70mph (Green)
Ceiling: 12,900ft
Notes: Harry Hawker used one example, No. 104, to set a British altitude record of 11,450ft on May 31, 1913

Bat Boat Type 1 and 2 (built 1912-1914)
Function: Two-seat amphibian / flying boat
Total built: 7 (1 x 'Bat Boat', 3 x Type 1, 3 x Type 2. Hulls by SE Saunders, superstructure by Sopwith)
Engine: Green, 70hp / Austro-Daimler, 90hp / Green, 100hp / Salmson, 200hp / Sunbeam, 200hp
Armament: None
Weight (empty/loaded in lb): 1200/1700 (Type 1), 2300/3120 (Type 2)
Endurance: 2 hours (Type 1) 4 hours, 30 minutes (Type 2)
Speed at altitude: 60-65mph (Type 1), 70mph (Type 2)
Ceiling: N/A
Notes: First Bat Boat built before September 1912. Second Type 1 delivered to Admiralty, third was amphibious and won the Mortimer Singer Prize on July 9, 1913. First Type 2 went to Germany, second to Greece, third to Admiralty

Type HT (Hydro Tractor) (built 1913)
Function: Two-seat general purpose floatplane
Total built: 3 (Sopwith)
Engine: Anzani, 100hp
Armament: None
Weight (empty/loaded in lb): N/A
Endurance: N/A
Speed at altitude: N/A
Ceiling: N/A
Notes: Given Navy serials 58, 59 and 60. No. 59 later converted to landplane

Type DM tractor hydro-biplane (built 1913)
Function: Two-seat competition floatplane
Total built: 1 (Sopwith)
Engine: Green, 100hp
Armament: None
Weight (empty/loaded in lb): 1600/2400
Endurance: N/A
Speed at altitude: 60-65mph
Ceiling: N/A
Notes: Built to compete in the Daily Mail's Seaplane Circuit of Britain contest

Type SPAz / Pusher Seaplane (built 1914)
Function: Two-seat pusher observation biplane
Total built: 10 (3 initial Greek order, 2 Admiralty order and 5 second Greek order. All Sopwith)
Engine: Anzani, 100hp
Armament: Option to fit machine gun
Weight (empty/loaded in lb): 1485/2200
Endurance: 2 hours, 30 minutes
Speed at altitude: 80mph
Ceiling: 4000ft
Notes: The SPAz was based on a one-off seaplane, the Type GPH, the sole example of which went into naval service as No. 93. The first three Greek SPAzs were delivered, the remainder impressed into British service

Type 137 and 138 (built 1914)
Function: Two-seat torpedo carrying trials aircraft
Total built: 2 (one of each, both Sopwith)
Engine: Austro-Daimler, 120hp / Salmson 2M7, 200hp
Armament: None or torpedo
Weight (empty/loaded in lb): 1980/2650
Endurance: 5 hours
Speed at altitude: N/A

Ceiling: N/A
Notes: Built to Admiralty order, served until January 1916

Type Ds / Sociable (built 1914)
Function: Dual control two-seat trainer
Total built: 1 (Sopwith)
Engine: Gnome, 100hp
Armament: None
Weight: (empty/loaded in lb): 960/1640
Endurance: 3 hours
Speed at altitude: 90mph
Ceiling: N/A
Notes: Ordered by Winston Churchill and specified as 'roomy' with leather upholstered seats. Also known as the 'Churchill' or 'Tweenie'

Type SS 'Tabloid' (built 1913-1914)
Function: Single-seat scout
Total built: 26 (27 including St.B two seat prototype, Sopwith)
Engine: Gnome, 80hp
Armament: None or 1 x side mounted Lewis gun firing through propeller
Weight (empty/loaded in lb): 730/1120
Endurance: 3 hours
Speed at altitude: 93mph
Ceiling: N/A
Notes: Also known as Sopwith Scout

Type SS in which 2nd Lt Norman Spratt flew the world's first fighter missions. *Ian David Roberts*

Special Torpedo Seaplane (built 1914)
Function: Two-seat torpedo bomber
Total built: 1 (Sopwith)
Engine: Salmson 2M7 (Canton-Unne), 200hp
Armament: 1 x torpedo
Weight (empty/loaded in lb): 3243/4324
Endurance: N/A
Speed at altitude: N/A
Ceiling: N/A
Notes: Trials were carried out before the Special Torpedo Seaplane was built using a mock-up torpedo dropping seaplane known as the Type TT

Type SPGn / Type 806 'Gunbus' (built 1914-1915)
Function: Two-seat pusher trainer
Total built: 36 (6 Sopwith, 30 Robey)
Engine: Sunbeam, 110hp or Sunbeam, 150hp
Armament: 1 x Lewis gun in nose
Weight (empty/loaded in lb): N/A
Endurance: 2 hours, 30 minutes
Speed at altitude: 80mph
Ceiling: 4000ft
Notes: The first Sopwith aircraft to be subcontracted

Type FTGn / Type 807 'Folder' (built 1914-1915)
Function: Two-seat observation floatplane
Total built: 12 (Sopwith)
Engine: Mono Gnome, 100hp
Armament: Option to fit machine gun
Weight (empty/loaded in lb): 1580/2440
Endurance: 3 hours, 30 minutes
Speed at altitude: 80mph
Ceiling: 3000ft
Notes: Nickname due to backwards folding wings for easier storage aboard ships. Seaplane version of D3 / D5 / Type 880 aircraft (see below)

Type 860 (built 1914)
Function: Two-seat observation floatplane
Total built: 22 (or 16 if 6 undelivered machines were never made, Sopwith)
Engine: Sunbeam Mohawk 225hp
Armament: Provision to carry 1 x 810lb 14in Whitehead torpedo. Option to fit 1 x Lewis gun above observer's cockpit
Weight (empty/loaded in lb): N/A
Endurance: N/A
Speed at altitude: N/A
Ceiling: N/A
Notes: A development of the earlier FTS.200 / Type C, the three examples of which entered service as Nos. 157-159. Designed to carry a torpedo and tested with one but seldom carried them in service. Orders for a further 24 cancelled

D3 / D5 / Type 880 (built 1914-1915)
Function: Two-seat observation biplane
Total built: 24 (26 including 1 x 1914 Circuit of Great Britain machine and 1 x Type 880 built for Greece. All Sopwith)
Engine: Mono Gnome, 100hp
Armament: Option to fit machine gun
Weight (empty/loaded in lb): 1310/1950 (with floats), 1160/1800 (without floats)
Endurance: 3 hours, 30 minutes
Speed at altitude: 69mph
Ceiling: 3000ft
Notes: Type D5, nicknamed 'Spinning Jenny' for its tendency to enter an unrecoverable spin, was a landplane version of the D3 / Type 880

Gordon Bennett racer (built 1914)
Function: Single-seat biplane racer / scout
Total built: 2 (Sopwith)
Engine: Mono Gnome, 80hp
Armament: Forward firing Lewis with bullet deflectors on propeller blades (No. 1214)
Weight (empty/loaded in lb): N/A
Endurance: N/A

Speed at altitude: 105mph
Ceiling: N/A
Notes: The two machines, which entered Admiralty service as No. 1214 and 1215, looked different from one another. 1214 was similar to a 'Tabloid', 1215 was much more streamlined

Type HS Schneider Cup racer (built 1914)
Function: Single-seat floatplane racer
Total built: 1 (Sopwith)
Engine: Mono Gnome, 100hp
Armament: None
Weight (empty/loaded in lb): 1220/1700
Endurance: 2 hours
Speed at altitude: 87mph
Ceiling: 7000ft
Notes: 1914 Schneider Cup entry, also operated as a land plane. HS stood for 'Hydro-tractor Seaplane'. Developed from the Type SS

Type HS 'Schneider' (built 1914-1915)
Function: Single-seat floatplane scout
Total built: 136 (Sopwith)
Engine: Mono Gnome, 100hp
Armament: Option to fit machine gun or drop 1 x 65lb bomb
Weight (empty/loaded in lb): 1220/1700
Endurance: 3 hours
Speed at altitude: 87mph
Ceiling: 7000ft
Notes: Developed from racer, developed into the Type 8200

Type 8200 'Baby' (built 1915-1917)
Function: Single-seat floatplane scout
Total built: 566 (100 Sopwith, 186 Blackburn, 50 Fairey, 130 George Parnall, 100 Ansaldo)
Engine: Clerget 9Z, 110hp or Clerget 9B, 130hp
Armament: 1 x Lewis gun, Rankin dart, Le Prier rockets or 2 x 65lb bombs
Weight (empty/loaded in lb): 1226/1580 (110hp), 1286/1715 (130hp)
Endurance: 2 hours (110hp), 2 hours, 15 minutes (130hp)
Speed at altitude: 100mph
Ceiling: 8000ft
Notes: Airframe cost £1072-10s, engine (Clerget 9B) cost £907-10s. Total price was £1980 (£172,000 in today's money). Fairey and George Parnall examples were heavily modified to become 'Hamble Babies'. Eight unlicensed Baby copies also made in Norway (see chapter 19)

Type LCT / Type 9700 '1½ Strutter' bomber version (built 1915-1917)
Function: Single-seat bomber
Total built (all types): 1196 (146 Sopwith, 100 Fairey, 100 Hooper, 75 Mann Egerton, Morgan 100, 350 Ruston Proctor, 150 Vickers, 100 Wells, 75 Westland)
Engine: Clerget 9Z, 100hp or Clerget 9B, 130hp
Armament: 1 x fixed Vickers gun and bombs
Weight (empty/loaded in lb): 1354/2362
Endurance: 2 hours, 15 minutes
Speed at altitude: 94mph
Ceiling: 8000ft
Notes: Airframe cost £842-6s, engine (Clerget 9B) cost £907-10s. Total price was £1749-16s (£129,000 in today's money). 100 Ship's Strutters converted from ex-French machines. Around

4500 1½ Strutters made in France plus more than 200 unlicensed copies made in Russia, made overall total built internationally circa 5995

Type LCT / Type 9400S and 9400L '1½ Strutter' fighter versions (built 1916-1917)
Function: Two-seat fighter
Engine: Clerget 9J, 110hp or Clerget 9B, 130hp
Armament: 1 x fixed Vickers gun, 1 x Lewis on wing, provision for 4 x 65lb bombs
Weight (empty/loaded in lb): 1160 to 1305/1910 to 2205 depending on type
Endurance: 4 hours (110hp), 3 hours, 15 minutes (130hp)
Speed at altitude: 96mph
Ceiling: 14,500ft (110hp), 15,500ft (130hp)

1½ Strutter of 43 Squadron, RFC, used to shoot down several Albatros aircraft. *Ian David Roberts*

1A2 (French made 1½ Strutter fighter) (built 1917-1918)
Function: Two-seat fighter
Total built (all types): Circa 4500 (Around 650 each by Amiot, Bessoneau, Darracq, Loire et Olivier, Hanriot, Sarazin and R E P)
Engine: Clerget 9Bc, 145hp or Le Rhone 9Jby, 130hp
Armament: 1 x fixed Vickers gun, 1 x Tour gun
Weight (empty/loaded in lb): 1380/2041
Endurance: 4 hours, 30 minutes
Speed at altitude: 97mph at 9850ft
Ceiling: 15,000ft
Notes: French production model

1B1 (French made 1½ Strutter bomber) (built 1917-1918)
Function: Single-seat bomber
Engine: Clerget 9Bb, 135hp
Armament: 1 x fixed Vickers gun, provision for 150lb bombs
Weight (empty/loaded in lb): 1322/2205
Endurance: 4 hours, 30 minutes
Speed at altitude: 102mph at 6500ft, 99mph at 15,000ft
Ceiling: 16,000ft

Type 9901 / Scout 'Pup' (built 1916-1917, 1918 as a trainer)
Function: Single-seat scout
Total built: 1846 (96 Sopwith, 80 Beardmore, 850 Standard, 820 Whitehead)
Engine: Le Rhone 9C, 80hp or Mono Gnome, 80hp or Clerget, 80hp or Monosoupape, 100hp
Armament: 1 x fixed Vickers
Weight (empty/loaded in lb): 787 to 856/1225 to 1297 depending on engine
Endurance: One hour, 45 minutes to three hours depending on engine
Speed at altitude: 104.5mph at 10,000ft
Ceiling: 20,000ft (Le Rhone), 21,000ft (Monosoupape)

Notes: Airframe cost £710-18s, engine (Le Rhone 80hp) cost £620. Total price was £1330-18s (£98,000 in today's money). Beardmore examples were Ship's Pups, Type 9901a. This cost more per airframe at £770. Also, see below

Pup of C Flight, 3 (Naval) Squadron – the first 'Black Flight'. *Ian David Roberts*

S.B.3F/D (Ship Board Type 3, built by Beardmore) or W.B.III (built 1916-1917)
Function: Ship launched fighter/scout
Total built: 100 (Beardmore)
Armament: 1 x Lewis gun
Weight (empty/loaded in lb): 890/1289
Endurance: 2 hours, 30 minutes
Speed at altitude: 91mph at 10,000ft
Ceiling: 12,400ft
Notes: Officially a Beardmore aircraft but in reality a heavily modified Sopwith Pup

Triplane (built 1916-1917)
Function: Single-seat scout
Total built: 156 (107 Sopwith including 10 for France, 46 Clayton & Shuttleworth, 3 Oakley)
Engine: Clerget 9Z, 110hp or Clerget 9B, 130hp
Armament: 1 x Fixed Vickers
Weight (empty/loaded in lb): 993/1415 (110hp), 1103/1543 (130hp)
Endurance: 2 hours, 30 minutes (110hp) or 2 hours (130hp)
Speed at altitude: 112.5mph at 6500ft or 116mph at 6000ft
Ceiling: 20,500ft (110hp), 22,000ft (130hp)
Notes: 9 examples had 2 x fixed Vickers

Triplane of Charles Dawson Booker, 8 (Naval) Squadron, RNAS, 1917. *Ian David Roberts*

Hispano Triplane (built 1916)
Function: Single-seat scout
Total built: 2 (Sopwith)
Engine: Hispano-Suiza, 150hp or Hispano-Suiza, 180hp
Armament: 1 x Fixed Vickers
Weight (empty/loaded in lb): N/A
Endurance: N/A
Speed at altitude: 120mph
Ceiling: N/A
Notes: Completely different fuselage and wing design to 'Clerget Triplane'

Camel F.1/FS1/TF.1 (built 1916-1918)
Function: Single-seat fighter
Total built: 5659 (503 Sopwith, 1425 Boulton & Paul, 146 British Caudron, 600 Clayton & Shuttleworth, 375 Hooper, 185 Marsh Jones & Cribb, 400 Nieuport & General, 300 Portholme, 1725 Ruston Proctor)
Engine: Clerget 9B, 130hp or Bentley BR.1, 150hp or Clerget 9Bf, 140hp or Le Rhone 9J, 110hp or Mono Gnome 9B-2, 100hp or Mono Gnome 9N, 150hp
Armament: 2 x Fixed Vickers
Weight (empty/loaded in lb): 889-1048/1422-1567 depending on engine
Endurance: 2 hours, 30 minutes
Speed at altitude: 101-121mph at 10,000ft depending on engine
Ceiling: 19,000-24,000ft depending on engine
Notes: Airframe cost £874-10s, engine (Clerget 130hp) cost £907-10s or (Bentley BR.1) £643-10s. Total price was £1782 (Clerget – £105,000 in today's money) or £1518 (Bentley – £89,000 today). The Bentley engine, most commonly found on RNAS Camels, gave the best performance of any Camel engine. Including 2F.1s, total Camel production was 5946

Camel 2F.1 (ship's Camel, built 1917-1918)
Function: Single-seat shipborne fighter
Total built: 287 (52 Sopwith, 35 Arrol Johnson, 140 Beardmore, 25 Clayton & Shuttleworth, 35 Hooper)
Engine: Clerget, 130hp or Bentley BR.1, 150hp
Armament: 1 x Fixed Vickers, 1 x Lewis
Weight (empty/loaded in lb): 956 or 1036/1523 or 1530
Endurance: 2 hours, 30 minutes
Speed at altitude: 114mph or 122mph at 10,000ft
Ceiling: 12,000ft or 17,300ft
Notes: Different wings from land Camel, four airbags fitted to rear of fuselage, rear fuselage removable for storage at sea

B.1 (built 1917)
Function: Single-seat bomber
Total built: 1 (Sopwith)
Engine: Hispano-Suiza, 200hp
Armament: 1 x Fixed Lewis plus up to 560lb of bombs
Weight (empty/loaded in lb): 1700/2945
Endurance: 3 hours, 30 minutes
Speed at altitude: 118mph at 10,000ft
Ceiling: 22,000ft
Notes: The single example made underwent two significant modifications changing wing size, height and propeller

T.1 Cuckoo (built 1917-1919)
Function: Single-seat torpedo bomber
Total built: 223 (1 Sopwith, 162 Blackburn, 50 Fairfield, 10 Pegler)
Engine: Sunbeam Arab, 200hp or Wolseley Viper, 200hp
Armament: 18in 1099lb torpedo
Weight (empty/loaded in lb): 2013 to 2585/3711 to 4350 depending on engine
Endurance: 4-6 hours
Speed at altitude: 98mph at 10,000ft
Ceiling: 12,000ft to 13,400ft depending on engine

Notes: Airframe cost £1613-10s, engine (Arab) cost £1017-10s. Total price was £2631 (£127,000 in today's money). In RAF service until 1923

Dolphin 5F.1 (built 1917-1918)
Function: Single-seat fighter
Total built: 1775 (1101 Sopwith, 365 Darracq, 309 Hooper)
Engine: Hispano-Suiza, 200hp (Dolphin I and III), Hispano-Suiza, 300hp (Dolphin II)
Armament: 2 x Vickers plus option of 1-2 x Lewis
Weight (empty/loaded): 1406/1881 (Dolphin I and III), 1566/2358 (Dolphin III)
Endurance: 2 hours
Speed at altitude: 120mph (Dolphin I), 140mph (Dolphin II), 117mph (Dolphin III)
Ceiling: 21,000ft (Dolphin I), 24,600ft (Dolphin II), 19,000ft (Dolphin III)
Notes: Airframe cost £1010-13s, engine (Hispano-Suiza 200hp) cost £1004. Total price was £2014-13s (£97,000 in today's money). A single two-seat conversion is known to have been made. Dolphin II had 300hp Hispano-Suiza engines, Dolphin III had 200hp engines ungeared

Snipe 7F.1 (built 1917-1919)
Function: Single-seat fighter
Total built: 2097 (604 Sopwith, 395 Boulton & Paul, 110 Coventry Ordnance Works, 30 Kingsbury, 135 Napier, 100 Nieuport & General, 153 Portholme, 570 Ruston Proctor)
Engine: Bentley BR.2, 230hp
Armament: 2 x Vickers plus option of 1 x Lewis
Weight (empty/loaded in lb): 1305/2015
Endurance: 3 hours
Speed at altitude: 125mph at 13,000ft
Ceiling: 19,000ft
Notes: The Snipe continued in service until 1926. Examples were tested with ABC Dragonfly engine, around 40 were converted to two-seaters

Snipe of 111 Squadron, RAF, Duxford, 1924. *Ian David Roberts*

Bulldog (built 1918)
Function: Two-seat fighter
Total built: 2 (Sopwith)
Engine: Clerget 11EB, 200hp / ABC Dragonfly, 360hp / Bentley BR.2, 230hp
Armament: 2 x Vickers, 2 x Lewis
Weight (empty/loaded in lb): 1441/2495 (Clerget)
Endurance: 2 hours
Speed at altitude: 109mph at 10,000ft
Ceiling: 15,000ft
Notes: Designed as a fighter but considered as a ground attack aircraft. The two prototypes were used during tests of the unreliable ABC Dragonfly engine.

Rhino 2B.2 (built 1918)
Function: Two-seat triplane bomber
Total built: 2 (Sopwith)
Engine: BHP (Beardmore Halford Pullinger), 230hp
Armament: 1 x Vickers, 1 x Lewis, bombs
Weight (empty/loaded in lb): 2185/3590
Endurance: 3 hours, 45 minutes
Speed at altitude: 103mph
Ceiling: 12,000ft
Notes: Used to test propellers when not adopted

Hippo 3F.2 (built 1917)
Function: Two-seat fighter
Total built: 2 (Sopwith)
Engine: Clerget 11EB, 200hp
Armament: 2 x Vickers, 2 x Lewis
Weight (empty/loaded in lb): 1867/2590
Endurance: N/A
Speed at altitude: 115mph at 10,000ft
Ceiling: 18,000ft
Notes: Designed as a 1½ Strutter replacement for the French

Buffalo (built 1918)
Function: Two-seat armoured contact patrol aircraft
Total built: 2 (Sopwith)
Engine: Bentley BR.2, 230hp
Armament: 1 x Vickers, 1 x Lewis
Weight (empty/loaded in lb): 2175/3071
Endurance: N/A
Speed at altitude: 105.5mph at 6500ft
Ceiling: 9000ft
Notes: Built using many Bulldog components

Swallow (built 1918-1919)
Function: Single-seat fighter
Total built: 1 (Sopwith)
Engine: Le Rhone 9J, 110hp
Armament: 2 x Vickers
Weight (empty/loaded in lb): 889/1420
Endurance: N/A
Speed at altitude: 113.5mph at 10,000ft
Ceiling: 18,500ft
Notes: Camel fuselage with monoplane wing based on Harry Hawker's aerobatic one-off, the Scooter

Snail 8F.1 (built 1917-1918)
Function: Single-seat fighter
Total built: 2 (Sopwith)
Engine: ABC Wasp, 170hp
Armament: 2 x Vickers, 1 x Lewis
Weight (empty/loaded in lb): 1390/1920
Endurance: N/A
Speed at altitude: 124.5mph at 10,000ft
Ceiling: N/A
Notes: Only one had monocoque fuselage

Snark (built 1918-1919)
Function: Single-seat high-altitude fighter
Total built: 3 (Sopwith)
Engine: ABC Dragonfly 1A, 360hp
Armament: 2 x Vickers, 4 x Lewis
Weight (empty/loaded in lb): Not available/2283
Endurance: N/A
Speed at altitude: 130mph at 3000ft
Ceiling: N/A
Notes: Triplane. First flew in April 1919

Salamander TF.2 (built 1918-1919)
Function: Single-seat armoured trench fighter
Total built: 158 (108 Sopwith, 50 Glendower)
Engine: Bentley BR.2, 230hp
Armament: 2 x Vickers, 4 x 20lb bombs, 1 x Lewis optional
Weight (empty/loaded in lb): 1852/2613
Endurance: 2 hours
Speed at altitude: 117mph at 10,000ft
Ceiling: 13,000ft
Notes: Originally based on Snipe but then developed independently

The first production Salamander, 157 Squadron, RAF, October 1918. *Ian David Roberts*

Snapper (built 1918-1919)
Function: Single-seat high-altitude fighter
Total built: 3 (Sopwith)
Engine: ABC Dragonfly, 360hp
Armament: 2 x Vickers
Weight (empty/loaded in lb): 1462/2190
Endurance: N/A
Speed at altitude: 139mph at 6500ft
Ceiling: 23,000ft
Notes: Biplane contemporary of the Snark

Dragon (built 1918-1919)
Function: Single-seat fighter
Total built: 130 (Sopwith)
Engine: ABC Dragonfly, 360hp
Armament: 2 x Vickers
Weight (empty/loaded in lb): 1405/2132
Endurance: N/A
Speed at altitude: 150mph
Ceiling: 23,000ft
Notes: Snipe with Dragonfly engine

Cobham (built 1918-1919)
Function: Three-seat bomber
Total built: 3 (Sopwith)
Engine: ABC Dragonfly 1A, 360hp / Siddeley Puma, 290hp
Armament: 2 x Lewis and bombs
Weight (empty/loaded in lb): Not available/6300
Endurance: N/A
Speed at altitude: N/A
Ceiling: N/A
Notes: Twin engine triplane

Gnu (built 1919-1920)
Function: Three-seat transport
Total built: 13 (Sopwith)
Engine: Bentley BR.2, 230hp or Le Rhone, 110hp
Armament: None
Weight (empty/loaded in lb): Not available/3350 (Le Rhone)
Endurance: 3 hours, 30 minutes
Speed at altitude: 93mph (BR.1) or 91mph (Le Rhone)

Ceiling: N/A
Notes: Initially built with closed cockpit, later changed to open

Dove (built 1919-1920)
Function: Two-seat tourer
Total built: 10 (Sopwith)
Engine: Le Rhone, 80hp
Armament: None
Weight (empty/loaded in lb): 1065/1430
Endurance: 2 hours, 30 minutes
Speed at altitude: 100mph
Ceiling: N/A
Notes: Two-seat civilian sports version of Pup

Atlantic (built 1919)
Function: Two-seat transatlantic challenge biplane
Total built: 1 (Sopwith)
Engine: Rolls-Royce Eagle VIII, 375hp
Armament: None
Weight (empty/loaded in lb): 3000/6500
Endurance: N/A
Speed at altitude: 118mph
Ceiling: 13,000ft
Notes: Featured detachable undercarriage

Wallaby (built 1919)
Function: Two-seat transport
Total built: 1 (Sopwith)
Engine: Rolls-Royce Eagle VIII, 360hp
Armament: None
Weight (empty/loaded in lb): 2780/5200
Endurance: N/A
Speed at altitude: 115mph
Ceiling: N/A
Notes: Similar overall dimensions to Atlantic

Antelope (built 1919)
Function: Three-seat commercial transport
Total built: 1 (Sopwith)
Engine: Wolseley Viper, 180hp
Armament: None
Weight (empty/loaded in lb): 2387/3450
Endurance: 4 hours
Speed at altitude: 110mph
Ceiling: N/A
Notes: Evolved from Atlantic and Wallaby

Grasshopper (built 1919)
Function: Two-seat dual-control trainer
Total built: 1 (Sopwith)
Engine: Anzani, 100hp
Armament: None
Weight (empty/loaded in lb): Not available/1670
Endurance: N/A
Speed at altitude: 90mph
Ceiling: N/A
Notes: The single example had four owners and flew until 1929

Schneider / Rainbow (built 1919-1922)
Function: Single-seat racing floatplane / aeroplane
Total built: 1 (Sopwith)
Engine: Cosmos Jupiter, 450hp / ABC Dragonfly, 320hp
Armament: None
Weight (empty/loaded in lb): N/A / 2200

SOPWITH MYSTERY MACHINES

While many Sopwith aeroplanes flown during the Great War wore the standard brownish green drab PC10, others were brightly painted in a variety of different colours.

Foreign users naturally applied their own colour schemes and markings, and even British units were sometimes allowed a degree of latitude in markings if not in colours.

After the war, and sometimes in training units, the attitude was almost 'anything goes'.

Contemporary photographs of machines have been examined and re-examined for decades to determine precisely which schemes were used on which machines by which units or individuals but every so often an image surfaces that stumps the experts.

Here are three such images. Can you shed any light on them? We would be most grateful for any information regarding location, date, unit or user.

* If you can help with these images, email dsharp@mortons.co.uk

Endurance: N/A
Speed at altitude: 175mph
Ceiling: N/A
Notes: Built as Schneider in 1919 and rebuilt in 1920-1922 as Rainbow

And finally... the Mouse

While numerous 'new' Sopwith machines were created by repair units putting together the salvagable remains of wrecked factory-made aircraft, one airman went a step further and used Sopwith bits to create an entirely new type.

Flight Lieutenant John Alcock was serving with the RNAS at Moudros, Greece, in the Aegean Sea in 1917 – a station equipped with the only Sopwith Triplane to serve in the region, N5431.

The Tripe was well used and destroyed five enemy machines in the hands of RNAS pilots before crashing into a wall while landing.

Alcock took the forward fuselage and lower wings and, along with some Pup upper wings, the tailplane of a Camel, and some components he'd made himself, and fashioned them into the Alcock A.1 Scout, aka the Sopwith Mouse.

It had a 110hp Clerget engine and a single Vickers machine gun. It first flew on October 15, 1917, but was written off in a crash in early 1918.

Alcock himself never flew it, having been forced down and taken prisoner by the enemy on September 30, 1917. ■

Flight Lieutenant John Alcock used parts of a Sopwith Triplane, a Pup and a Camel to compose a 'new' type – the Alcock A.1 Scout. The enemy captured him before he could fly it.

It has been suggested that the large '6' painted on the side of this Camel was a racing number but this does not match the entries of any Camels in contests such as the Aerial Derby or the King's Cup of the early 1920s. If this is a civilian Camel, would it still have its guns? Keeping them, perhaps with firing gear removed, would certainly have been helpful in maintaining the aeroplane's delicate weight balance and centre of gravity. It appears as though a military serial on the tail may have been painted over or otherwise removed/obscured.

The spectacular dragon emblazoned along the side of this Camel may have been Welsh – and painted a vivid red – but that doesn't go very far towards identifying the machine's unit or the location where this shot was taken. Camels wearing more conventional colour schemes are ranged across the background of the image, could this machine have been an officer's personal hack, or that of an instructor at a training base?

It has been speculated that the stripes on this Triplane, which may have been in use at Beaulieu Aerodrome, Hampshire, in 1918, were red, white and blue. Further, did the other side of the fuselage have identical vertical stripes, or were they horizontal? Most Triplanes had crashed, been retired or had otherwise been scrapped by 1918 so this would be a relatively rare survivor. The uniform of the officer standing beside the machine appears to be RAF, rather than RFC, dating the photograph to some time after April 1, 1918.

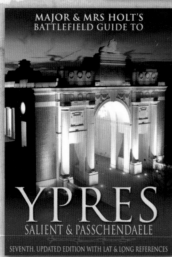
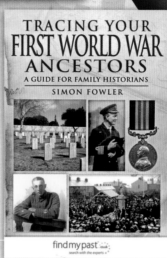
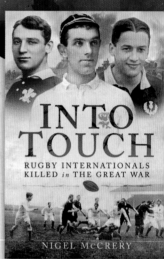
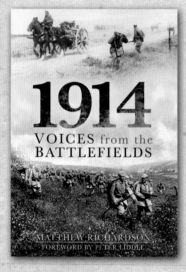
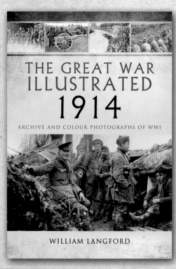
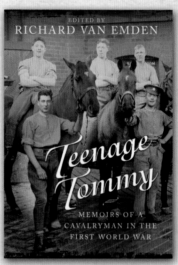
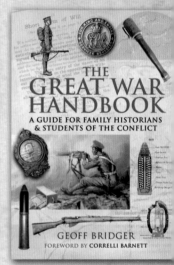